PATTERN PLAY

A ZENTANGLE® CREATIVITY BOOSTER

ACKNOWLEDGMENTS

All art in this book is the property of the artist who created it. It has been reproduced with permission of the respective artists, and every effort has been made to ensure credits are accurate. If not specified, all artwork is done by the authors. (Look for our chop to see which of us did which.)

PUBLISHED BY

Cris Letourneau, CZT, Pickerington, Ohio

TangledUpInArt.com

ISBN-13: 978-0-9903798-0-5
ISBN-10: 0990379809

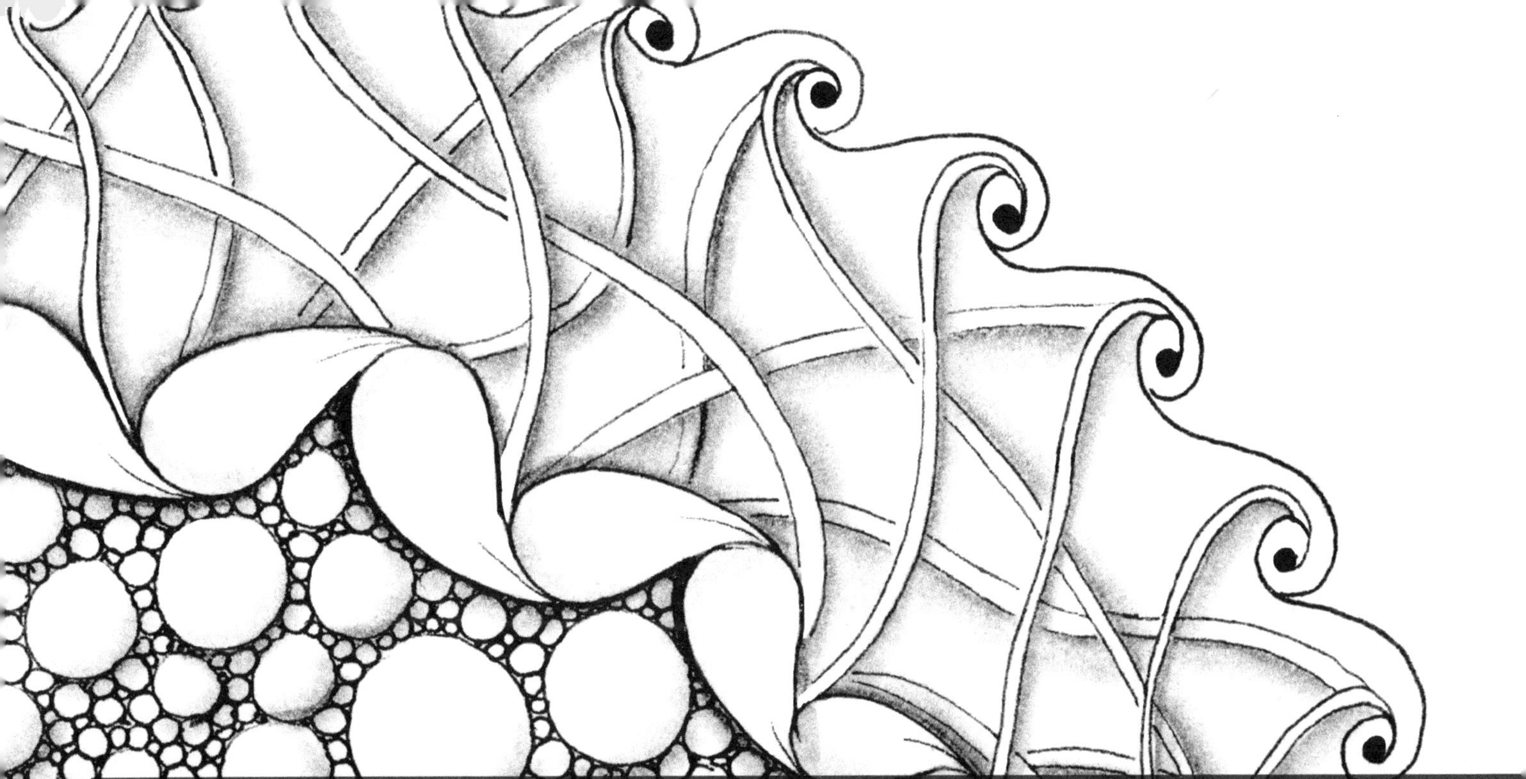

PATTERN PLAY

A ZENTANGLE CREATIVITY BOOSTER

Written and illustrated by Cris Letourneau, CZT and Sonya Yencer, CZT

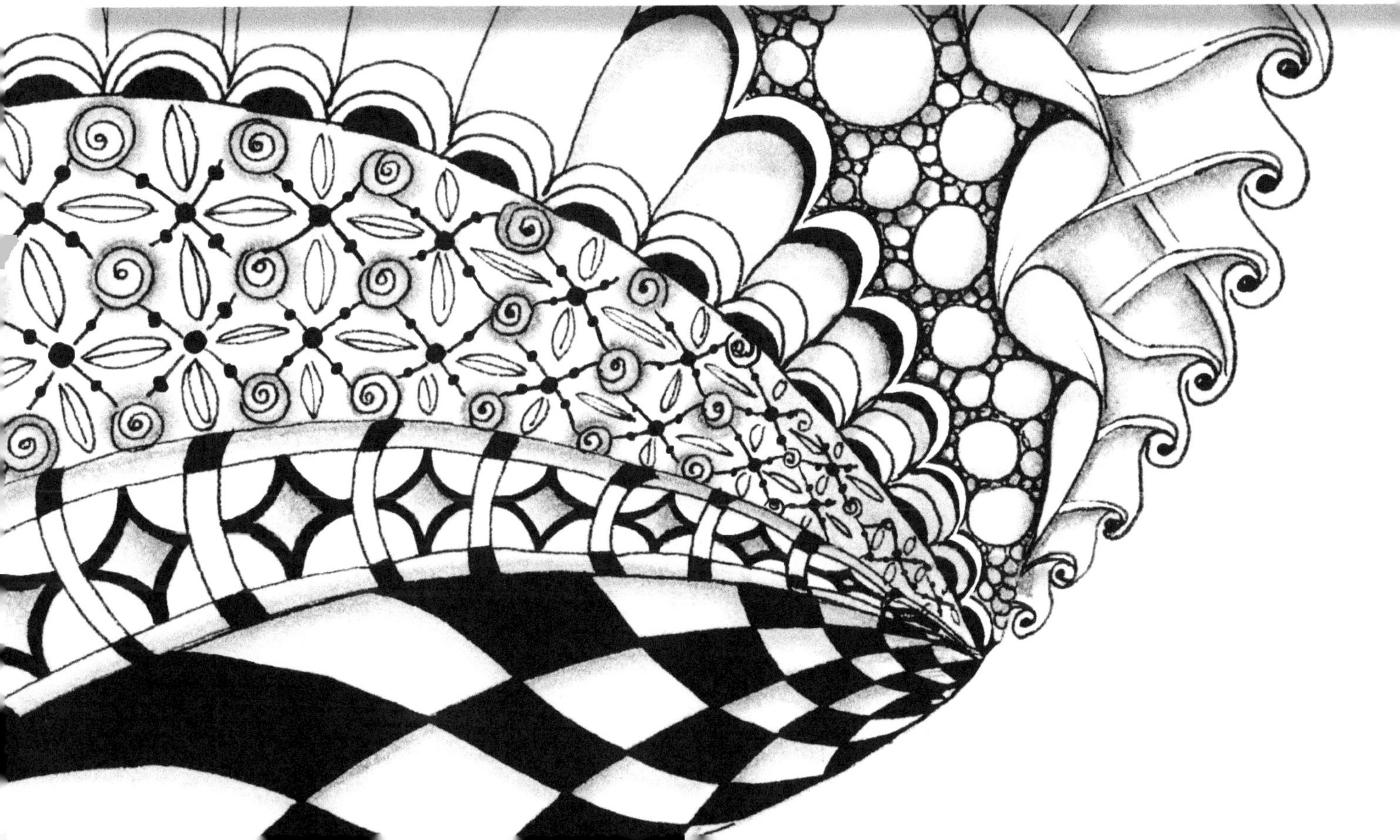

CONTENTS

CHAPTER 4

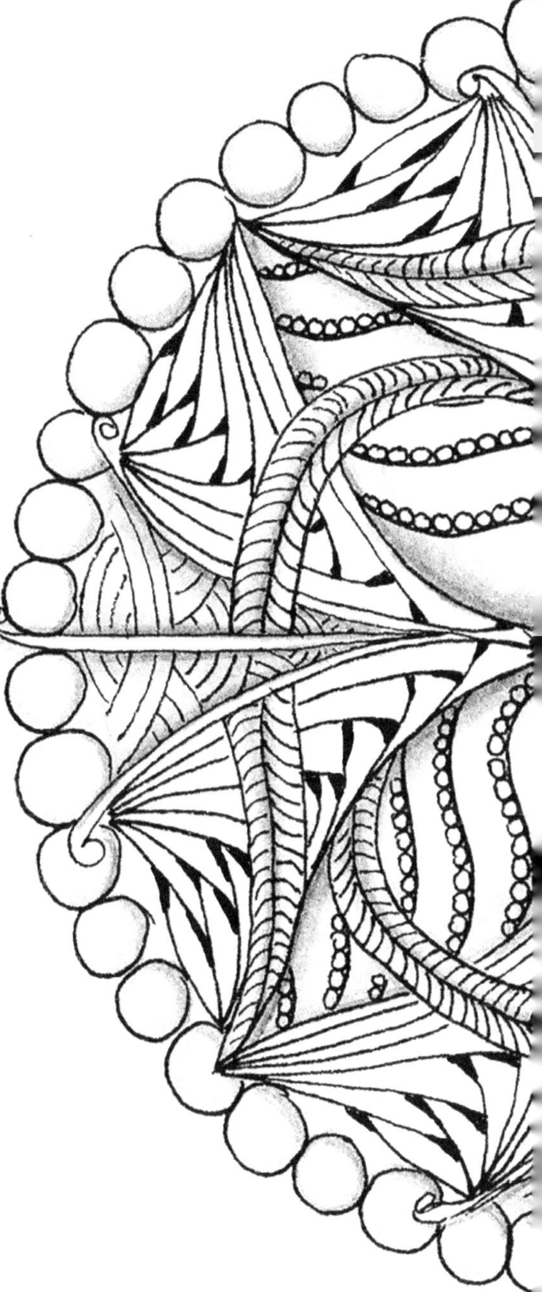

about *the* authors

Although this is the pair's first book together, they have been friends for over 10 years, weathering multiple cross-country drives, Girl Scout duties, vacations, fund-raisers, and the daily challenges of raising teenagers. After all of that, writing a book together was a piece of cake!

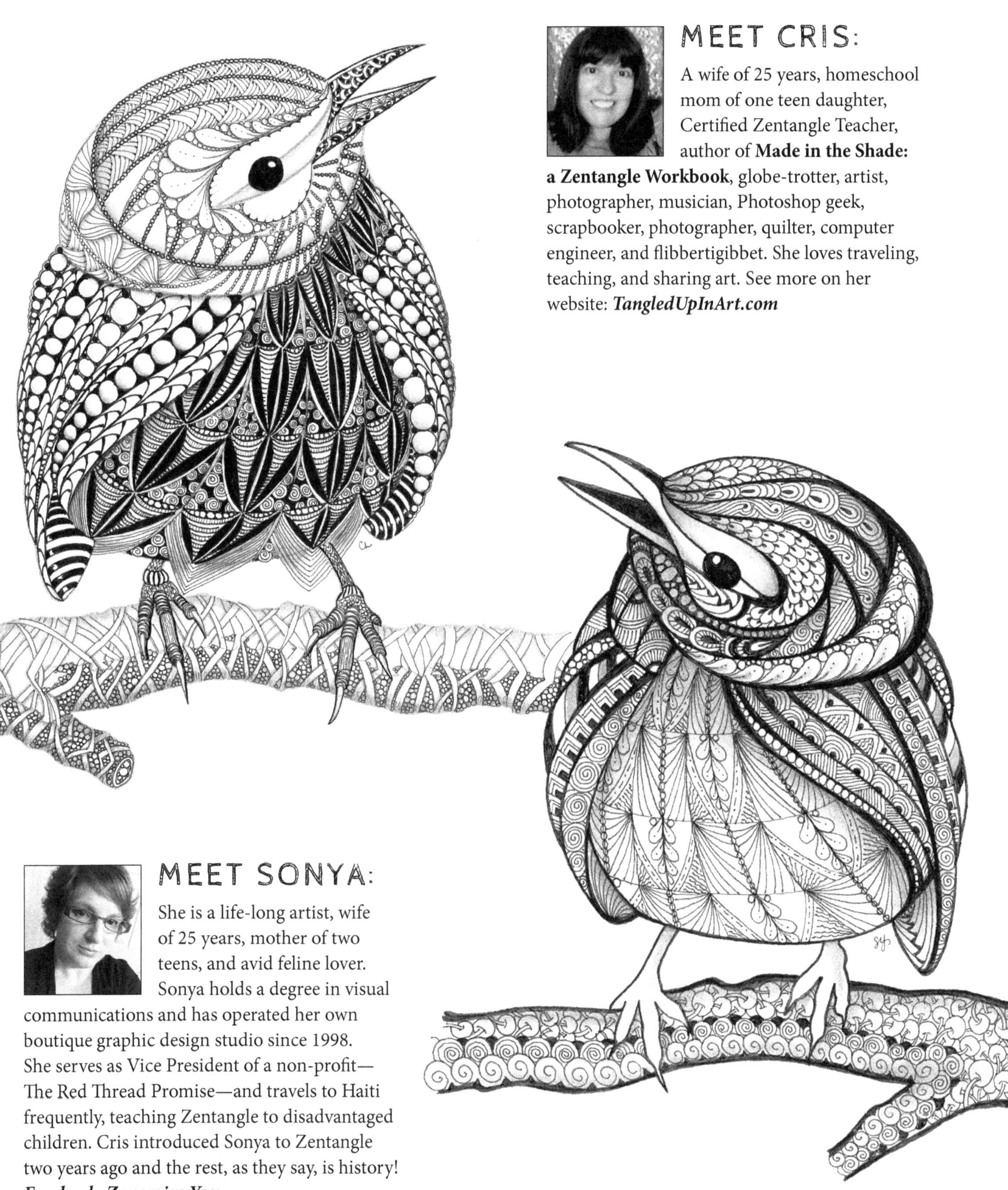

MEET CRIS:

A wife of 25 years, homeschool mom of one teen daughter, Certified Zentangle Teacher, author of **Made in the Shade: a Zentangle Workbook**, globe-trotter, artist, photographer, musician, Photoshop geek, scrapbooker, photographer, quilter, computer engineer, and flibbertigibbet. She loves traveling, teaching, and sharing art. See more on her website: ***TangledUpInArt.com***

MEET SONYA:

She is a life-long artist, wife of 25 years, mother of two teens, and avid feline lover. Sonya holds a degree in visual communications and has operated her own boutique graphic design studio since 1998. She serves as Vice President of a non-profit—The Red Thread Promise—and travels to Haiti frequently, teaching Zentangle to disadvantaged children. Cris introduced Sonya to Zentangle two years ago and the rest, as they say, is history! ***Facebook: Zenergize You***

Prairie Warbler template: ©Ben Kwok

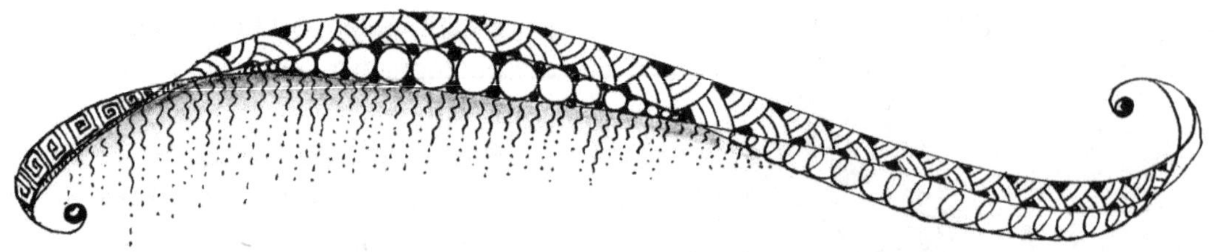

WHEN YOU CREATE IN A ZENTANGLE WAY, YOU CREATE A BEAUTIFUL PIECE OF ART. YOU ALSO CAN DELIBERATELY CREATE

A MOOD, A FOCUS, A STATE OF MIND.

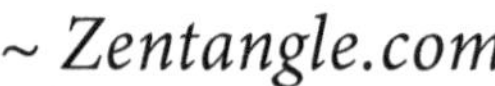

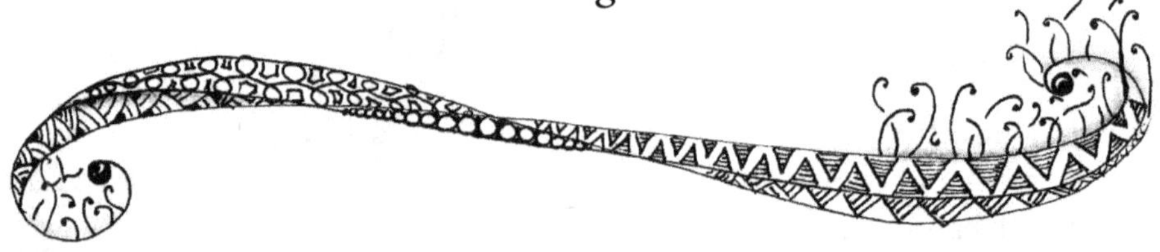

CHAPTER 1

ABOUT ZENTANGLE

From its infancy a decade ago in rural Massachusetts, the rapidly growing art form known as Zentangle® has become a global phenomenon. There are Certified Zentangle Teachers® (CZT®s) in most of the United States, as well as numerous countries worldwide.

Throughout human history, evidence can be found that the need for self expression is deeply rooted in our being. Zentangle satisfies that primal need, using ancient patterns that are still popular today. The satisfaction experienced in the act of creation makes it appealing to everyone from the young to the old—from artists to scientists, and everyone in between. The calming deliberateness of each pen stroke has an even greater appeal when one lives in a high-stress, fast-paced, "plugged-in" world. In an era of instant everything, creating Zentangle art conjures up a bygone era, a time when people were not constantly busy—before the age of smart phones and 24-hour news, movies-on-demand and the internet—when people would relax in the evening and spend time with each other without electronic interference.

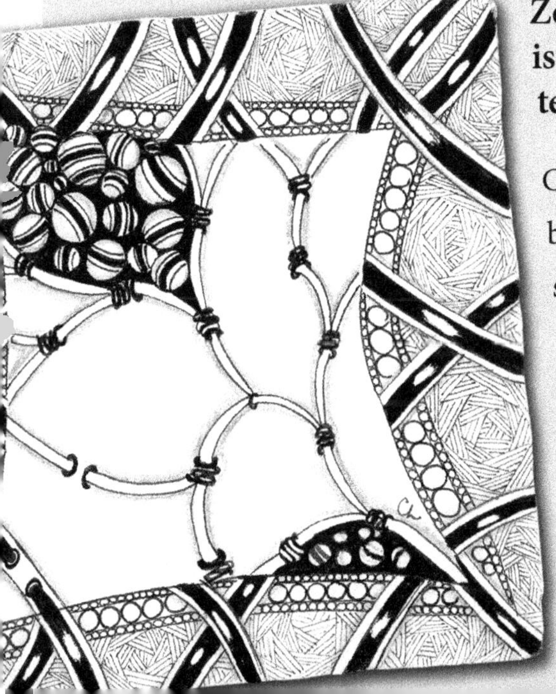

Zentangle reawakens an inner sense of calm that is so vital to combat everyday stress in this hectic, technological age.

Creators Rick Roberts and Maria Thomas understood the busyness of modern life and created the ***Zentangle Method*** specifically so that it can be done in whatever short bits of time you can carve out of your day. Since there is no need for fancy tools, a dedicated space, planning, preparation, or clean-up, creating Zentangle art can be enjoyed anywhere, anytime.

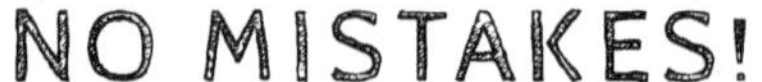

NO MISTAKES!

Perhaps one of the biggest surprises to people who discover Zentangle art is that you do not have to be an artist to do it. There are no preconceived ideas or rules to follow so there is no wrong way to do it. Each piece of art will be as unique as the person who created it. Cris always tells her students,

"Do not worry. You cannot fail. If you sit down to make a Zentangle you will end up with a Zentangle."

Zentangle art is meant to be a surprise, even to its creator. Since you do not sit down with the end in mind, there is no goal or ruler you can use to judge the result. CZT Margaret Bremner says, *"The child-like process of just seeing what happens is a key element of Zentangle. There are no mistakes that cannot become something more interesting."*

NO EXCUSES!

The Zentangle Method was designed to remove obstacles, so that most anyone can do it. You do not need a lot of time, money, space, or talent. Zentangle materials are small, lightweight, inexpensive, and do not need to be plugged in, so it does not matter where your short bits of time are found: waiting in the car or the doctor's office, watching a child's sporting event, or even in front of the television with your family.

All you need is enough light to see what you are doing and a firm surface on which to work. The numerous benefits of finding that five minutes may surprise you.

©Carla Jennings

BENEFITS OF ZENTANGLE PRACTICE

Despite its simplicity, practicing Zentangle can have profound results similar to other mindful activities, like yoga and meditation. People who embrace the Zentangle Method have often reported that they:

- Feel peaceful and less stressed
- Manage pain better
- Feel more confident
- Become more observant and aware of the patterns and beauty that surround them
- Become less judgmental
- Trust their instincts more
- Improve hand-eye coordination
- Become better problem-solvers
- Fall asleep faster and awake feeling refreshed
- Feel more creative and expressive
- Have a sense of accomplishment and believe they can finish things
- Concentrate longer with increased focus
- Meditate more deeply

Understandably, some people are skeptical of these claims, clinging to the "sounds too good to be true" philosophy. *We invite you to try it for yourself and discover the truth.*

Practicing the Zentangle Method has no known harmful side effects. What have you got to lose?

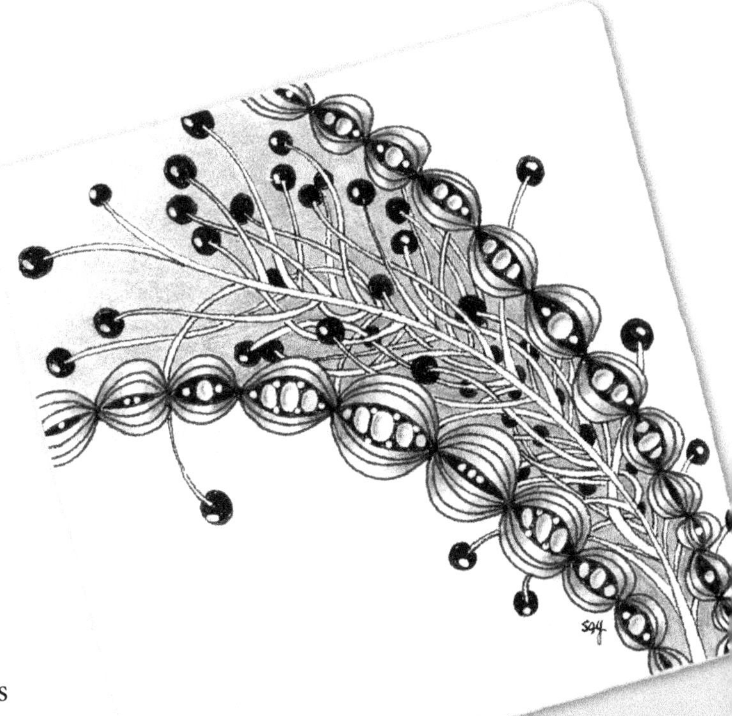

NOTE: *Zentangle is not a verb. It is the name of the company and the trademarked process. When you draw patterns, you are tangling, and the result is Zentangle art.*

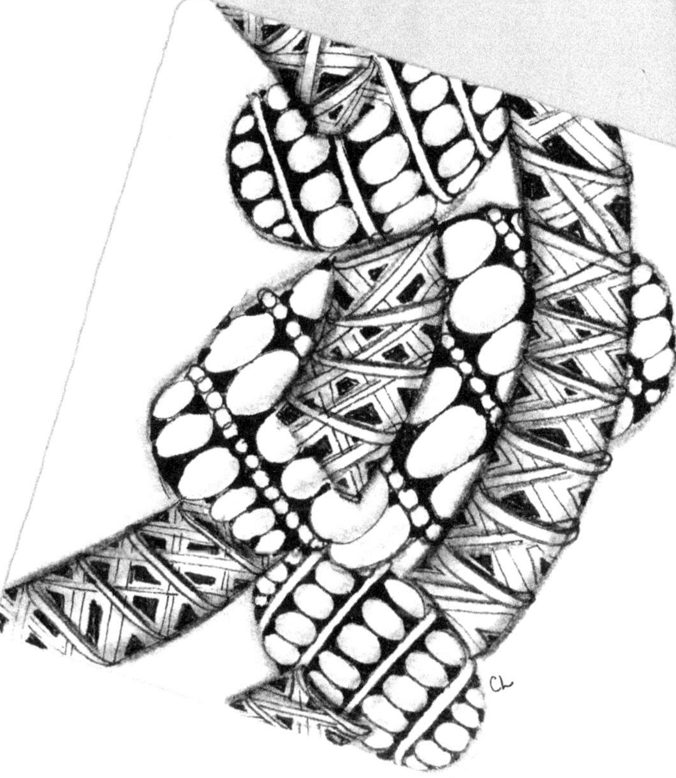

ZENTANGLE CLASSES

The best way to learn the Zentangle Method is to take a class with a Certified Zentangle Teacher (***CZT***[†]). Much can be accomplished in a group setting with quality instruction, open dialogue, and interaction with classmates.

Students come into class with varying attitudes and expectations. Some are cautious, concerned about "doing it right" and not wanting to make a mistake. Others worry that their art will not look like what is being demonstrated or created by fellow students. Regardless of how they begin, the most profound moments in class are often experienced at the very end. This is when everyone's completed tiles are arranged into a grid creating the class ***mosaic***.

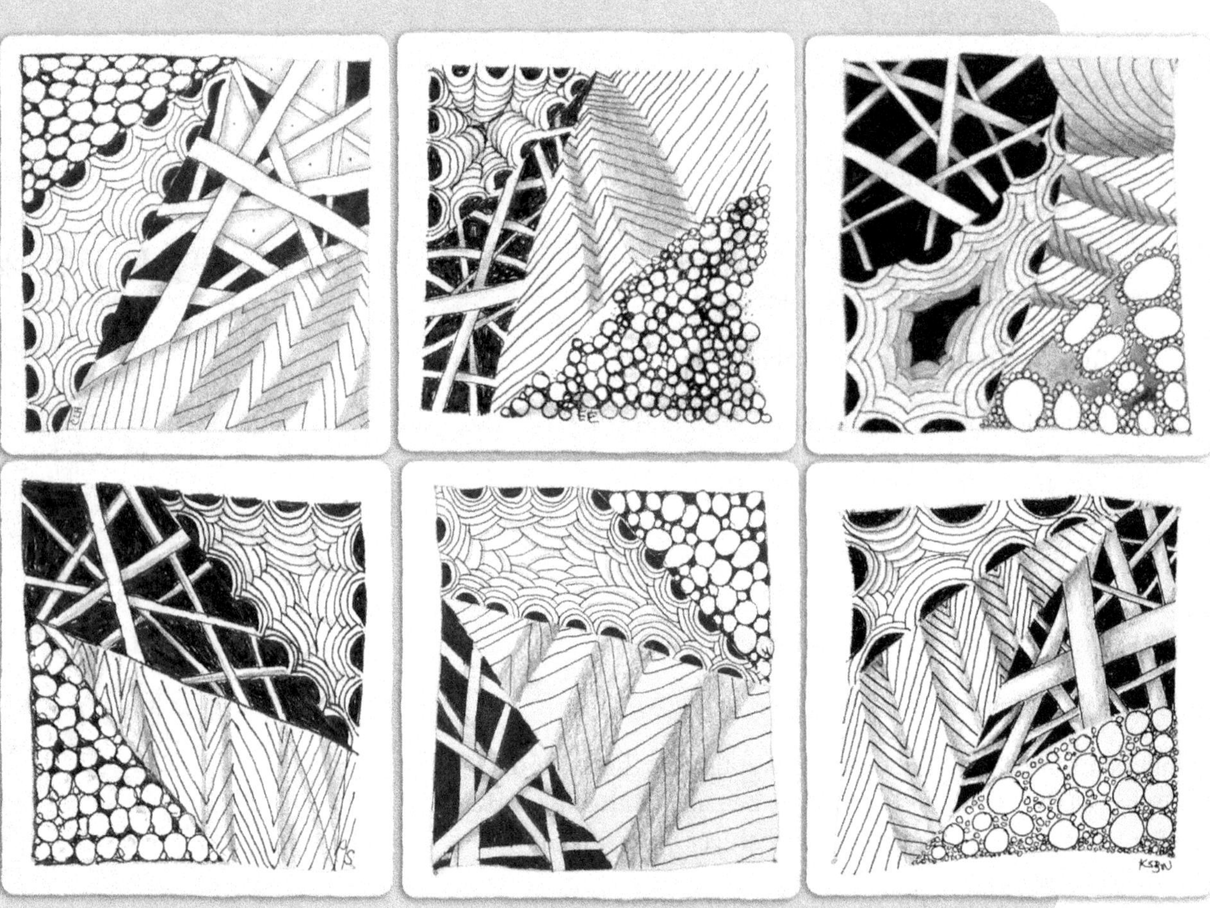

A TYPICAL BEGINNER CLASS MOSAIC

Students' reactions to the mosaic are priceless! They no longer ask, "Did I do it right?" or "Is mine good enough?" Instead, they *ooh* and *aah* over the variety in the tiles, marveling at the unique qualities of each person's art and celebrate the differences they see.

Finally, and most importantly, they observe that their art fits in with all of the others. They finally *believe* in their hearts that it is okay that their tile does not look like anyone else's. And they celebrate it!

[†] *All words in **bold italic** are defined in the glossary starting on page 132*

HOW-TO BOOKS

The classroom experience described on the previous page is unique and, unfortunately, something that cannot be duplicated by reading a book, *not even this one*. However, by reading and completing the exercises described in Chapter 2: *Zentangle 101*, you can get a feel for the instruction received in a beginner class. While classes are the best way to learn the process, books are a fantastic tool to introduce new tangles and strings, provide inspiration, and help you develop your own style.

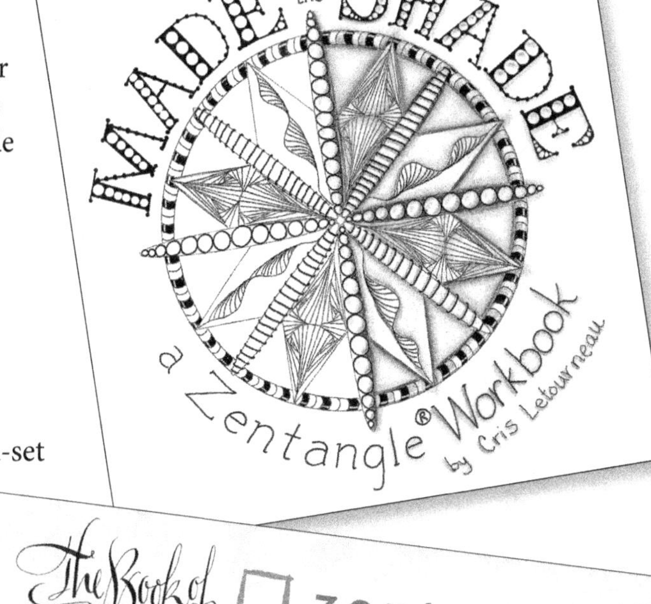

When admiring a beautiful tangle in a book, it is quite natural to want to duplicate it. That is the goal of most traditional art instruction books. They contain step-by-step instructions and projects teaching the techniques needed to replicate the artist's style. However, this is not a traditional how-to book.

If potential students approach Zentangle art with the same mind-set used for traditional art books, *"I want to produce this exact piece of art, just like the author did in this book,"* the process ceases to be relaxing, creative, or in the true Zentangle spirit.

Why? On one hand, if the project does look just like the one in the book, the readers may feel that they have mastered the tangle and move on. This imposes limits on creativity from the beginning—only experiencing what the author has demonstrated—never exploring what else that tangle could be if they used their own imagination. On the other hand, if the tangle does not look like the author's, then they may feel that they have done something wrong and become frustrated, questioning their own abilities and miss out on the relaxing, mindful Zentangle experience as it was created to be.

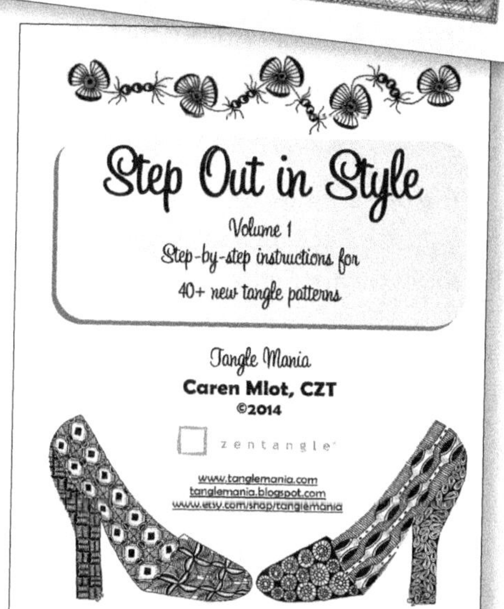

The Zentangle Method is more than just copying a piece of artwork. It is a process that allows you the opportunity to explore and develop your own creativity, accept what comes, and relax as you create art with no expectations.

In *The Joy of Zentangle*, it says *"every tangle pictured in this book is merely a suggestion or starting point. You can adapt and change any tangle to make it your own."* This is exactly what the Zentangle Method is about, yet it is rarely explored in books—until now.

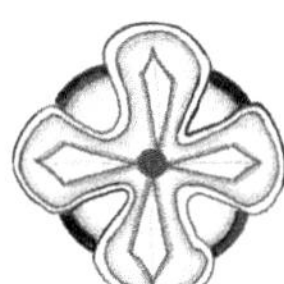

In this book, we will show you a minimum of six different ways to explore each tangle we present. We encourage you to play with each pattern and to develop your own unique style.

ZENTANGLE IS NOT

The Zentangle Method is an easy-to-learn, relaxing, and fun way to create beautiful images by drawing structured patterns. It is a ritual, a ceremony, and a process. The beautiful art is just a wonderful side effect. Because it is simple and the results may resemble mindless doodles, it is quite understandable that people sometimes get the wrong impression. We would like to set the record straight.

Zentangle is ***not*** representational.

Because you are not attempting to copy an object from the physical world* or even an image in your mind, there is no way to make a mistake. Each stroke is an opportunity to see what happens next. There is no need to worry about the outcome. It will always look like a Zentangle!

Zentangle is ***not*** mindless doodling.

It is a focused, mindful activity. CZT Kelley Kelly explains that doodling is to Zentangle what stretching is to yoga. Both are valuable, but for different reasons.

NOTE: *Think you are not creative? Potential students tell Cris this all the time. If you are one of them, think about this:*

"It is not who we are that holds us back, it is who we think we are not."

~ Michael Nolan

Following the Zentangle Method means that each stroke is made with intention and deliberate focus. That makes it so relaxing. The only way to truly forget about everyday worries is to think about something else. Kelley teaches, "*Our worries are like an elephant in the room. If you are told not to look at it, that is the only thing you will see. But if you focus on doing other things, the elephant gets bored and leaves. For a lot of us, the left brain is overused. We need to let it rest. Free the right brain from the cage you have put it in and let it breathe.*"

Children (and adults) know all too well that the more they try to forget about the monster under the bed, the harder it is to do. Whether your monster is simply your ever-expanding to-do list or something more serious, tangling will give your brain a welcome rest.

* *Zentangle-Inspired Art, like the peacock on page 10, is a popular extension of the Zentangle Method in which the artist incorporates tangles into representational artwork. The patterns give the piece a unique sense of energy and movement not easily attained by traditional art techniques.*

Zentangle is ***not*** complicated.

Although the results often look complex, ***tangles*** (patterns) are broken down into simple, repeated strokes that anyone can learn. Once you understand how the strokes flow and connect, you may find yourself lost in the patterns! It is almost like magic when you finish your tile and see the results—a welcome surprise—especially if you doubt your artistic abilities.

Zentangle is ***not*** just for artists.

You do not need artistic training or special talent to tangle. The simple strokes used in tangling are the same ones used to draw a stick figure or write your name. Picasso said, *"Every child is an artist. The problem is how to remain an artist once we grow up."* Even if you do not think of yourself as an artist now, Zentangle will change your mind as you rediscover the childlike wonder and joy in expressing yourself through art.

Zentangle is ***not*** just a collection of patterns.

Many tanglers are so excited about the beautiful patterns that they inadvertently start a second hobby: collecting tangles. Time spent on a quest for new patterns leads to even more time needed to file, organize, and search through their ever-expanding collection. We want to help you avoid this time drain by encouraging you to rely on your own creativity. You will not feel the need for a reference book of every tangle in existence. Your creative spirit will be nurtured through in-depth exploration of tangles you already know. The results will inspire you to continue finding and refining your style. The bottom line is this: while you cannot have Zentangle without patterns, *the patterns are not the point.*

Having a lot of tangles is like using a huge box of paints. If you only use the colors straight from the box, you will always be limited in your choices. However, when you learn to mix the paints to create your own unique colors, the only limit is your imagination. The same is true of tangles. Learning how to take the existing tangles in your "box" and make them your own will allow your art to have infinite variety.

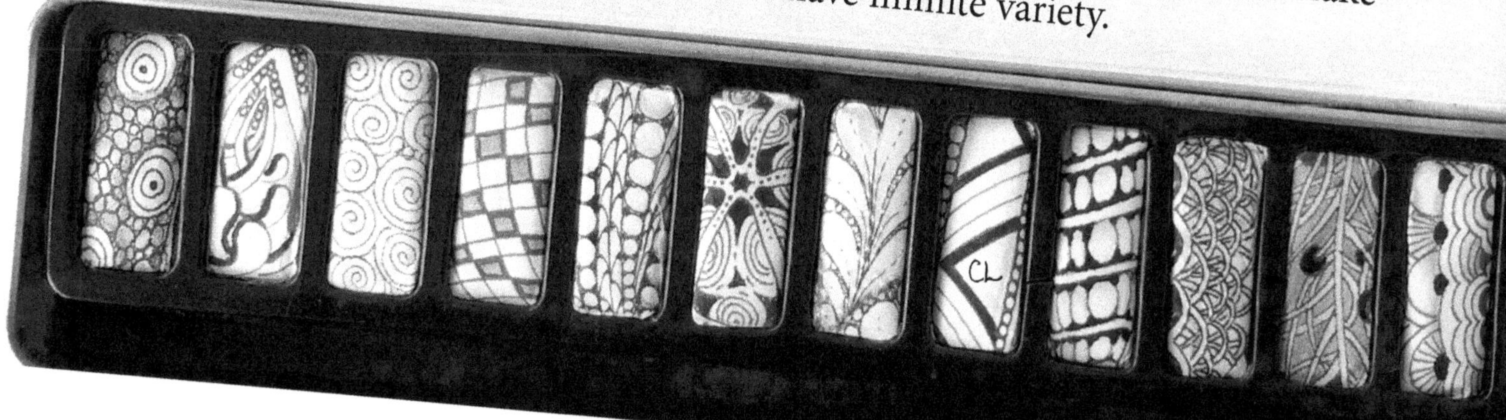

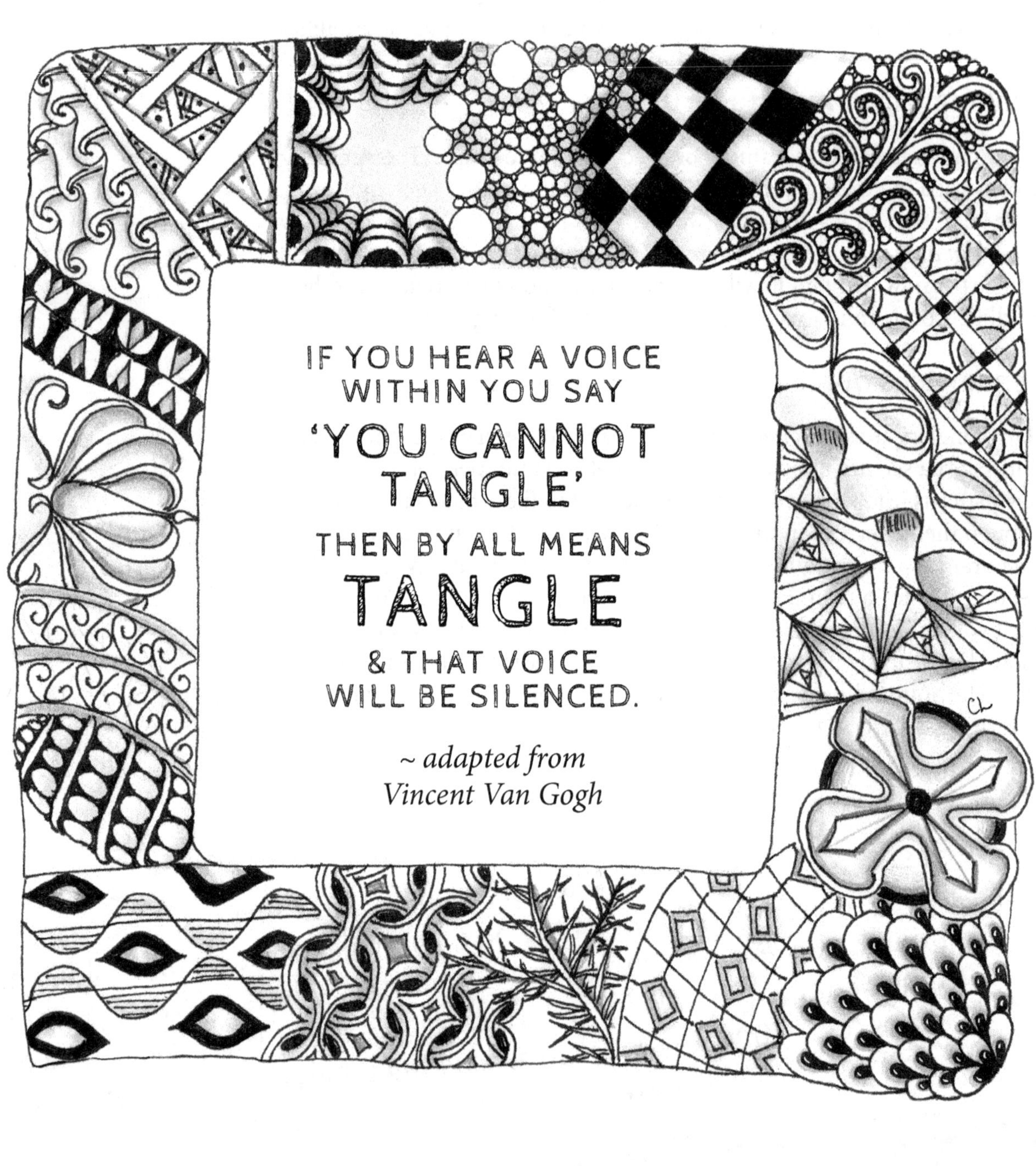
IF YOU HEAR A VOICE
WITHIN YOU SAY
'YOU CANNOT
TANGLE'
THEN BY ALL MEANS
TANGLE
& THAT VOICE
WILL BE SILENCED.
~ adapted from
Vincent Van Gogh
CL

CHAPTER 2

ZENTANGLE 101

If you have never taken a class with a CZT, or if could use a refresher on the basics, this chapter is for you. In it, we guide you through six simple steps to creating a tile as if you were taking a Zentangle 101 class. For the experienced tangler, it is a refresher, helping you to refocus on the benefits of tangling mindfully. We encourage you to follow the steps and create a tile, whether it is your first or your fifty-first.

As you begin your journey, remember that when you are creating Zentangle art, the process is more important than the product. Focus on **how** you are tangling rather than **what** you are tangling.

Keep the process in mind and let the art take care of itself.

Let your journey begin!

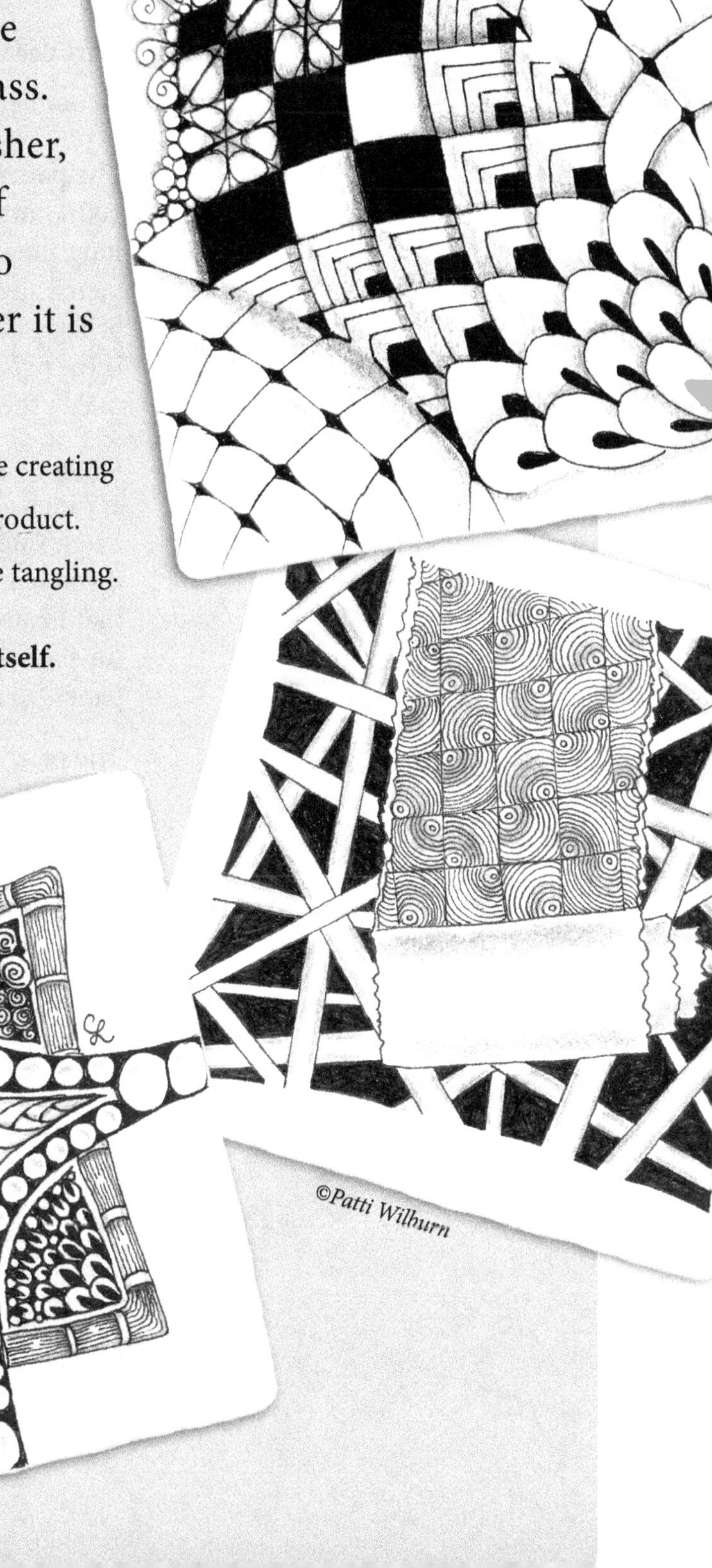

©Marty Deckel

©Patti Wilhurn

NECESSITIES

One of the many benefits of the Zentangle Method is that it requires very few materials. All you need is a pen, paper to write on, and a pencil. These simple materials allow you to begin right away. It is possible to tangle on anything, but using the best possible tools and high quality materials helps you get in the right frame of mind to begin. Using high-quality materials and tools affirms that you are creating art, not just killing time.

Your art deserves the best.

We recommend the following:

NOTE: "Tiles" get their name from their stone or ceramic counterparts. They can be combined into dramatic larger pieces called mosaics.

- **The paper.** Official Zentangle tiles are the preferred paper. Made of 100% cotton Fabriano® Tiepolo™ printmaking paper imported from Italy, they have just the right amount of **tooth** (texture) to accept pencil and ink beautifully. Their soft white color provides a beautiful background for your art. Their small size, just 3 1/2 inches square, is the perfect size to hold in your hand and rotate as you work. It makes them easy to transport and quick to complete.

  If you do not have an official tile, do not let that stop you! Cut a 3 1/2 inch square out of cardboard (a cereal box works well) to make a template. Trace the template onto paper that has a slight texture if you have it, like watercolor or drawing paper, and cut it out. Note that the texture of your paper will affect your line work and the finished tile. This is an opportunity for exploration. Try different papers to see the impact that paper choice has on your tangling.

- **The pen.** The pen recommended by most Zentangle enthusiasts is a black Sakura® Pigma® Micron® pen, size 01 (.25 mm). They contain archival-quality pigment ink that will not bleed, fade, or smear. With these pens, your artwork will withstand the test of time. The fine tip size allows you to create delicate and intricate art.* If you do not have a Micron, use the thinnest black pen you have.

Beginning Zentangle classes use only black for a good reason: it eliminates the need to stop and think about what color to use. By eliminating decision-making, you allow the right side of your brain to continue making art with no interruptions from the already overused analytical left side of your brain. Fewer interruptions means increased focus. More focus translates into a greater sense of relaxation and accomplishment.

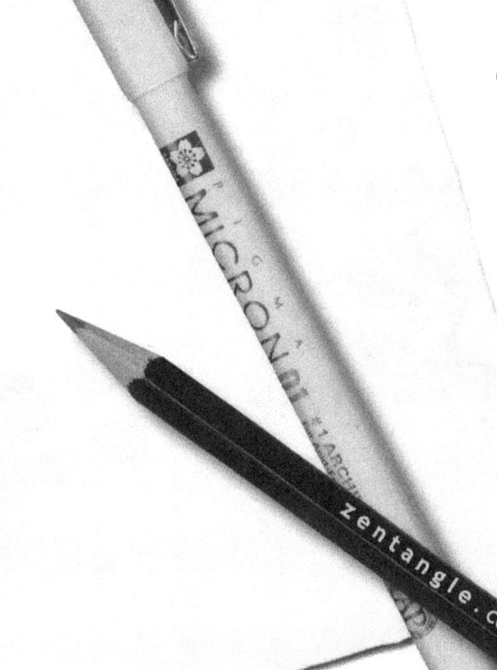

* *Smaller and larger tip sizes are available if you prefer finer lines for details or thicker lines for filling in large spaces. However, neither is necessary.*

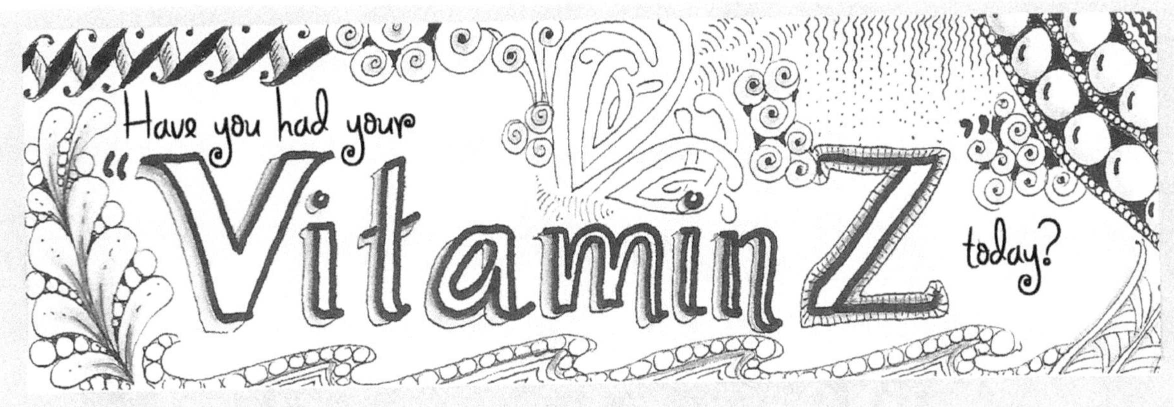

This is the bookmark that Cris gives her students to remind them that tangling is a healthy habit.

- ✏ **The pencil.** Any pencil can be used to begin your tile, but try to find one without an eraser so you will not be tempted to erase "mistakes." Pencils are also great tools to add depth and dimension to your art through shading. If you want to learn more about pencils and shading, see Cris's book *Made in the Shade: a Zentangle Workbook.*

- ✏ **Your work area.** If you have the opportunity, create an environment that is distraction-free. Clear your desk or table top; turn off the television; put on some relaxing instrumental music.

  However, if you do not have the luxury of a dedicated, peaceful workspace, do not let that be a reason to not tangle. You do not need a lot of room, technology, or heavy machinery. All you really need is something sturdy to write on and enough light to comfortably see what you are drawing. As you tangle, you may notice that any noise and minor disturbances fade away.

- ✏ **Your mindset.** Before you pick up your pencil, close your eyes for just a moment. Take a deep, calming breath, and appreciate the opportunity to spend a few minutes doing something creative.

  Let go of expectations! Zentangle is about the process, not the patterns. As long as you keep that in mind you cannot fail. If you are sitting down with some other expectations then you are setting yourself up for potential disappointment if the results do not meet your expectations. Only once you learn to "let go and let Zentangle" will you begin to experience the joy, wonder, and peacefulness that is inherent in the Zentangle Method.

Are you ready to begin? Relax. Breathe. Smile.

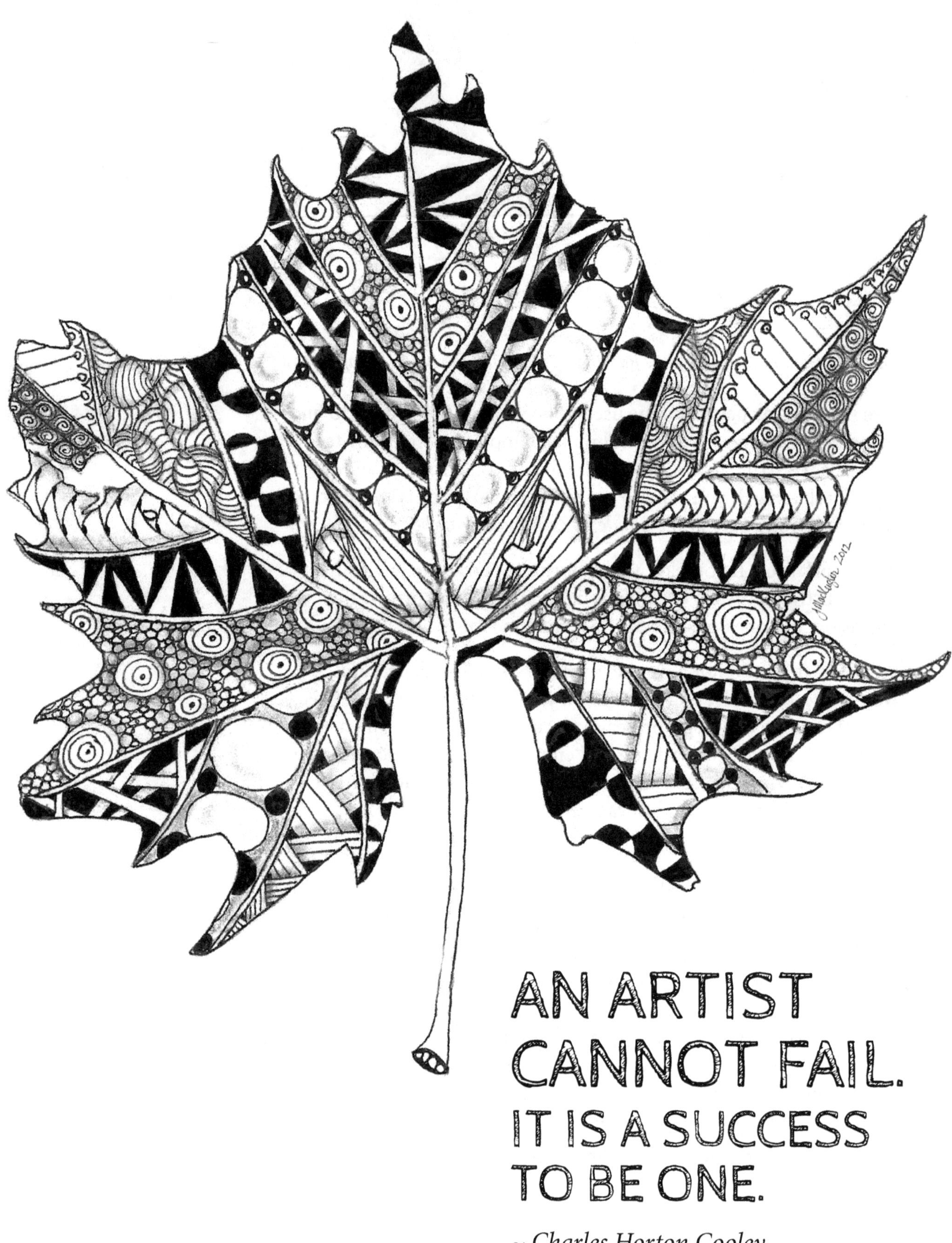

AN ARTIST CANNOT FAIL.
IT IS A SUCCESS TO BE ONE.

~ Charles Horton Cooley

TANGLING AT A GLANCE

The Zentangle Method is simple yet powerful and can be described by six easy-to-remember steps: **Still, Frame, String, Fill, Shade, Finish. (SFSFSF)***

As you work through the process on the following pages, keep in mind that **the Zentangle Method is meant to be a tool to help you relax, focus, and let your creativity blossom.** To get the most out of your Zentangle time, make a habit of following all of the steps. They do not take a lot of time and will make this practice much more rewarding. They are not laws that must be obeyed, but tools to allow you to gain the most benefits from your tangle time.

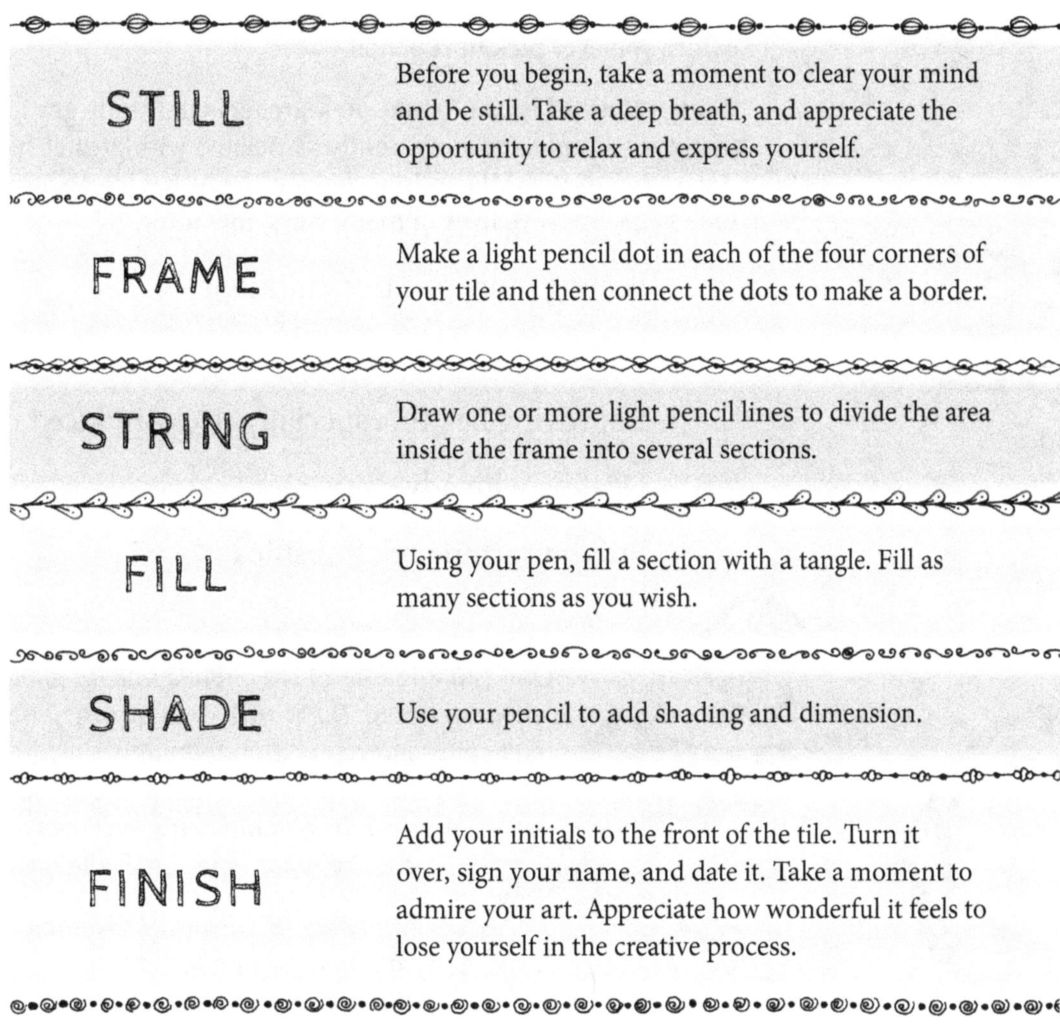

STILL	Before you begin, take a moment to clear your mind and be still. Take a deep breath, and appreciate the opportunity to relax and express yourself.
FRAME	Make a light pencil dot in each of the four corners of your tile and then connect the dots to make a border.
STRING	Draw one or more light pencil lines to divide the area inside the frame into several sections.
FILL	Using your pen, fill a section with a tangle. Fill as many sections as you wish.
SHADE	Use your pencil to add shading and dimension.
FINISH	Add your initials to the front of the tile. Turn it over, sign your name, and date it. Take a moment to admire your art. Appreciate how wonderful it feels to lose yourself in the creative process.

* *The six steps described in this book capture the essence of the Zentangle Method, but have been nicknamed to make them easier to remember.* STILL *is step 1:* ***Gratitude and Appreciation.*** FRAME *is steps 2 & 3:* ***Corner dots &Border.*** FILL *is step 4:* ***Tangle.*** FINISH *is steps 7 & 8:* ***Initial and Sign & Appreciate.***

Still

Step 1: Still your mind and get ready to tangle.

Clear your mind of the day's business. Even if you cannot be in a relaxing environment, you can close your eyes for a moment and take a deep, calming breath. Take a moment to relish and be thankful for the opportunity to do something creative.

This step often gets overlooked in the excitement to begin, but it may be the most important of all. We encourage you to strive to make it a habit before you ever pick up a pencil.

WELL BEGUN IS HALF DONE.

~Aristotle

Being thankful is important. Researchers who study gratitude find that it is strongly and consistently associated with greater happiness. According to WebMD and *Psychology Today*, having an attitude of gratitude helps improve lives in many ways, including:

- Feeling more positive emotions
- Relishing good experiences
- Improving health, especially stress-induced diseases
- Dealing with adversity
- Building strong relationships

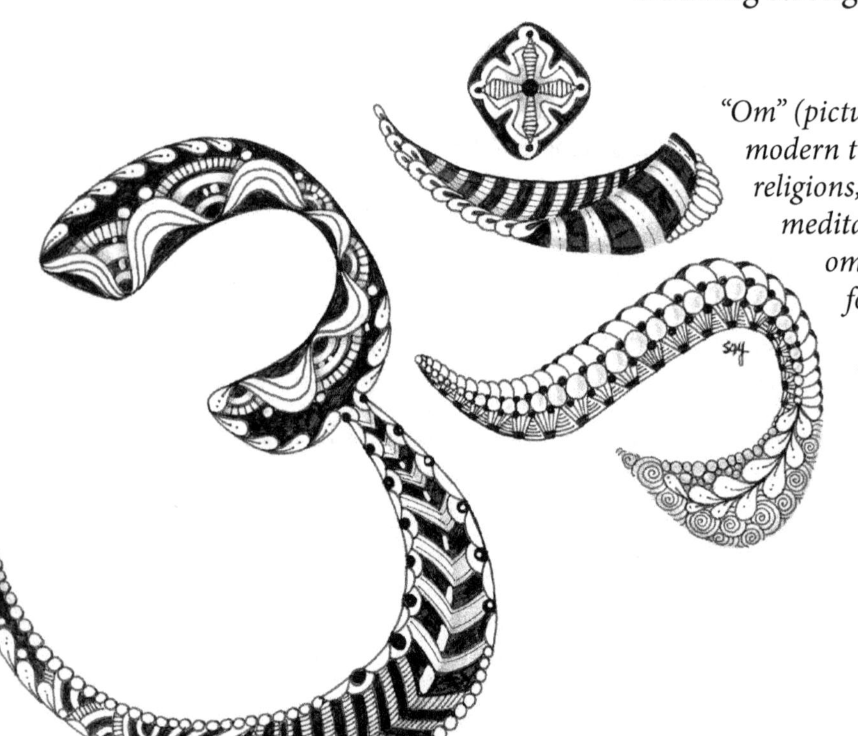

"Om" (pictured here) is symbolic in both ancient and modern times. The word's roots are attributed to various religions, but today it is commonly used in yoga and meditation practices. When pronounced repeatedly, om's calming sound helps melt away distractions, focus the mind, and center the speaker's energy.

Practicing the Zentangle Method can achieve a similar sense of relaxed focus; no particular spiritual belief is required.

Frame

Step 2: Draw four dots and a border.

When CZT Barb Round teaches a beginner class, she introduces the ritual of Zentangle by saying, "*The fear of a blank page must be right up there with fear of public speaking.*" Her students agree. The blank tile has **so much** potential that making that first stroke can be quite intimidating. Similar to authors experiencing writer's block, artists often do not know where to begin. The Zentangle Method eliminates this hesitation because you know exactly where to start: the frame.

On the front of your tile, use your pencil and draw four light dots, one near each corner of the tile. The dot should be just dark enough for you to see it.

Next, using your pencil, connect the dots, loosely following the edges of the paper. Do not reach for a ruler. Your frame is not supposed to be perfectly square, and your lines need not be straight. This is an organic, rather than a geometric, art form. Draw the lines just dark enough for you to see. The frame is a guideline, a place to start your artwork, nothing more. If the lines are too dark, you may hear that little voice inside your head that tells you to stay inside the lines. Light lines remind you that they are suggestions rather than rules that must be followed.

Goodbye, intimidating blank tile.

String

Step 3: Draw your "string."

NOTE: The string got its name from Rick's childhood experience of watching his grandmother drop strings into sugar water and pull out beautiful rock candy, like the lollipops below.

In Zentangle lingo, a ***string*** is a merely a light pencil line that divides your tile into sections. It is from these strings that your beautiful tangles grow. CZT Mary Sergeant explains that your string is your foundation: "*Because of the foundation, you do not have to think about where to go with a Zentangle.*"

She explains how this simplifies the process, "*As an abstract painter, composition is sometimes an overwhelming challenge, so much so that thoughts about composing (and other formal elements) take precedence over other aspects of a painting, like newness, discovery, immediacy, and freshness. With a string, the composition happens almost effortlessly.*

The string sits in the background as a gentle guide from which to build your masterpiece. Because there is no need to keep thinking about what goes where, freshness and delight come alive with little effort."

Relax! There is no wrong way to draw a string. Unlike tangling, which is done deliberately, strings are drawn lightly and quickly without a lot of thought or planning. Pre-strung tiles are available if you do not want to draw your own. Or you can trace a shape or copy someone else's string. **Even when two or more people use the same string and the same tangles, each person's art is a reflection of his or her own unique self.**

In beginner classes, students start with the same string, usually a 'Z' shape. Inside your frame, draw your string. To follow along with your fellow students in this virtual class, draw a 'Z' or 'N' like the one shown on the tile to the left.

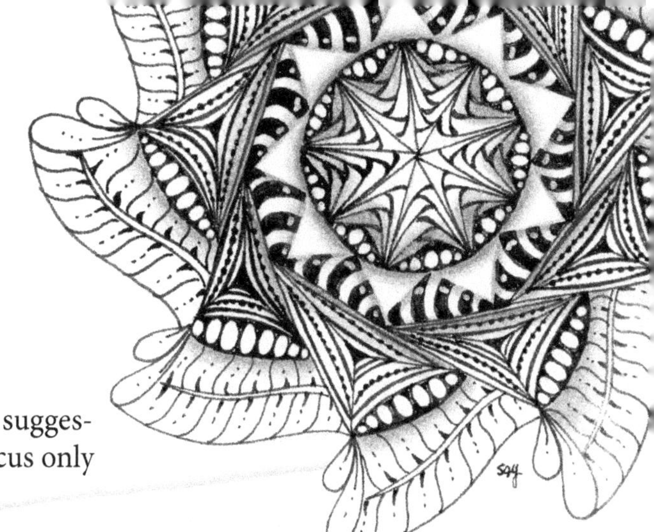

The string is drawn lightly because, as with the border, it is just a suggestion. As you fill the different sections in the next step, you can focus only on stroking your tangles. There is no need to stop to see if you have done enough. For artists who are used to constantly keeping in mind design, composition, and balance, it is so refreshing to be able to just create art without distractions. Simply continue until you reach the string. Since it is just a suggestion, you can cross the line if you wish.

Zentangle strings are like gentle alarm clocks: if you have to wake early, and do not have an alarm clock, you wake frequently in the night to check the time, so restful sleep becomes difficult. But, when you have a trusted alarm clock, you do not have to keep waking up to check the time. However, once it goes off, you can hit the snooze and go back to sleep. Similarly, when you get to the edge of a string, you do not have to stop. You can keep tangling if you want.

Even though strings are not erased, it is often difficult to find them once the tile is complete. They fade into the background, and only the artist can know for sure what it looked like in the beginning. As you look at the art in this book, try to discover the strings in various tiles. You may be surprised how hard they are to uncover.

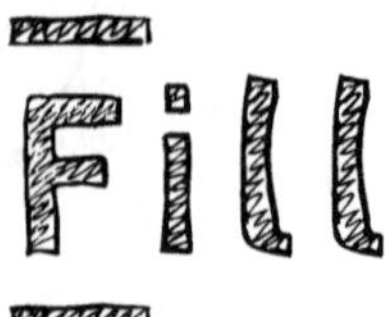

Step 4: Fill the sections with tangles.

This step is where the magic starts—when you forget your worries as you focus on the art you are creating. Your string is in place as a guide, so you are free to focus on each stroke and immerse yourself in the beauty of the automatically unfolding patterns.

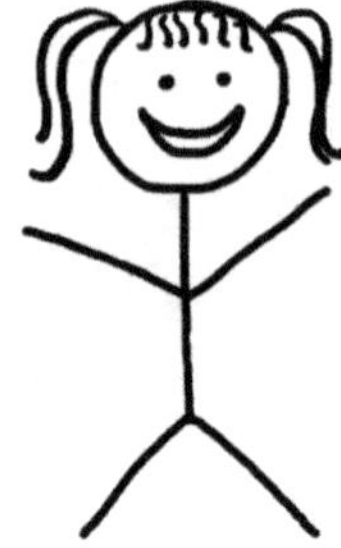

Because the finished results look so complicated, you may be surprised to find that they are simple to create. Every pattern is ***deconstructed*** into a few repeated strokes. The strokes are basic, those used in ordinary handwriting or in creating a simple stick figure. These strokes are then reassembled into a unique, specific sequence called a ***tangle***. Instructions that show the sequence of strokes to recreate each tangle are graphically represented in a step-out. ***Step-outs*** contain simple drawings and require little to no explanation. Follow the arrows and add the strokes shown and you can learn to draw any number of tangles with a little practice.*

- • Dots
- | Lines
- ( ) Curved lines
- O Orbs
- S Squiggles

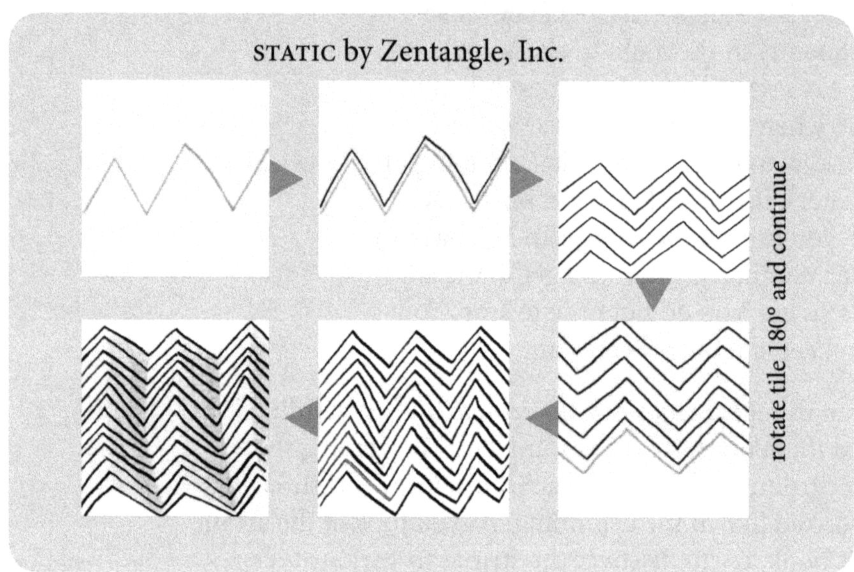

If you search online and find a "tangle" with more than six steps or that need explanations, proceed with caution. If there are many steps, or if the strokes are complicated, you may become frustrated instead of relaxed. Most true tangles have few steps and they all use simple strokes that are easy to draw. Not every pattern can be a tangle.

Pick a tangle, choose a section, and begin tangling. Do not labor over size or shape or making everything symmetrical. Simply focus on the beautiful ink flowing onto your tile until you reach the string and are gently reminded that this may be a place to change tangles (or not!). Be deliberate with your strokes, not tentative. Allow them to flow naturally. If your line is a bit wobbly, acknowledge it without judgment or attempts to correct it, and move on. By directing all of your attention to each stroke of the pen, you can release other thoughts and concerns. Do your best to let go of planning and judgment. (Be patient with yourself; this takes practice!) Let the final result be a surprise.

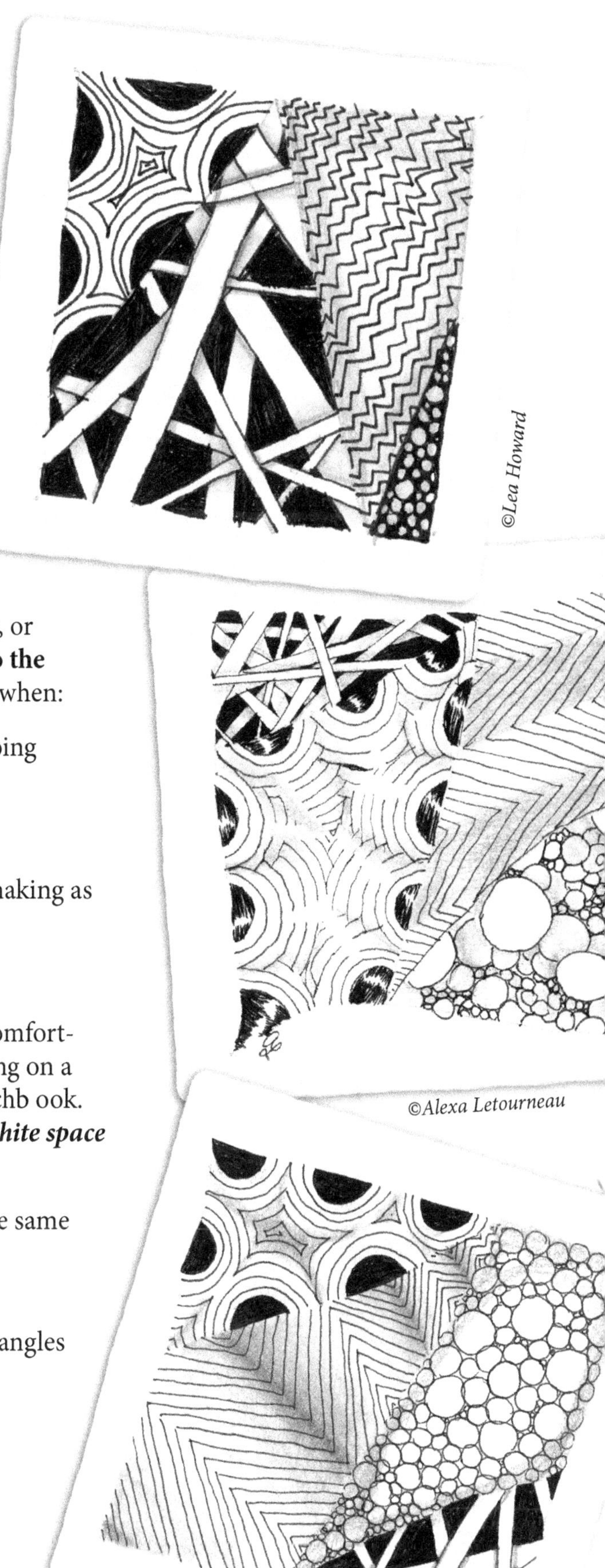

©Lea Howard

©Alexa Letourneau

To be truly present in the moment, you must move beyond expectations and focus only on each stroke as you are creating it. By doing so, you can achieve a state of relaxed focus, or ***mindfulness****. In this state, **you are actively paying attention to the moment you are living in**. You can tell you are in the moment when:

- Your mind is not off wandering while your hands are doing something else.
- You are not multitasking.
- You are actively paying attention to the marks you are making as you tangle.
- You are not judging, but simply being.

As you tangle, turn your tile in whatever direction feels most comfortable for you to draw. This is easy and natural to do when working on a small tile, but can be more challenging when working in a sketchb ook. It is not necessary to fill every section every time. Sometimes ***white space*** (empty space) is a nice resting spot for the eyes.

The examples above show different people's interpretation of the same four tangles: STATIC (as shown on the left), HOLLIBAUGH (page 54), CRESCENT MOON (page 58), and TIPPLE (page 50).

If you are participating in the virtual class, do these same four tangles on your tile.

**Mindfulness can help reduce stress-induced inflammation, which could benefit people suffering from chronic inflammatory conditions like rheumatoid arthritis, inflammatory bowel disease, and asthma. (Reference: articles.mercola.com, Dr. Mercola, 4/3/13)*

Shade

Step 5: Add interest and dimension with shading.

At the end of step 4, you may be tempted to declare your tile done, however, this is not the end. Now it is time to shade your tile. Once you see the wonderful effects you can achieve, you will never skip this step.

Shading is done with a pencil and, if desired, a smudging tool (i.e. a cotton swab, fingertip, or a paper stump). It can be as simple as adding a bit of gray as a third color for interest or as complex dramatic shading to add dimension, contrast, and movement. Tangle step-outs usually have shading ideas included, but these are only suggestions. Feel free to shade your tangle as you see fit.

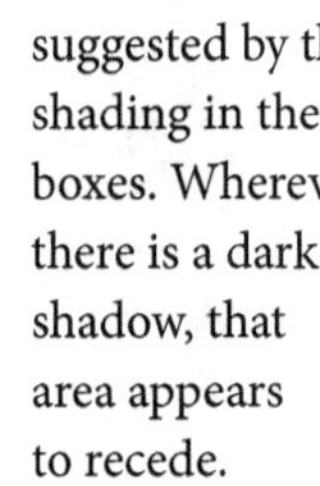

Note the different dimension suggested by the shading in the boxes. Wherever there is a dark shadow, that area appears to recede.

You do not have to learn a lot of rules to begin shading, but it helps to understand a few basic concepts:

- Darker colors tend to recede; adding shadow to a part of a tangle will make it look like it is sinking down into your tile.
- Soft-edge shadows on objects (form shadows) look more natural than hard-edge shadows.
- Just as there is no up or down, right or left in Zentangle art, there is no need for a consistent light source.

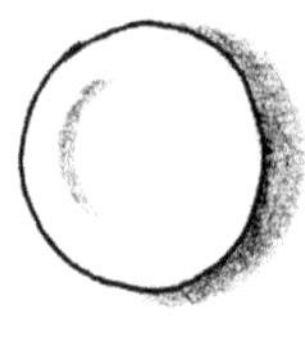

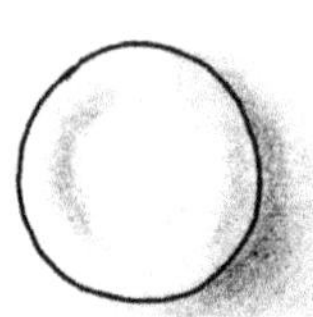

Shadows can have a hard edge (top) or soft edge (bottom). Most tanglers use a soft-edged shadow, but feel free to explore both to find your preference.

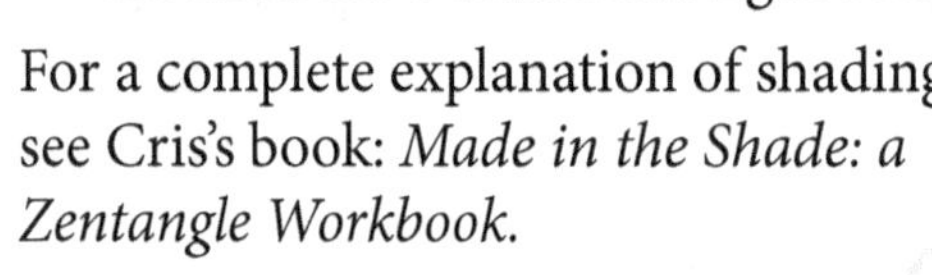

For a complete explanation of shading, see Cris's book: *Made in the Shade: a Zentangle Workbook.*

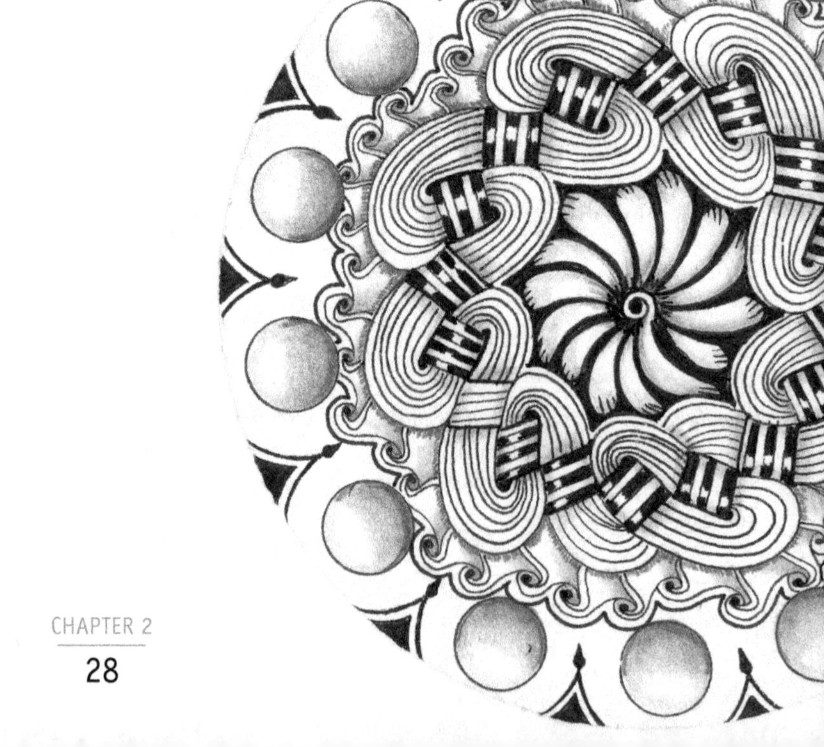

Finish

Step 6: Sign and reflect.

Always sign your art. It shows that you value your creative process. Begin by putting your initials on the front. Since a Zentangle tile has no up or down, hold it at arm's length and turn it in each direction to choose where to place your initials. See what a huge impact a little change in perspective can make.

As you continue on your Zentangle journey, you may develop a stylized way to draw your initials, like branding livestock to identify the owner. In Asian countries, such a signature seal is colloquially called a ***chop***. These signature seals are used to sign art and important documents. Interestingly, chops often have a mark designating the preferred orientation of the piece. This is left out of a Zentangle chop since there is no top or bottom.

If you are using a tile or other small paper, turn it over and sign your name and write the date on the back. Consider writing a comment or two about the piece or anything special that was happening when you drew it. You can then use your tiles as a visual journal. Over time, you will enjoy looking back on your collection of tiles, remembering events, and appreciating how your style has evolved.

Before you turn your tile back over, let go of judgment. When you look at the front again, take a moment to appreciate what you have done and be thankful for the opportunity to have created something beautiful. As you turn your tile and examine it, you may be surprised by what has revealed itself in your art.

Now, if you have made a tile, add it to the virtual class mosaic on the following pages.

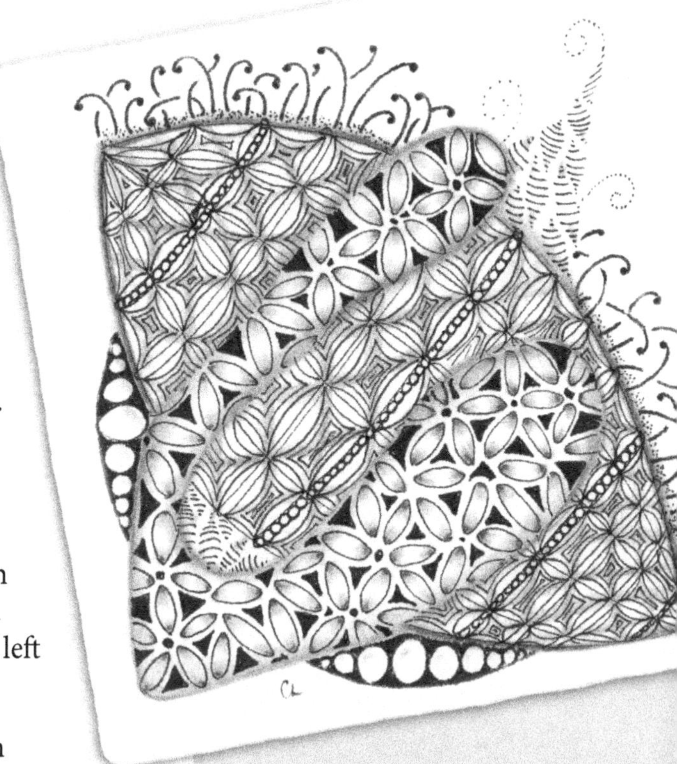

THE ESSENCE OF ALL BEAUTIFUL **ART**, ALL GREAT ART, IS GRATITUDE.

~ Friedrich Nietzsche

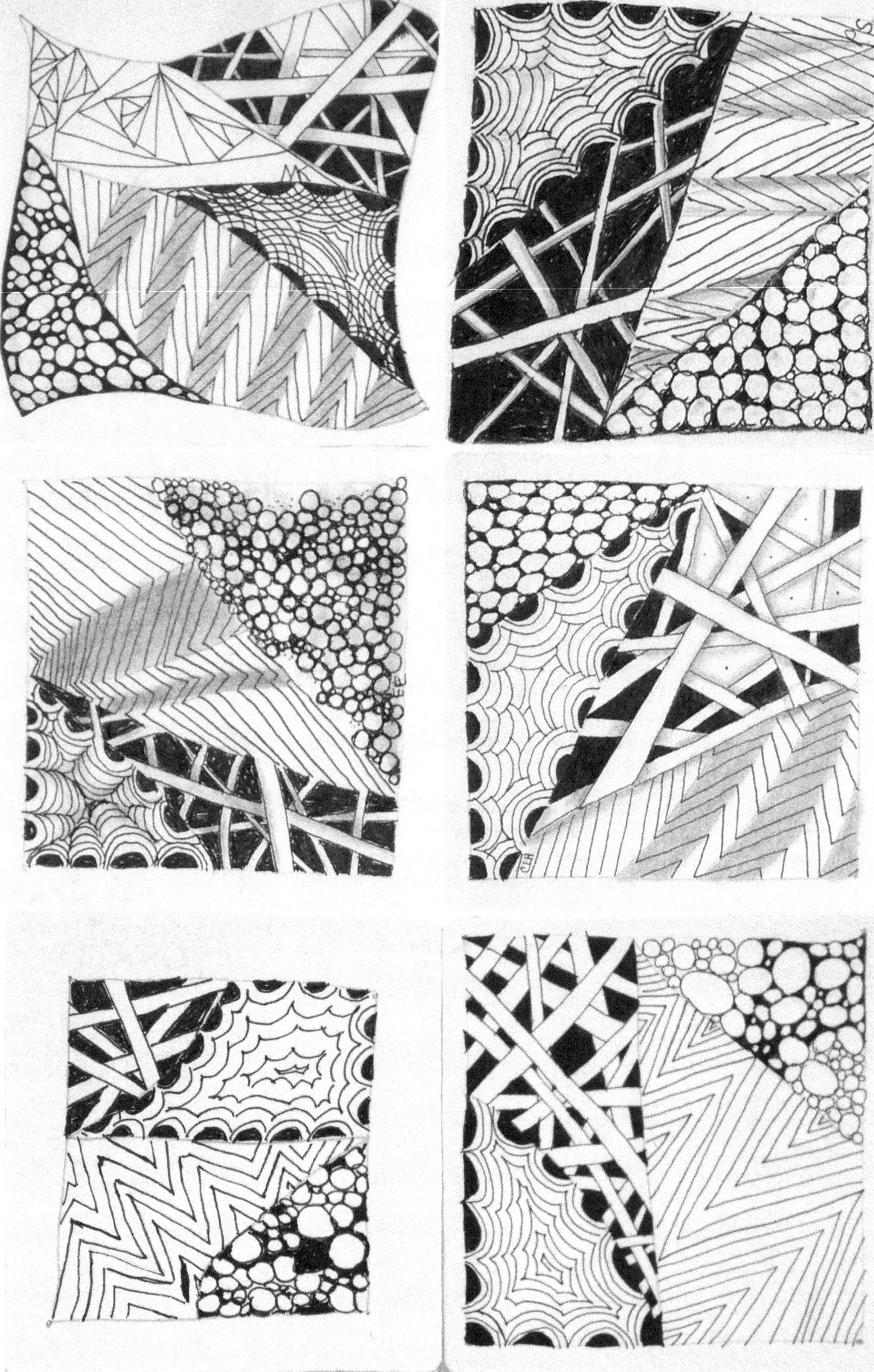

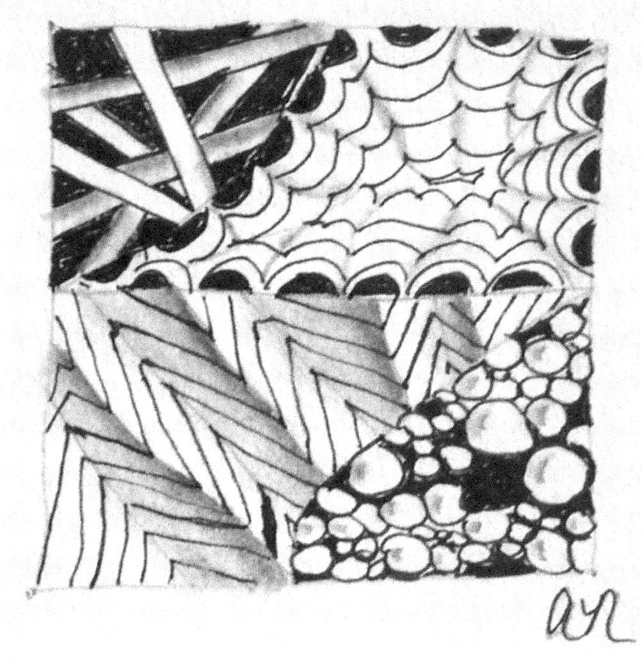

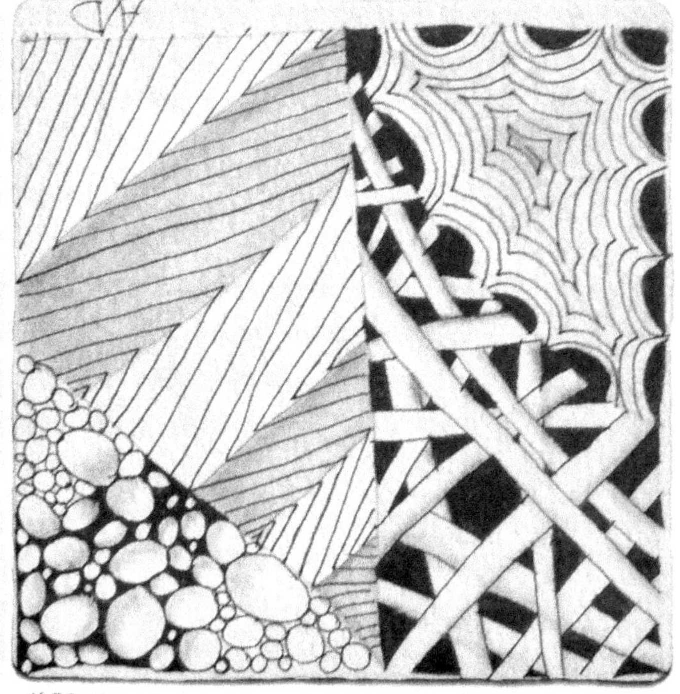

PUT YOUR TILE HERE IN THIS VIRTUAL CLASS MOSAIC.

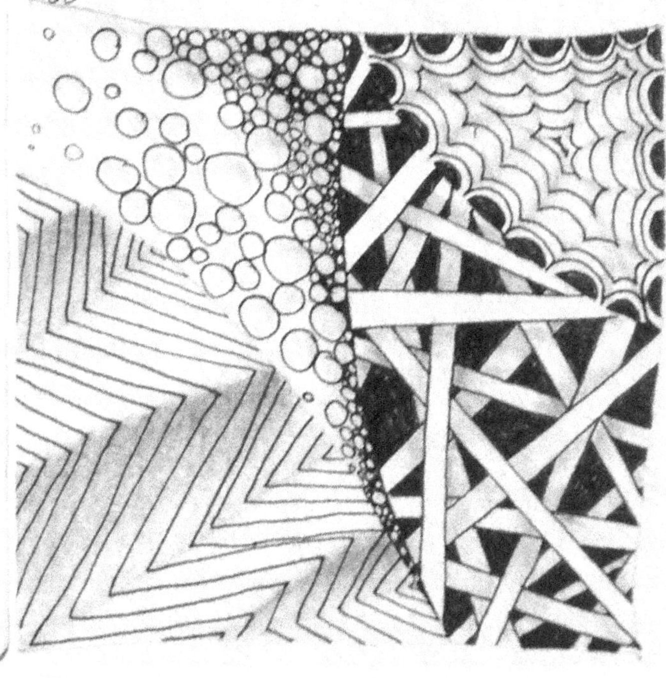

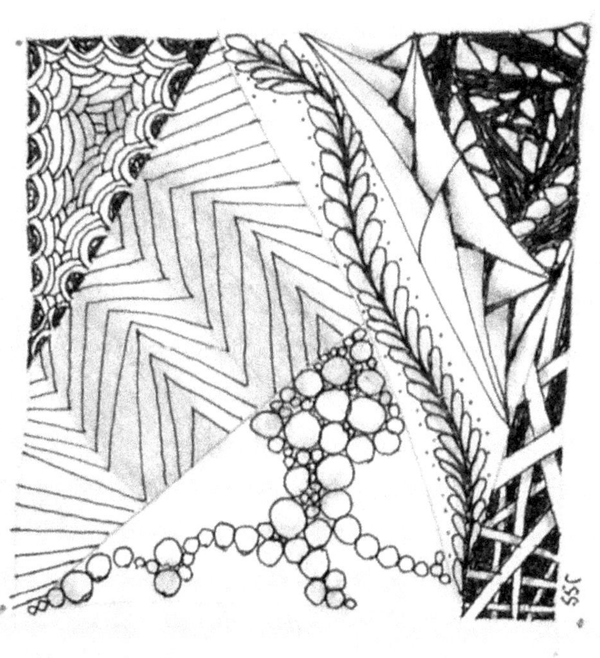

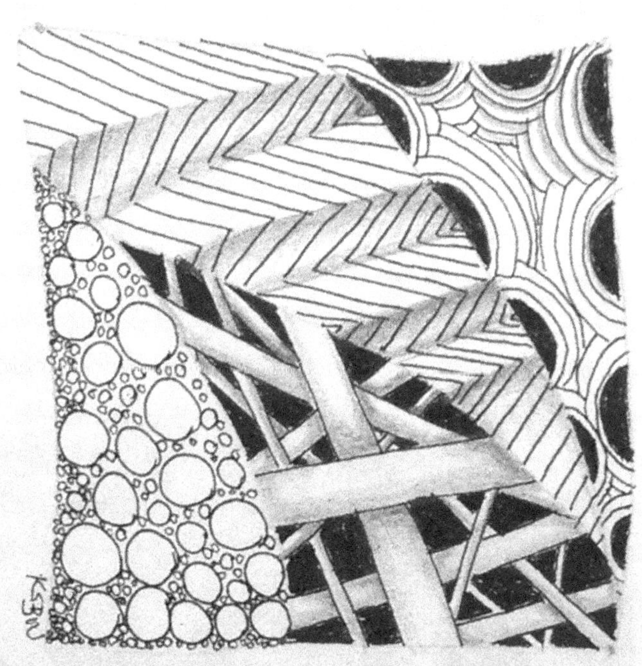

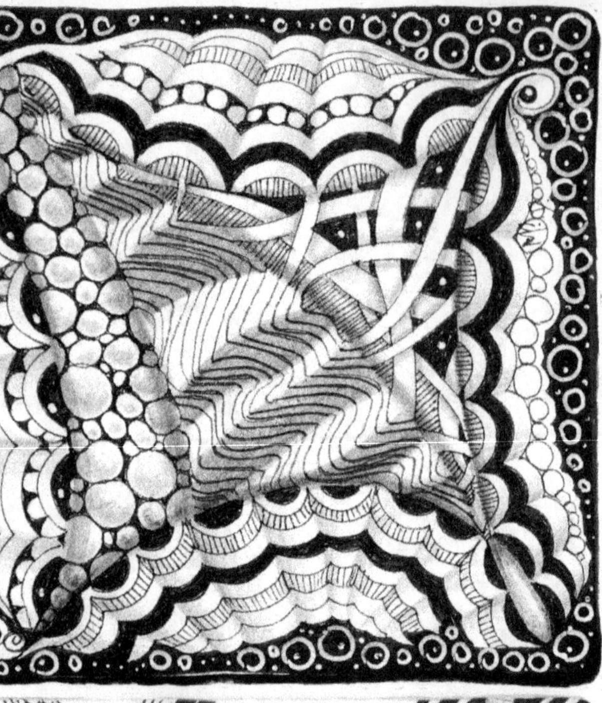

©Marty Deckel

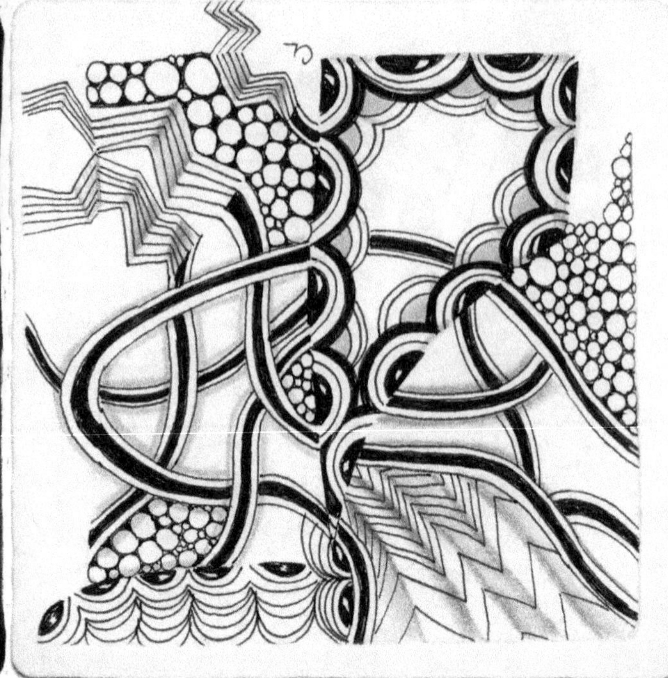

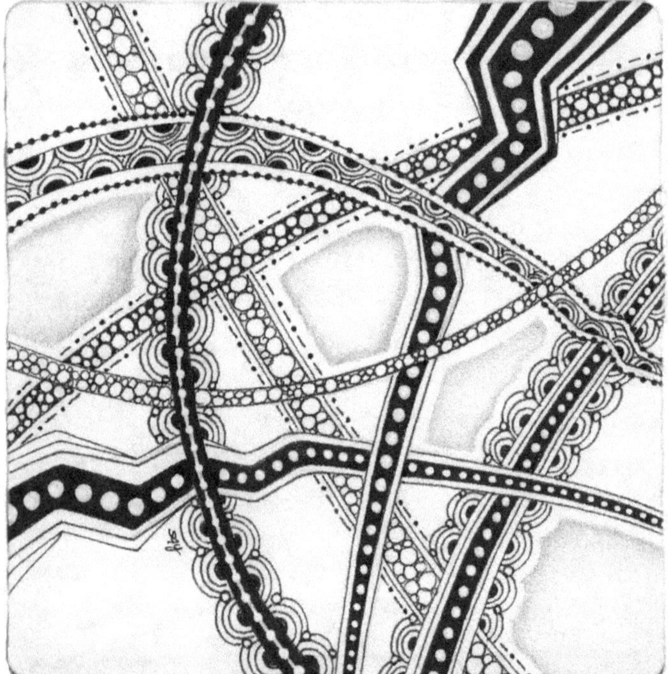

SEASONED TANGLERS TACKLE THE SAME TANGLES.

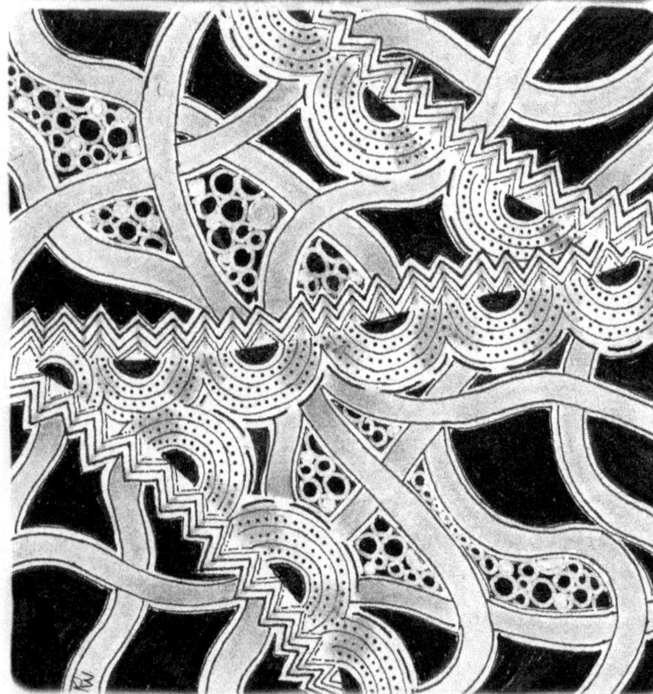

©Patti Wilburn

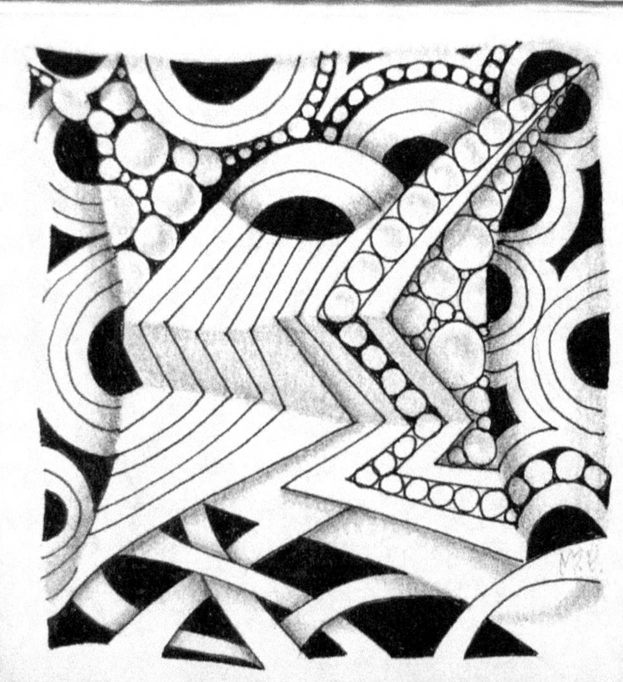

©Marty Deckel

CHAPTER 3

UNTANGLING TANGLEATIONS

New students walk out of a Zentangle 101 class excited and eager to learn all they can about the new world of Zentangle. They often think the best way to accomplish this is to gather and master more and more patterns. We urge you to resist the temptation of collecting patterns, at least for a while. Too many choices can steal your zen. CZT Sinda Wood tells her students, "*It is the zen that is so important, not more designs to draw.*"

tan-gle-a-tion
(tan-gəl-ā-shən)
noun

1. **A noticeable variation of an existing tangle.**
2. **Adding your own personality to a tangle.**

Before learning any more tangles, we invite you to explore this chapter and learn about tangleations. Tangleations are a valuable tool to help you develop your own style. CZT Beckah Krahula says that tangleations are the key to unlocking a tangle's full potential.

Compare the tiles on these pages, created by seasoned tanglers, with the mosaic on page 31. Can you believe they all use the same simple Z string and tangles?

Notice the variations in pen strokes, combination of patterns, and shading techniques. Your personal style will evolve as you learn and practice, giving your art character and personality. These differences of expression are celebrated and are part of what makes tangling so interesting. While it takes time to learn all of the techniques demonstrated here, this chapter presents tools to start you on your journey. **Use it as a springboard to fuel your exploration.**

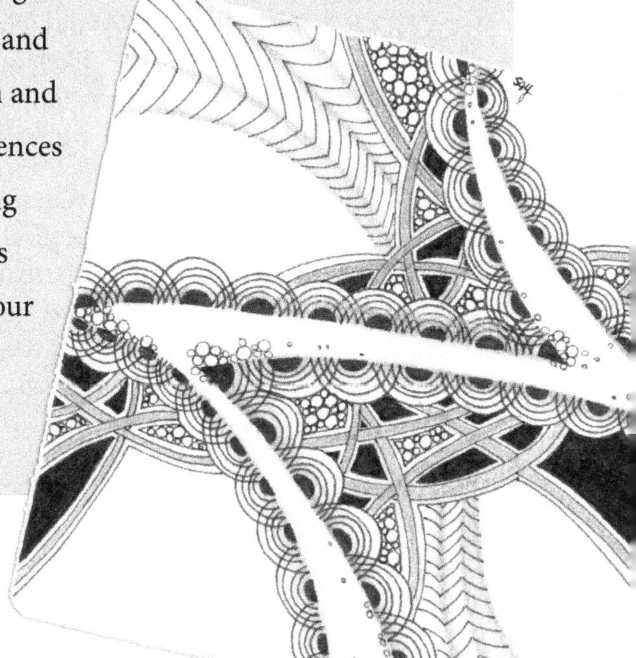

THERE ARE NO RULES.

THERE IS NO JUDGMENT.

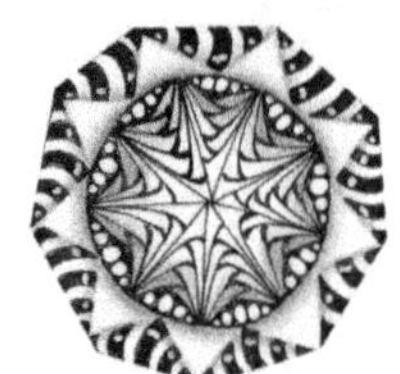

THERE ARE NO TANGLE POLICE.

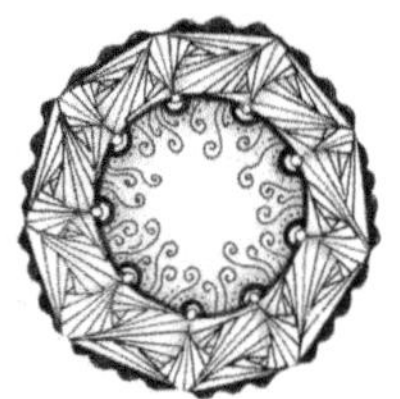

TANGLES, TANGLEATIONS, AND TANGOS. OH, MY!

Tangles are named patterns that have been deconstructed into a series of elemental strokes so that they can be created one stroke at a time. They are named to make it is easier to share and discuss your art. Instead of saying, "*I like that curvy thing you did in the middle,*" you can say, "*I like your* MOOKA." Tangle names are intentionally non-representational so you can use your imagination when drawing them.

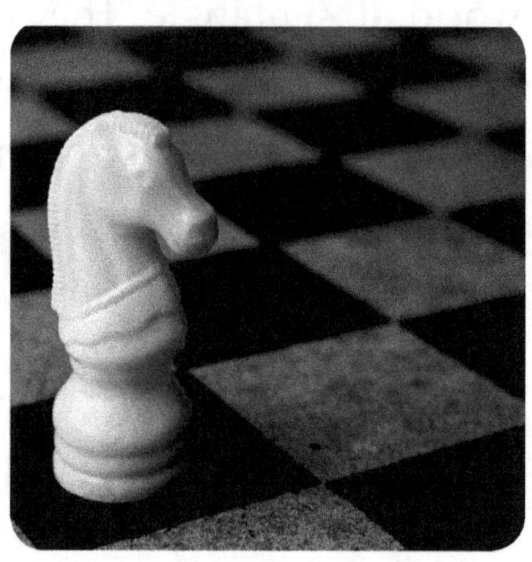

*You **do not** draw a chessboard, which has a precise definition: 64 perfect squares in rows of 8, alternating black white.*

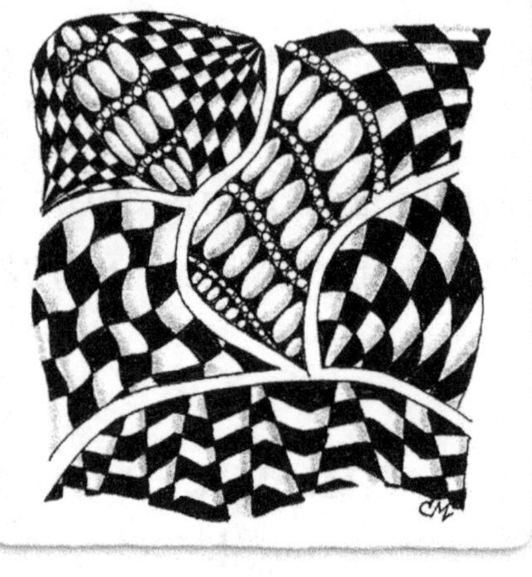

©Caren Mlot

*Instead, you **tangle** KNIGHTSBRIDGE (PAGE 46). You get to decide if your squares are perfect, how many there are, and how to fill them!*

If you try to draw a chessboard, you would probably need a ruler or graph paper. These are not necessary for the Zentangle Method, because just as chess knights* do not move in a straight line, neither do the strokes used in tangling.

If you want your KNIGHTSBRIDGE to have curvy lines and random black and white squares, no one can tell you it is wrong. Instead, they will likely say, "That is a cool ***tangleation***. I wish I had thought of it!" Doing a tangle your own way is not a mistake! It is a tangleation, and it is something we encourage.

When Rick and Maria introduced the term tangleation, they quite accurately predicted, "*This will no doubt inspire lengthy classification discussions around Zentangle dinner tables as to what is a new tangle and what is 'just' a tangleation.*" We cannot vouch for dinner tables, but there continue to be many discussions on CZT mailing lists and Facebook pages debating this question.

* *Knights are the horses in chess (pictured above). They move in an "L" shape: two squares in one direction and one in the other.*

A tangleation is structurally based on the original tangle; in other words, it has the same fundamental approach, but it looks different. The question usually arises as to when the differences are great enough to merit a new name. There is no definitive answer to this question. It is a matter of opinion. As Edmond Burke says, *"It is the nature of greatness to not be exact."*

Tangleations can be formed by combining two tangles. In this case, they are called a ***tango****, because it is as if the two tangles are dancing with each other. We used tangos as borders on many of the sketchbook pages in Chapter 4, as shown below.

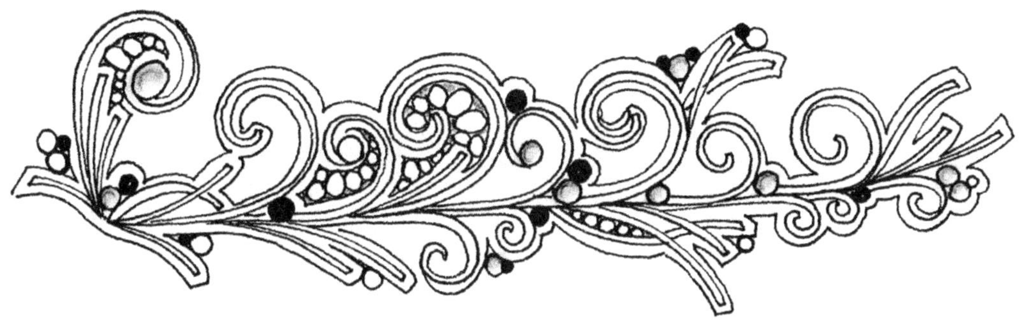

(above) OPUS *and* VERDIGOGH
(below) MI2 *and* HOLLIBAUGH

Tangleations are empowering!

Despite the repeated insistence of CZTs, some students still feel as if they are doing something wrong when their tangle looks different from the teacher's example. When the teacher sees the student's unexpected result and announces to the class, *"Hey, look at this beautiful tangleation!"* their shame turns to pride. CZT Laura Harms, better known as "the Diva," says it this way: "One of the wonderful parts of Zentangle is how it is always growing and changing to become something beautiful and new. Part of the way this happens is through tangleations or variations of tangles."

Tangleations inspire us to celebrate our creativity. It is another tool that Rick and Maria gave us to help us relax as we tangle. **The possibility of creating a new tangleation means that the pressure to conform to someone else's interpretation is gone.**

* *Alternately, tangoes are referred to as entangled tangles.*

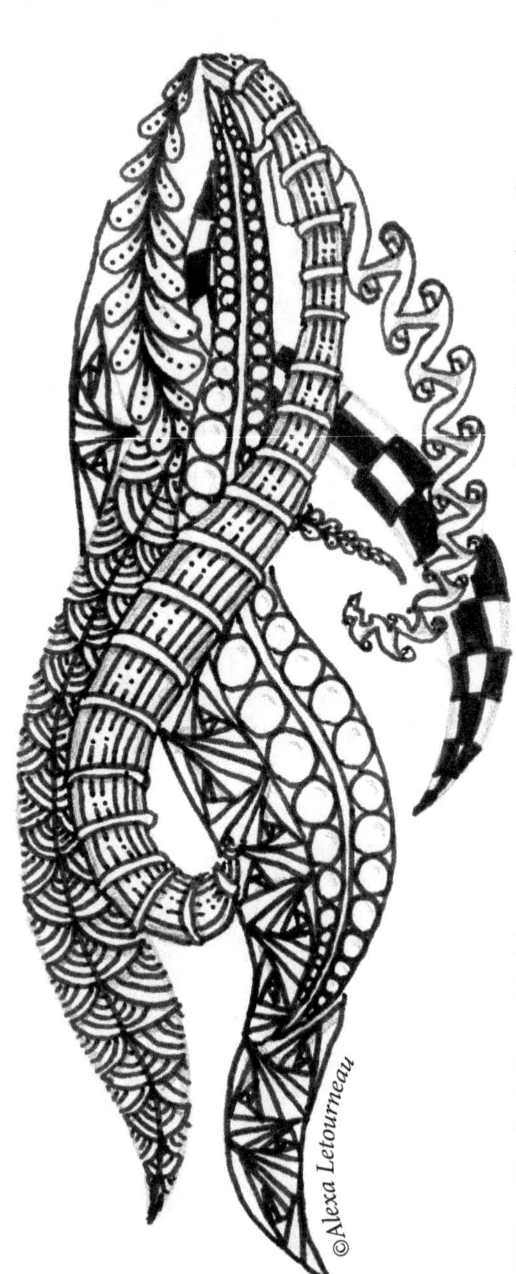

CREATIVITY IS CRUCIAL

A quick Internet search shows hundreds of citations on the importance of creativity. Article after article stresses that creativity is not only for artists, but also for business professionals, and for people in the business of living. It is a critical part of everyday life. Dr. Amanda Alders Pike provides a thoughtful summary:

*7 Ways that Creativity Enhances Lives**

- Provides a novel and fun way for people to socialize
- Stimulates the brain to think up original ideas
- Gives a sense of pride in having a finished product
- Makes people feel like part of a community
- Uses images to aid communication
- Exercises fine and gross motor skills
- Relieves stress and focuses attention on here and now

Be creative today and every day. It is important for your brain activity, your general health, and your emotional well being!

SAY YES TO TANGLEATIONS!

There are many reasons why people do not create tangleations. Most fit into one of the following three categories:

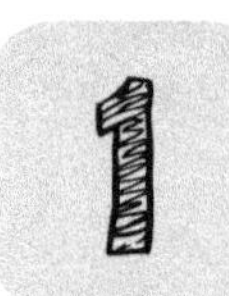

They need permission.

Some tanglers do not truly believe that they are allowed to deviate from the patterns. They assume that the tangles are supposed to be drawn the exact way they are taught, and it never occurs to them to change the design. If you have read this far, we hope you have taken our words to heart and that this is no longer an obstacle for you.

You still might have to practice letting go of expectations and giving yourself permission to think outside the box (or string), but knowing that there are no Zentangle judges waiting to tell you did something the wrong way should quiet your own inner critic's negativity.

* *Alders Pike, A. (2013). Digital Newsletter: September. http://eepurl.com/EjRi5, used with permission.*

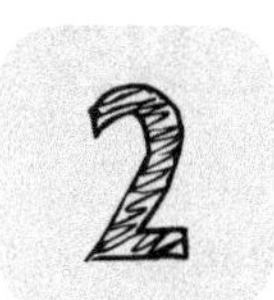

They are afraid.

While some people regularly nurture their creative spirit, others are so vulnerable to criticism that they are afraid to try anything new. They are paralyzed by fear of failure. They may have been beaten down by criticism to the point that they have forgotten that creativity even resides inside them. Fear inhibits their capacity to find their zen and express themselves genuinely.

People have different needs for variety and consistency, freedom and control. Some are content to recreate a tangle exactly as they were taught. They find pleasure in consistency and are uncomfortable starting down a path when they do not know where it will lead. By contrast, others thrive on variety and are happy to do things differently every time. They are energized by the exploration of new things and embracing the unknown.

While there is nothing wrong with drawing a tangle the same way every time, people who add their own twist often say that this is part of what makes tangling so much fun. The freedom and self-expression that comes from breaking the rules is empowering although not always easy to do. It takes trust in your own creativity to allow yourself to conquer the fear of the unknown and believe that it is okay if things turn out differently than you had planned.

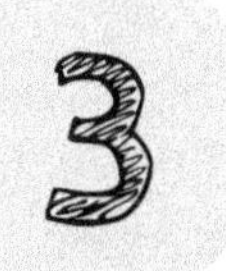

They do not know how.

Just as some people can play an instrument by ear, others need lessons. Both can make beautiful music! The same can be said of creating tangleations; for some it comes naturally while others need instruction.

Tangleations are born in a variety of ways. Some occur unintentionally. Eager beginners start to work before the teacher finishes demonstrating. Experienced tanglers try a tangle they have not used in a while and do not quite remember the steps. Distractions cause artists to go off in unexpected directions. Sometimes they are the result of going with the flow and seeing where it leads you. Creating tangleations may also be intentional, especially if you are creating a ***monotangle*** (a piece of art using only one tangle) and are exploring variations in a single pattern.

Learning to make tangleations requires a thorough understanding of the tangle, a willingness to let go of expectations, and giving yourself permission to think outside the box. As with any creative endeavor, this can take some practice, but the rewards are well worth it.

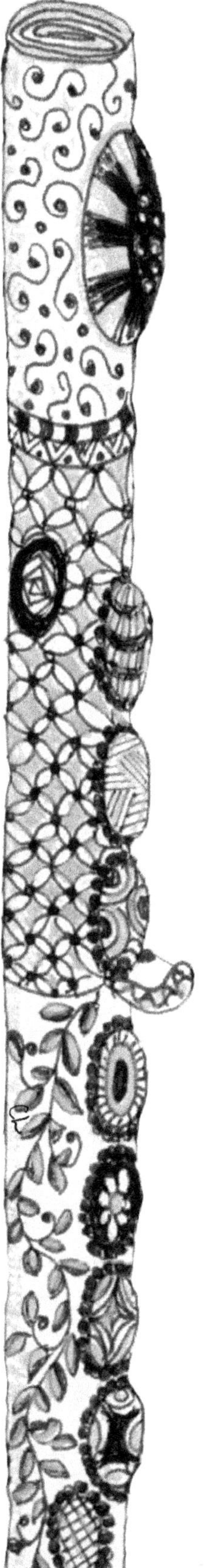

DECONSTRUCTING TANGLEATIONS

Tangleations are created the same way as any other tangle: one stroke at a time. Instead of looking at a tangle and wondering what to change, deconstruct it first. This means to take it apart and break it down into its elemental strokes. Luckily, tangles come that way!

FLUKES
by Zentangle, Inc.

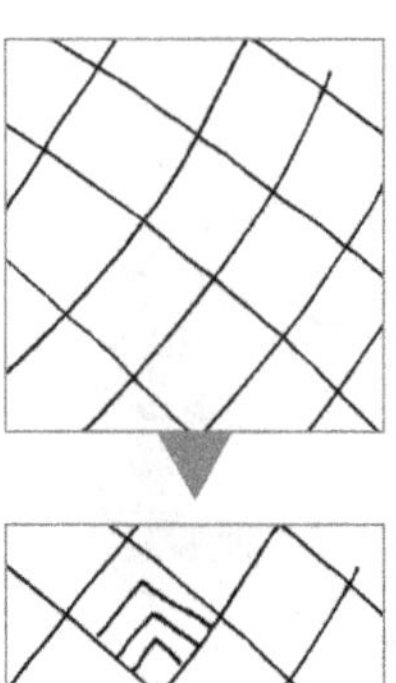

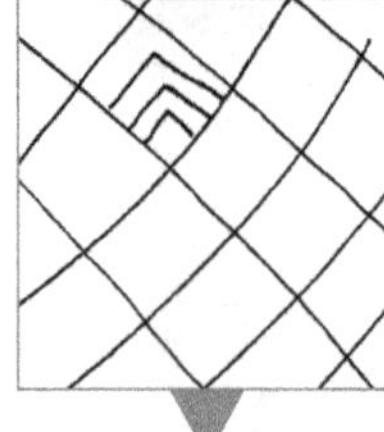

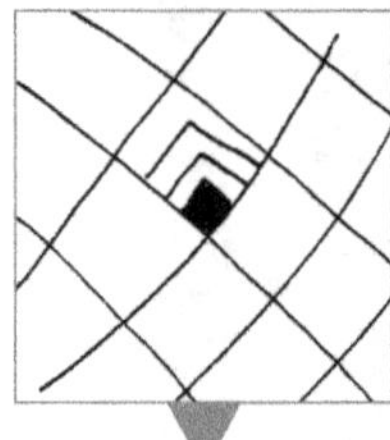

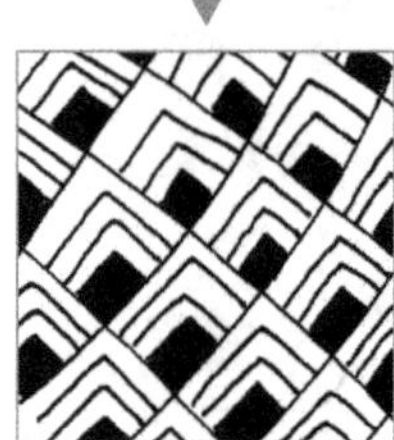

Take FLUKES for example. Examine the step-outs (far left). It has three basic elements: a large square formed by the grid, a small black square, and a series of L-shaped bent lines. We will examine each element in turn to see how even a slight change can make a big difference in the overall appearance of the tangle.

DIFFERENT STROKES FOR DIFFERENT FOLKS

We will start by playing with the simplest element: the L-shaped bent lines. You may be surprised how many ways you can change those lines.

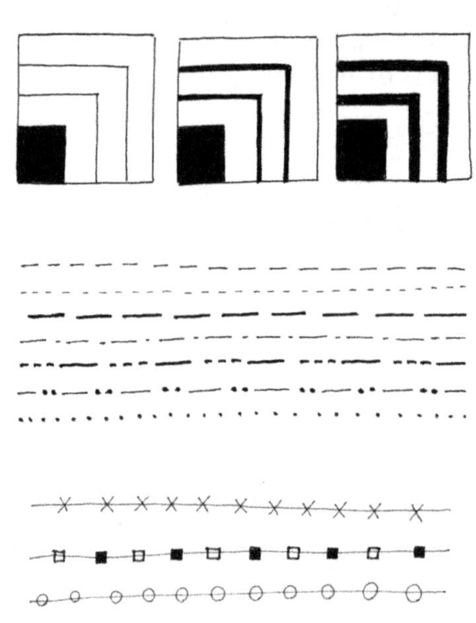

It can be as simple as using a thicker or thinner pen or varying the pressure of your stroke to change the ***weight*** (thickness) of your line.

How about changing the line style? Make it dashed, dotted, or a combination of both. Clearly, there is no end to the variations you can create by a simple change in the line appearance.

Try adding embellishments to your lines. Perhaps dots or X's or squares. Any variety of small elements can really alter the visual effect.

You can even double them up. Keep both strokes the same or mix and match.

Note the impact of these changes on the look of a square of FLUKES.

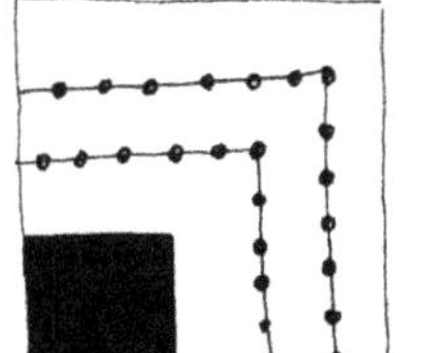
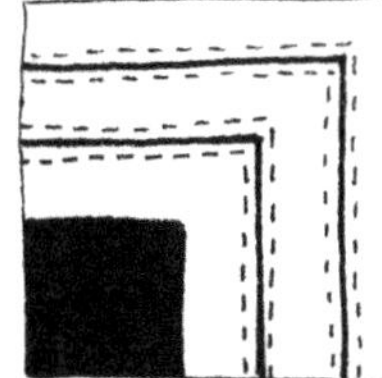
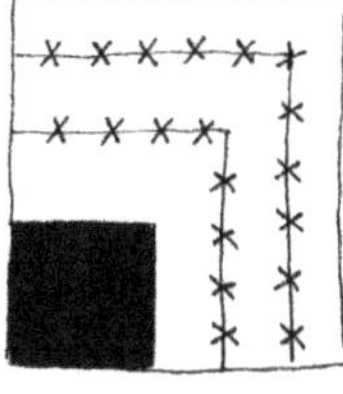
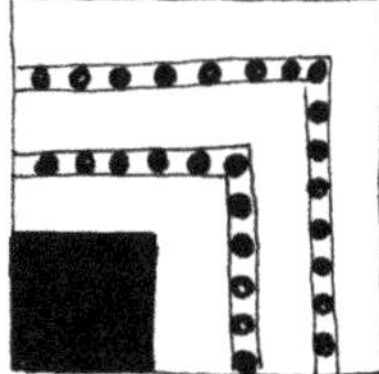

By combining different line techniques, you can really change FLUKES and give it your unique flair. A small change to a single line may not be noticeable, but apply that same tiny change to many lines and watch how they all add up. The difference can be subtle or dramatic, depending on the choices you make. Try your hand at some tangleations to complete the grid below.

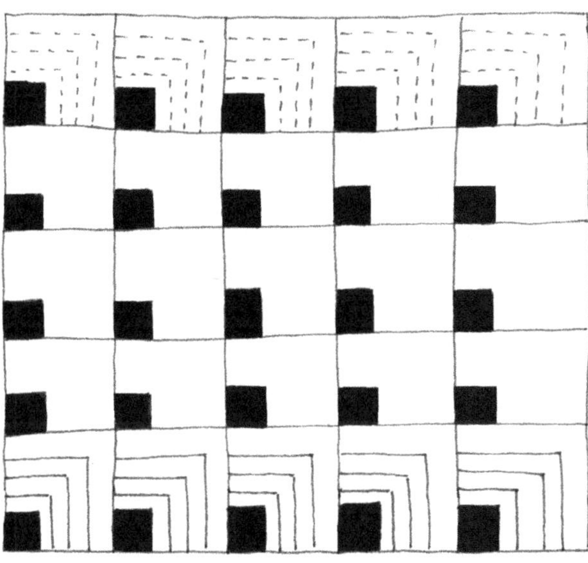

Look for more inspiration in the monotangle at the right that features many creative tangleations of FLUKES.

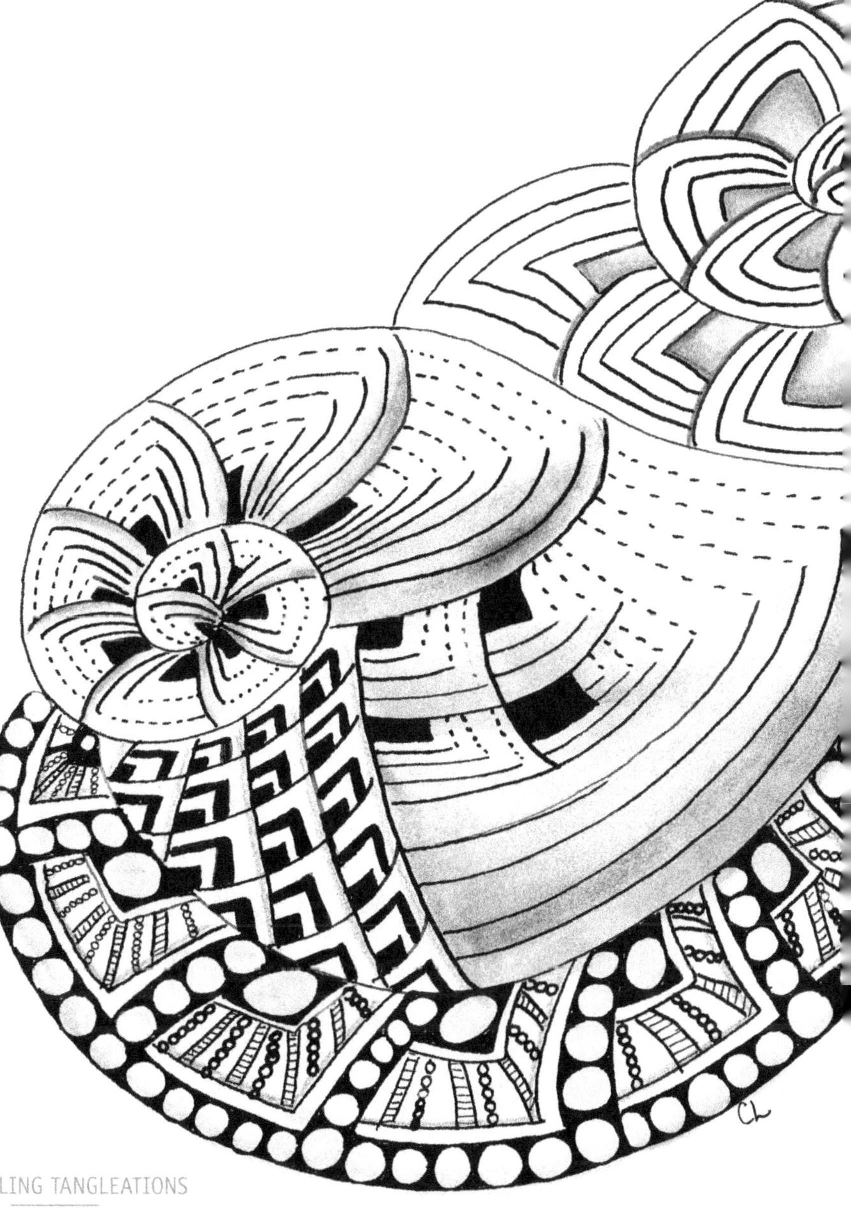

FILL 'ER UP

When one section of a tangle is darker than others, it will draw your eye toward it. In art terms, this is called the ***focal point***. In FLUKES, the solid black square is an attention-grabber so a small change to it can make a big difference in the overall look of the finished piece.

Have fun when you change fill patterns. Try stripes, polka-dots, different shading techniques, and maybe even small versions of a tangle. Here are a few ideas to get you started:

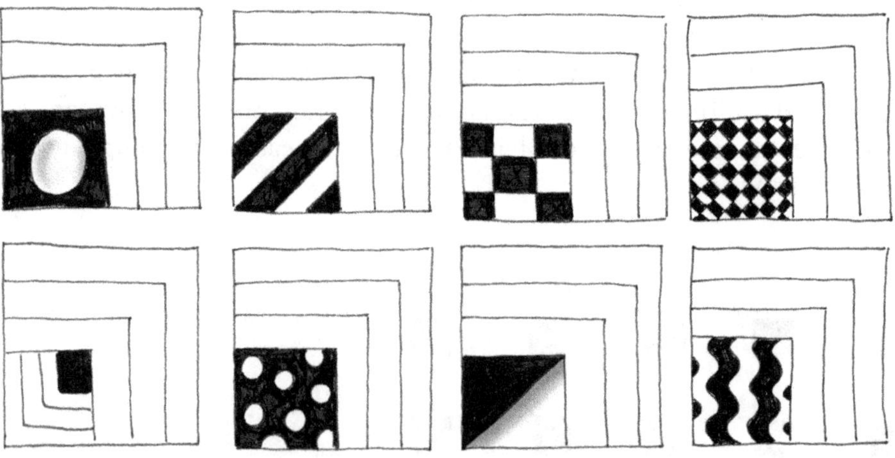

You can use the same fill pattern for each square or use a variety in the same piece of artwork. This opens another area of limitless possibilities. Will you alternate the fill patterns in checkerboard fashion, apply them in rows for a striped effect, or place them randomly?

Your turn!

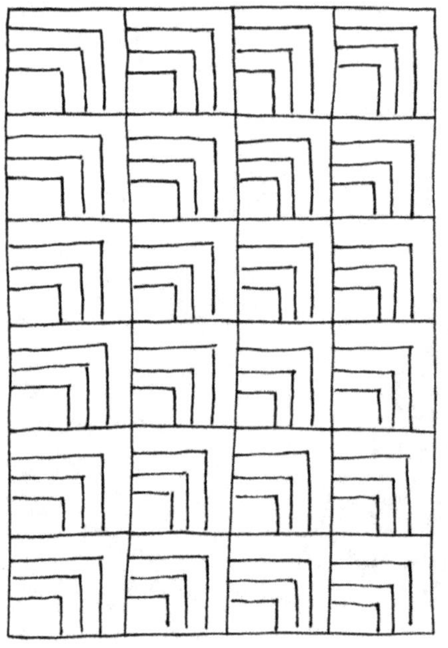

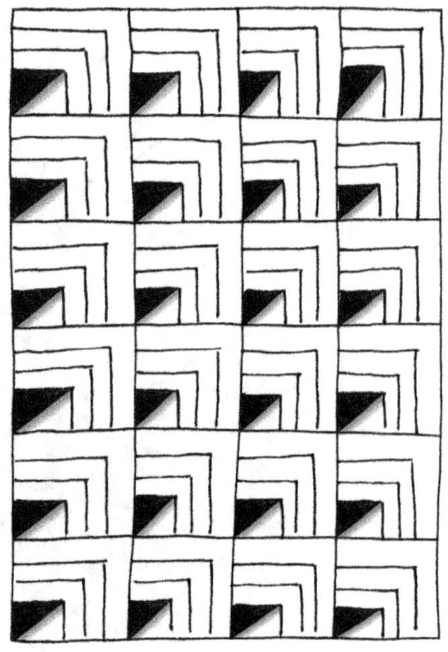

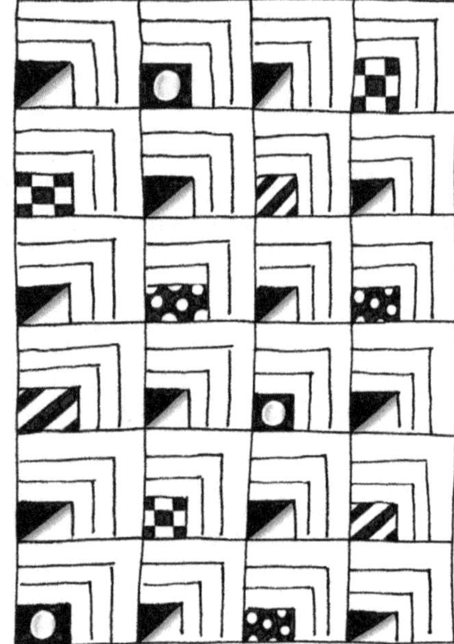

UNLOCK THE GRID

The final element that can be changed in this tangle is the large squares making up the grid. Because grids do not have to consist of straight lines and right angles, you are free to curve the lines, change how close together or far apart they are, and draw the lines at any angle you wish.

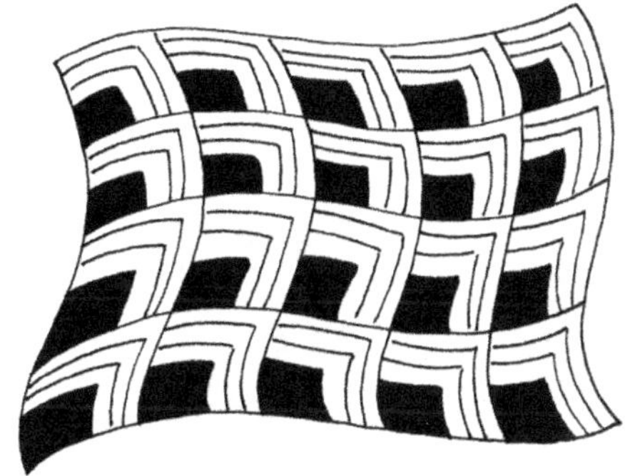

A few subtle curves can give an illusion of movement.

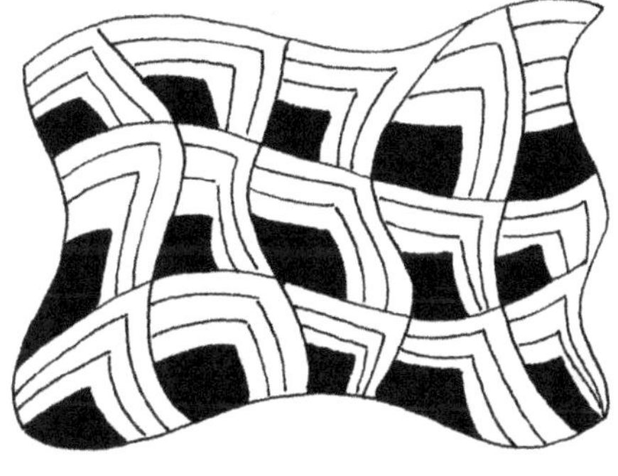

Exaggerated, uncontrolled curves simulate chaos.

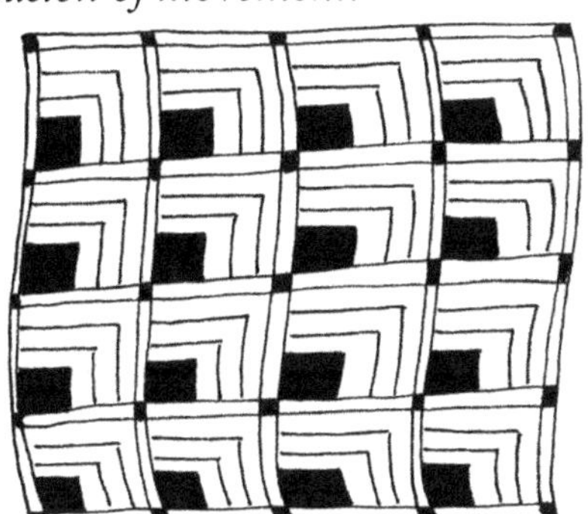

Using a double line grid adds another level of detail.

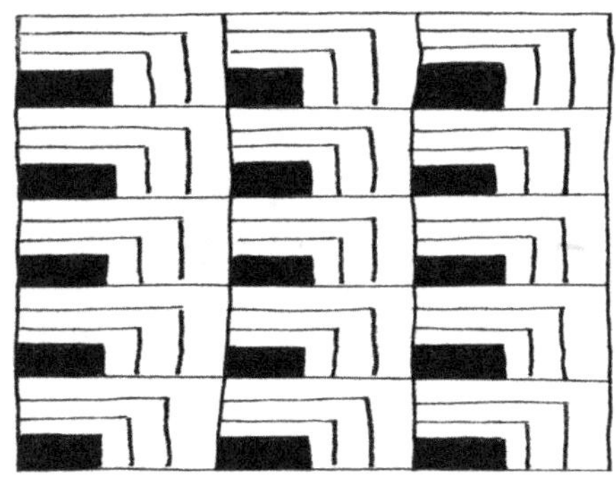

Spreading the lines further apart in one direction forms rectangles.

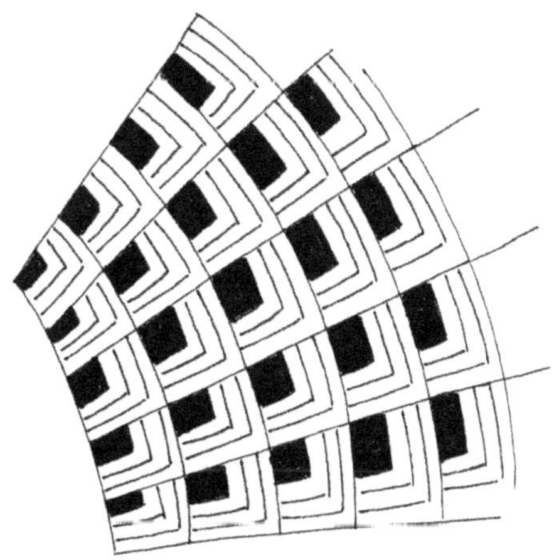

Combining divergent and curved lines makes the pattern appear to be expanding.

All of the changes demonstrated so far are confined to a single element. But, **there is no rule that says you can only change one element at a time**. Explore combining different grids, fill patterns, and line styles for something easy, fun, and different.

Use the space in the margins to see what you can do.

KICKING IT UP A NOTCH

When changing multiple elements of a tangle simultaneously, it helps to think of how the parts of the tangle relate to each other in terms of ***scale*** (size), spacing, and position. Dramatic differences can be created when you experiment with these changes.

Look at what happens when you vary the scale of the black square and spacing of the L-shaped lines.

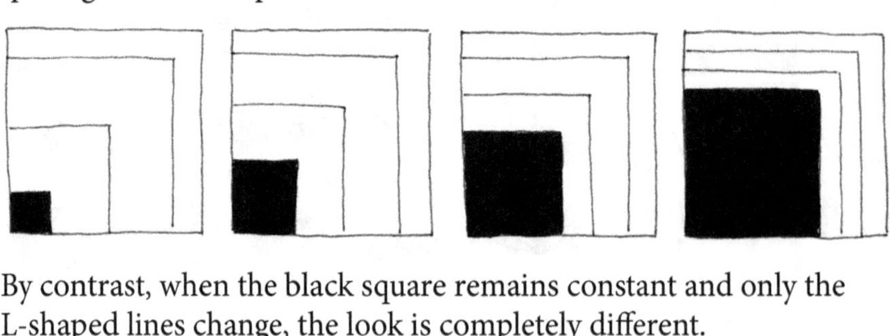

By contrast, when the black square remains constant and only the L-shaped lines change, the look is completely different.

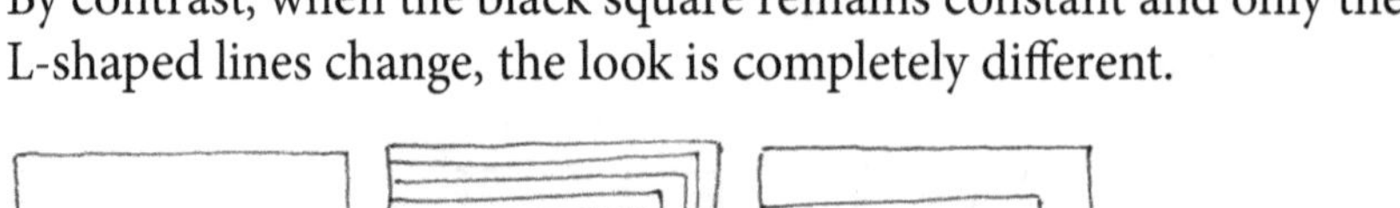

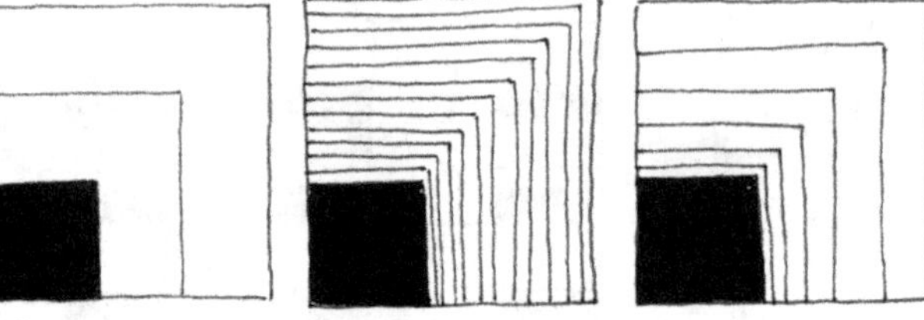

You can also make changes that are more structural. Why not change the shape of the black square to something new?

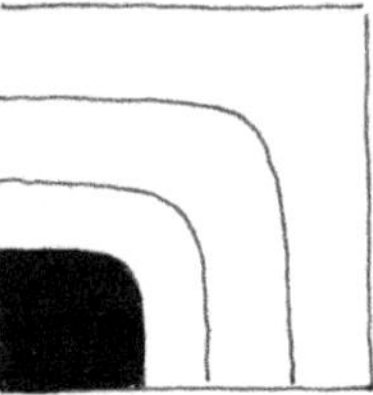

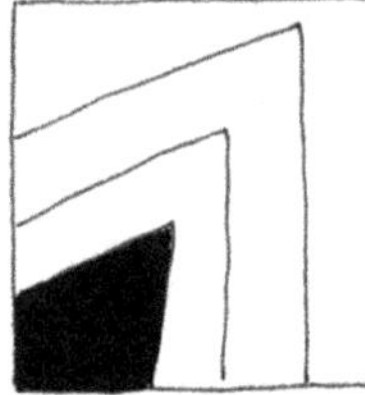

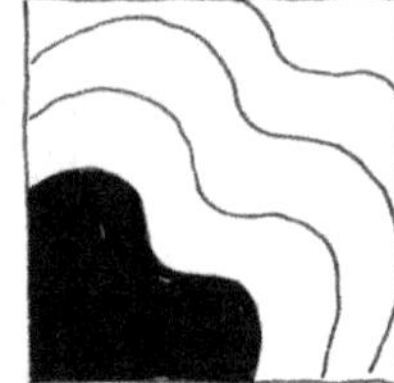

Last, but not least, what if you rotated the pattern within the grid or even removed the grid altogether for free floating FLUKES?

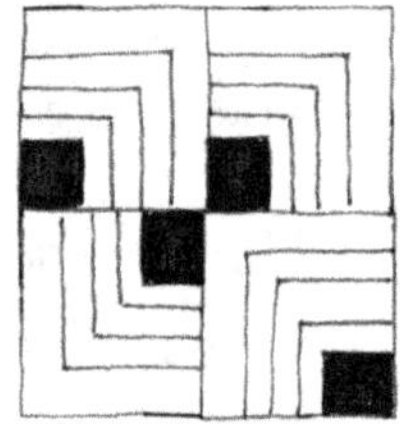

At this point, you are probably creating a new tangle rather than a tangleation, but the process and result are the same: **you have now successfully used your creativity to create a unique piece of art in your own unique style.**

SPICING THINGS UP WITH AURAS

There are six ***tanglenhancers*** (techniques to enhance a tangle) defined by Rick and Maria: shading, auras, rounding, perfs, dewdrops, and sparkles. Here, we will focus on possibly the most popular one: auras.

While tanglers are often familiar with auras, it seems that the word can mean something different from person to person. During our research, we were delighted by the origin of the word. Aura comes from the Greek meaning breath of air. If you want to give your tangles a breath of fresh air, try using an aura.

In Zentangle art, an ***aura*** is a halo or outline of an object. CZT Emily Classon explains, "*I think it is helpful to think of an aura as the ripples created by skipping a stone across a river. Each line mimics and expands the shape.*"

- Have a tangle that you want to show off? Add a couple of auras to enlarge it.

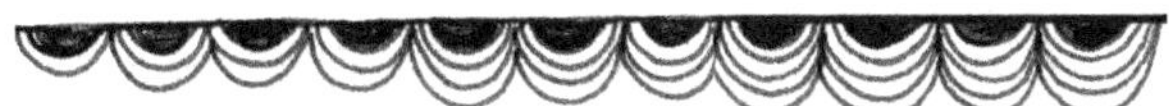

- Want a light and airy look? Keep your auras delicate and further apart. Maybe use dotted or dashed lines.

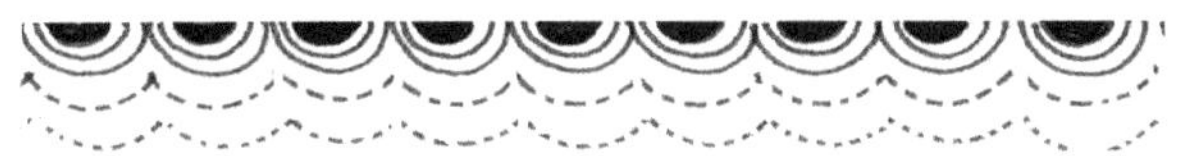

- Looking for something bolder? Fill in every other aura with one of the following or make up your own: solid black, checkerboard pattern, tiny lines, or dots.

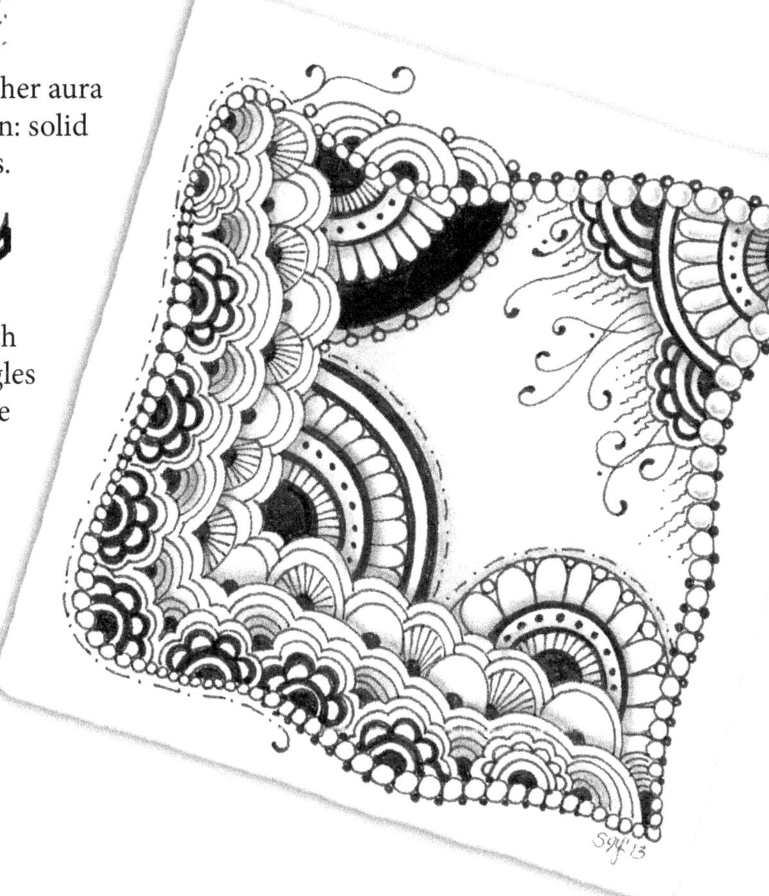

Some tangles have auras as part of their step-outs, such as AURAKNOT and CRESCENT MOON, but even the tangles can be enhanced by additional auras! Look at all of the ways auras are used to beautify CRESCENT MOON in this tile. It is difficult to think of a tangle that cannot use an aura or two (or a dozen) to change the look and add your own personal signature.

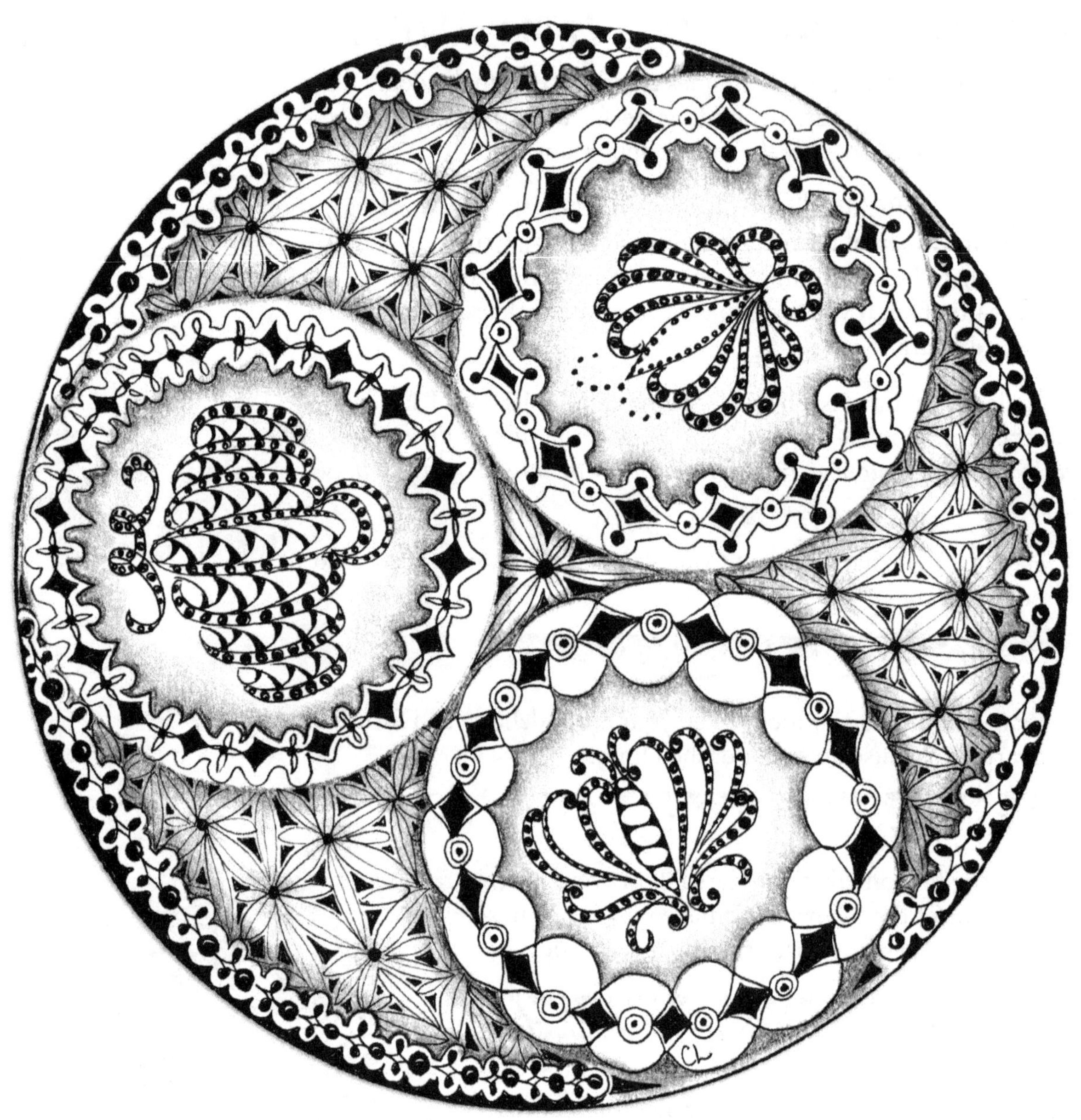

THERE ARE
NO MISTAKES.
ONLY NEW PATHS
TO EXPLORE.

~ Gregory David Roberts

TANGLES TO EXPLORE

In this chapter, we present 21 tangles for you to learn, play with, and make your own. There are a variety of tangles: classic official tangles, brand new ones, and a few of our favorites. Some are simple and some require a bit more concentration. All of them are ripe with creative opportunities. If all of the books in the library can be written with only 26 letters of the alphabet, think of the possibilities within these pages.

Each chosen tangle is thoroughly described in two introductory pages and two sketchbook pages. The introductory pages contain background, step-outs, how-to drawing tips, six tangleations for you to explore, as well as beautiful finished pieces of art to inspire you. The sketchbook pages contain tangling tips, suggestions for even more opportunities to personalize the tangle, and, of course, lots of room for you to draw.

We encourage you to take your time and have fun flexing your creative muscles on these pages. Focus on one pattern at a time. By doing so, you will become so familiar with its structure that the basics become automatic, freeing your mind to add your own style.

There is no such thing as the "perfect" tangle. Instead of spending time looking for it, pick a tangle and make it perfectly yours.

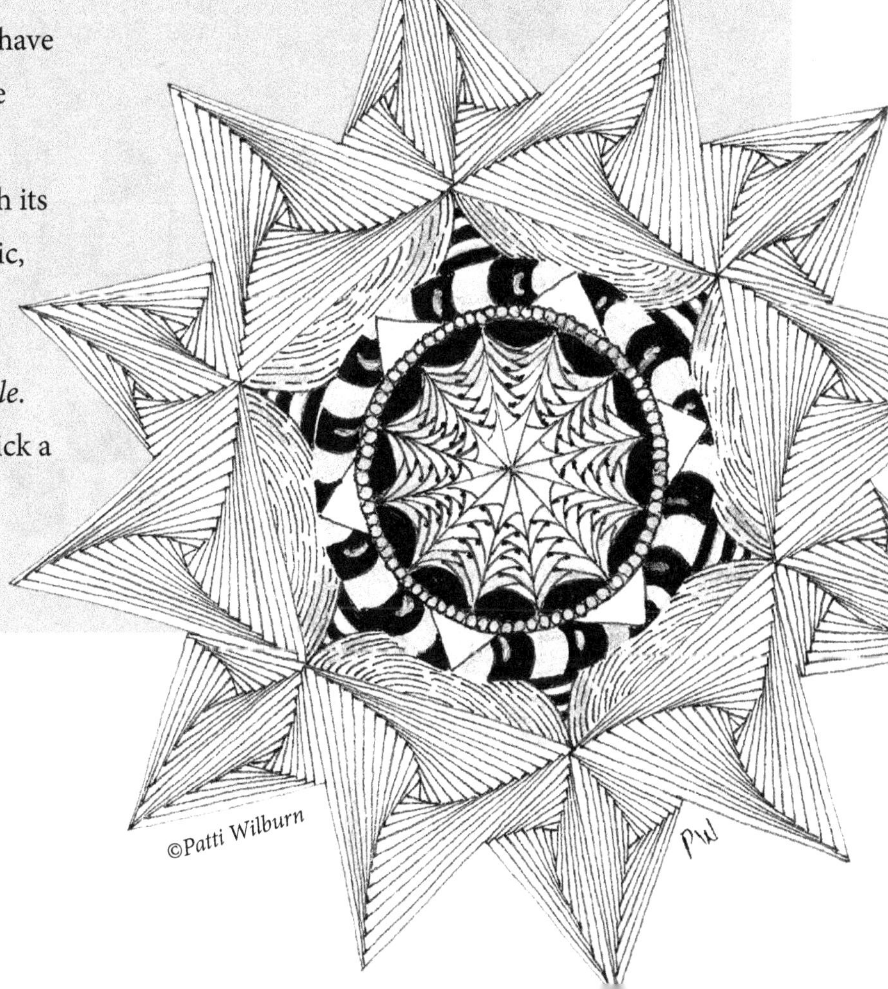

©Patti Wilburn

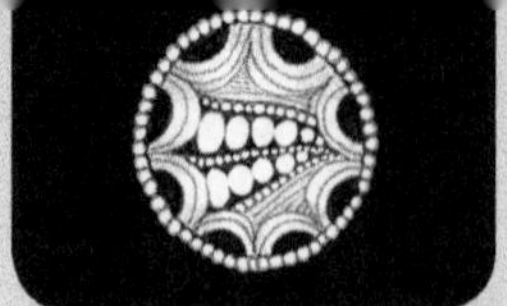

KNIGHTSBRIDGE

by Rick Roberts & Maria Thomas

KNIGHTSBRIDGE *is beautiful, bold, and graphic. Students often ask "Why not just call it a chess board? We know what that looks like." Therein lies the problem: expectations.* KNIGHTSBRIDGE, *like all tangles, is not "supposed" to look like anything. It is defined anew each time it is created.*

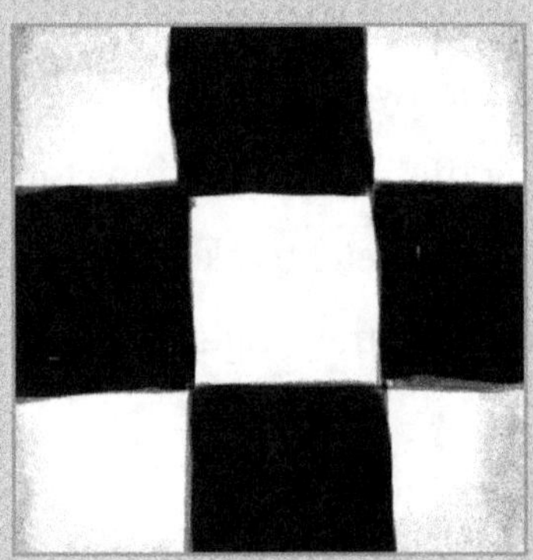

an official Zentangle tangle

Creating tangleations for KNIGHTSBRIDGE can be challenging because it has so few elements that can be changed. However, it is worth the effort because any tangleation of KNIGHTSBRIDGE can be used as a base for a tangleation of any other grid-based tangles.

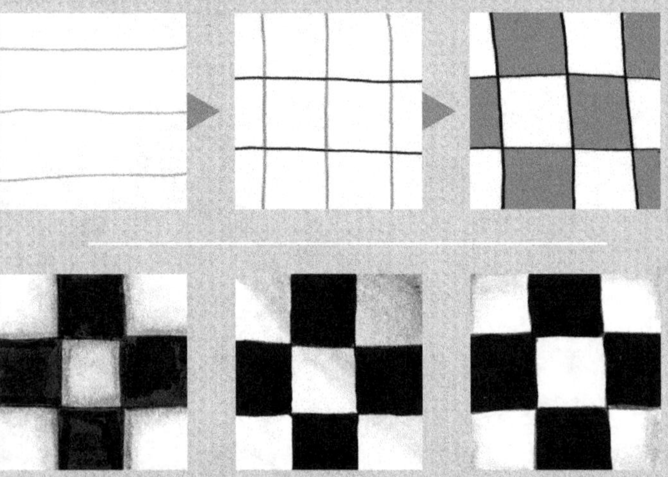

Shading is another way to personalize tangles as shown above. For an in-depth look at shading, see ***Made in the Shade*** *(p. 134).*

TANGLEATION 1

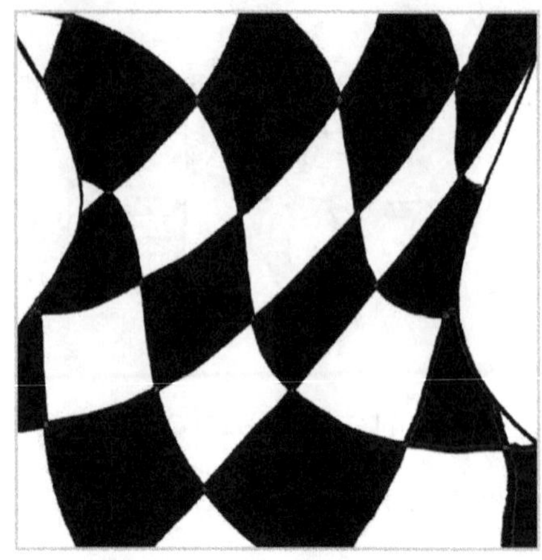

Curve the lines, and turn the grid on an angle to add movement and liveliness.

TANGLEATION 2

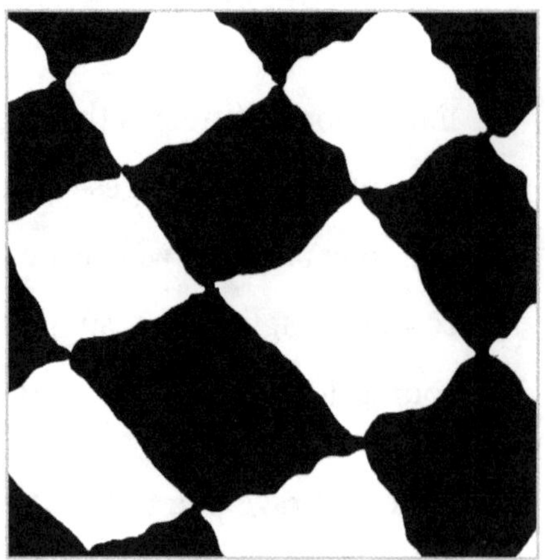

Make intentionally wobbly lines for an organic take on this geometric tangle.

TANGLEATION 3

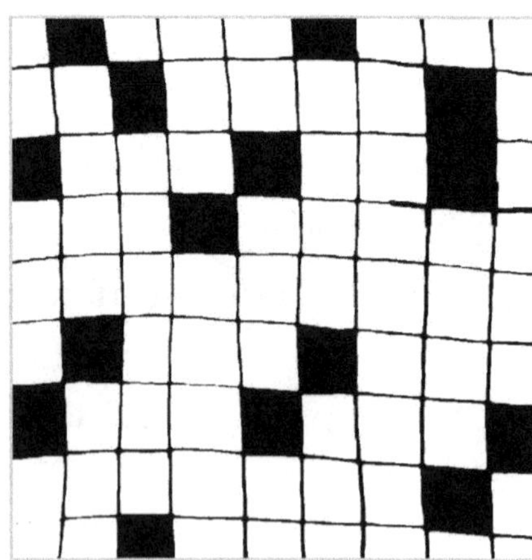

Fill in random squares to give a crossword-puzzle effect. (For the serious crossword-puzzle fanatic, make sure that your design is symmetrical.)

TANGLEATION 4

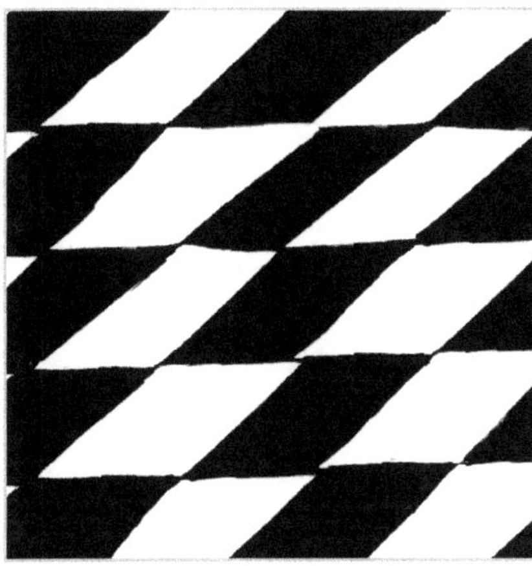

Draw the vertical strokes at an angle to produce a harlequin pattern that has been popular for over 400 years.

TANGLEATION 5

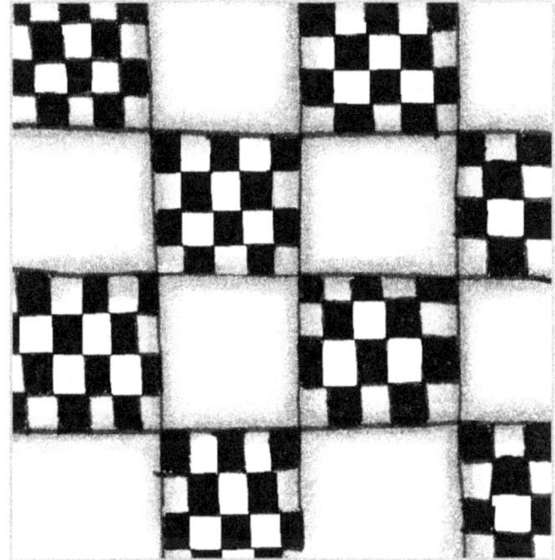

Use **KNIGHTSBRIDGE** as a string. Fill the large black squares with smaller **KNIGHTSBRIDGE** (or another tangle).

TANGLEATION 6

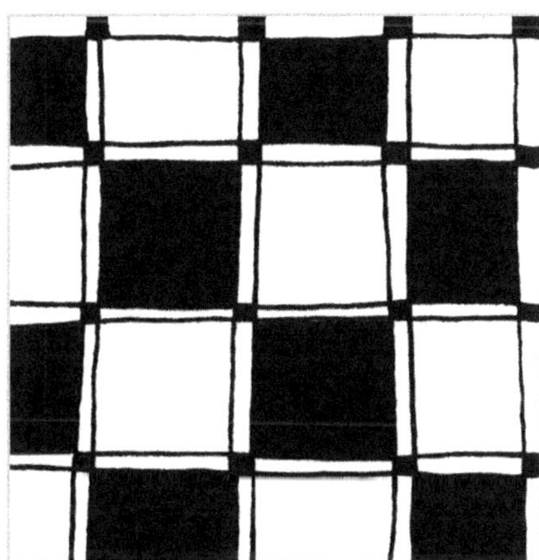

Draw a double grid. Fill the small squares and every other large square to create a plaid effect.

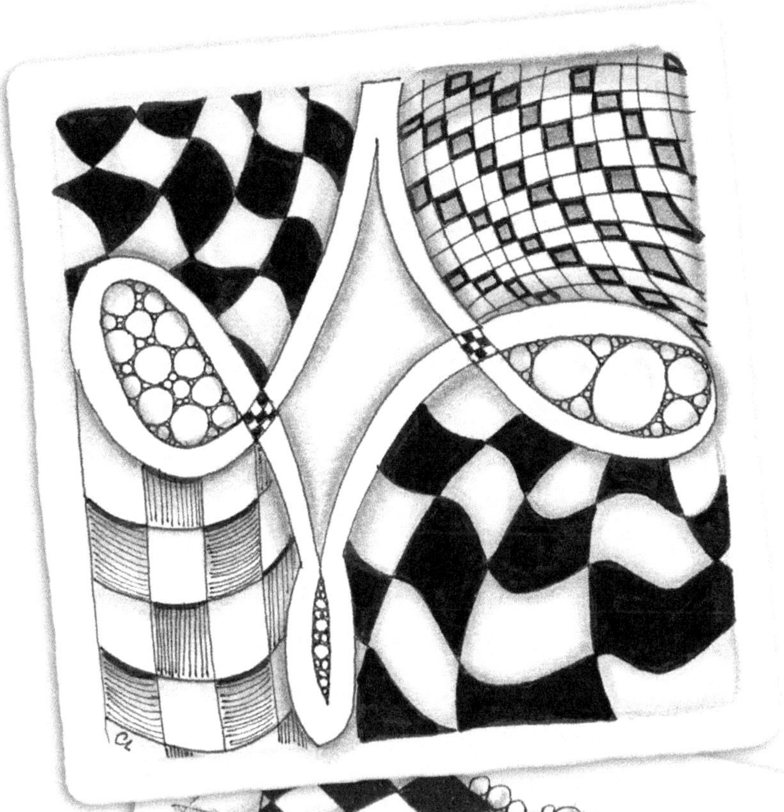

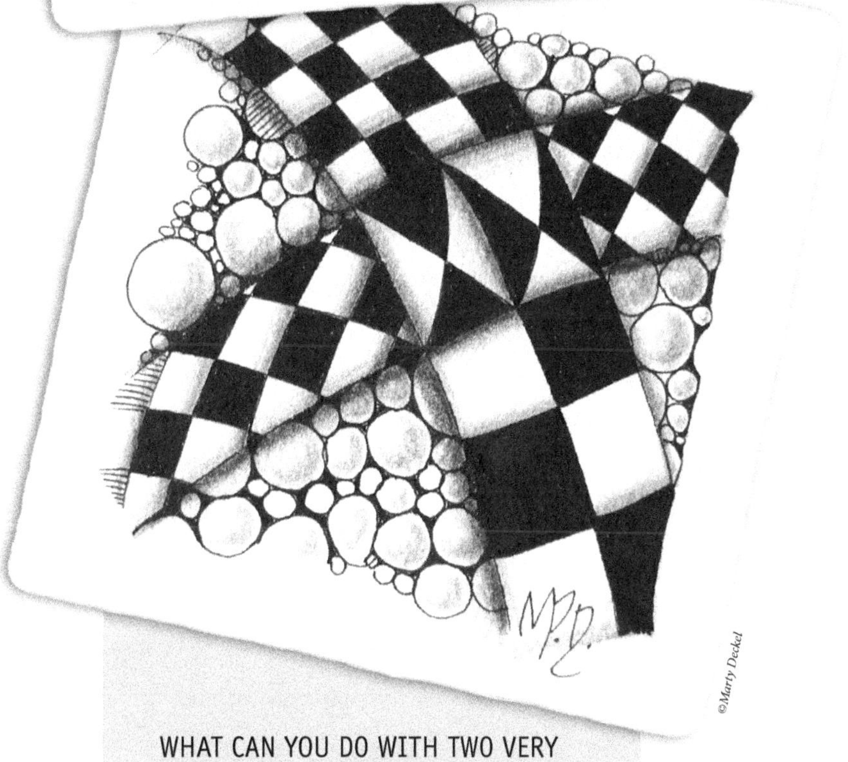

©Marty Deckel

WHAT CAN YOU DO WITH TWO VERY SIMPLE TANGLES AND SOME IMAGINATION? AS DEMONSTRATED ABOVE, QUITE A LOT! BOTH TILES USE ONLY **KNIGHTSBRIDGE** AND **TIPPLE**, YET THE VARIETY IS REMARKABLE.

IDEA STARTERS

Draw some of the tangleations we drew or try some of these:

- See how many ways you can put KNIGHTSBRIDGE inside an orb.
- Fill squares with light and dark tangles.
- Fill a curvy border.
- Start your grid in one corner, and fan it outwards.
- Fill the grid with solid black and many shades of gray.

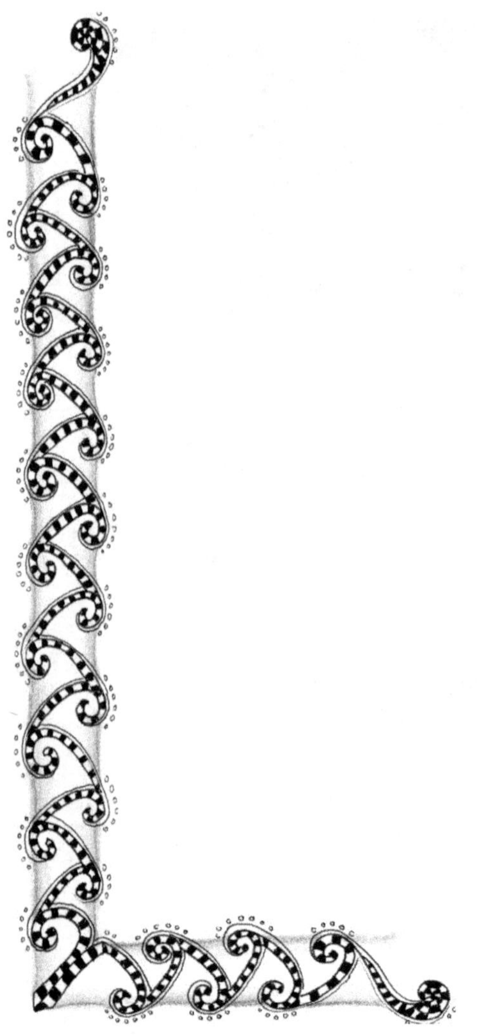

✏ Idea starters are just suggestions. If you have other ideas, use those! Creativity is like a muscle that gets stronger the more it is used. It is a spark from within that flames when nurtured.

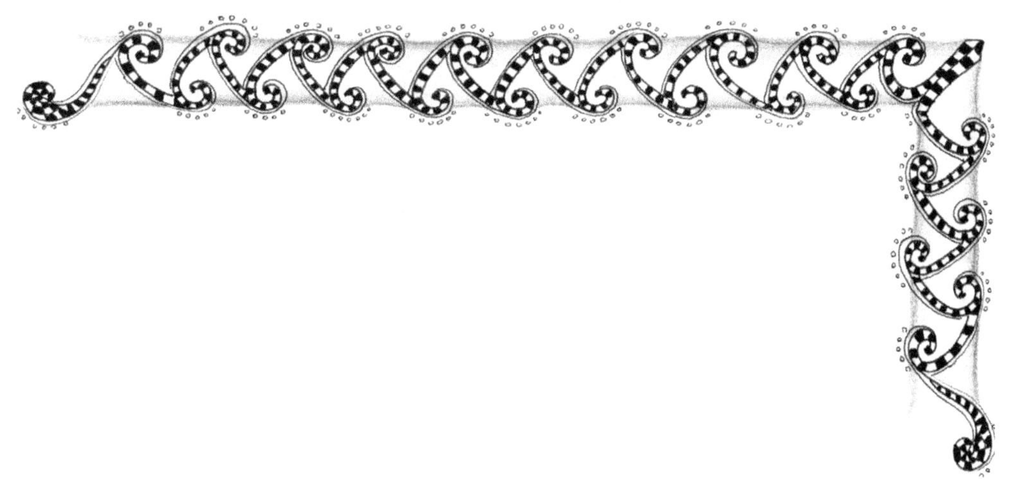

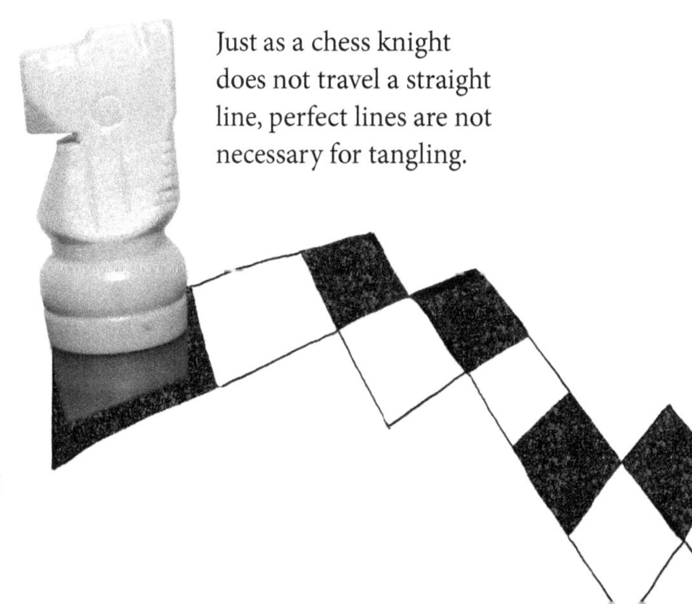

Just as a chess knight does not travel a straight line, perfect lines are not necessary for tangling.

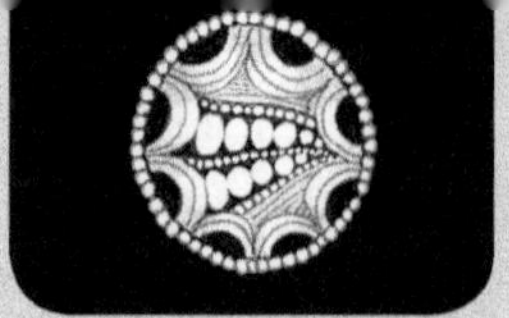

TIPPLE

by Rick Roberts & Maria Thomas

A Zentangle staple, TIPPLE *is another tangle that consists of a single stroke: the orb. Instead of "drawing circles," which must be perfectly round, we "tangle orbs," which are more like pancakes: round, but not perfect. Rhythmically and deliberately inking each orb as you fill a space with* TIPPLE *may help you find your Zen.*

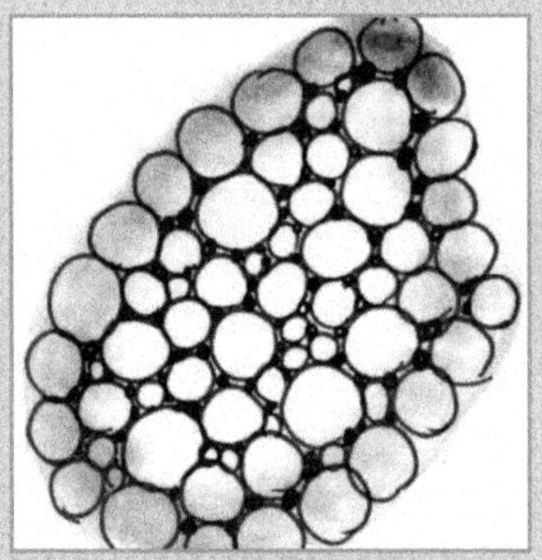

an official Zentangle tangle

Just because TIPPLE is simple does not mean it is boring. The possibilities are endless when you explore variations in size, fill, spacing, and shading.

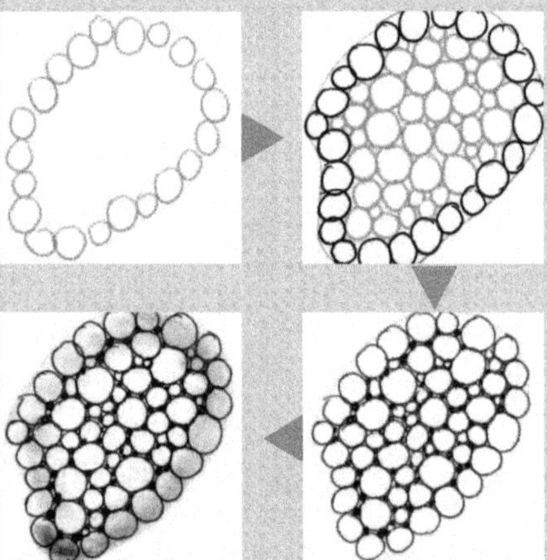

TANGLEATION 1

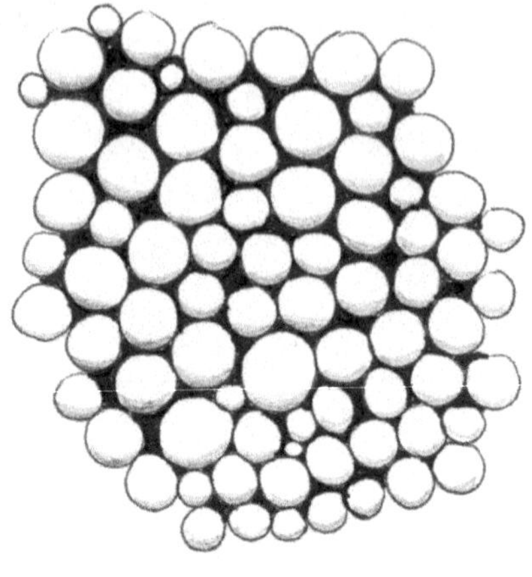

Start from the center of your space and work outwards, the opposite of the step-outs below. Fill the background solid black, and shade each orb separately for a tidy, 3D effect.

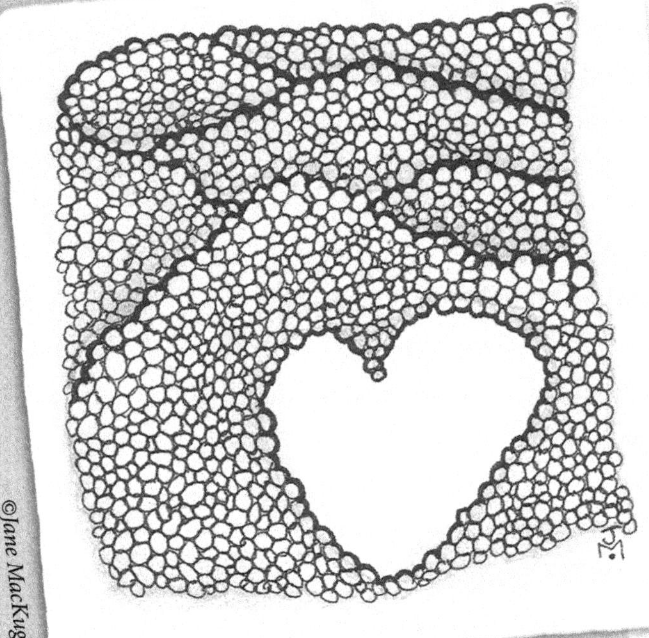

©Jane MacKugler

BOTH OF THE FEATURE TILES USE TIPPLE EXCLUSIVELY. THE EFFECTS ACHIEVED BY EACH ARTIST WITH ONLY ONE TANGLE SHOWCASE THE IMPACT OF SCALE AND SHADING.

TANGLEATION 2

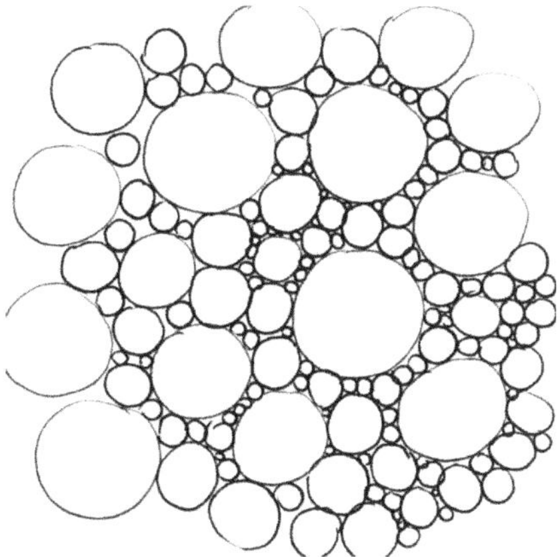

Draw the large orbs first. Add smaller orbs in between, being careful not to completely fill every space.

TANGLEATION 3

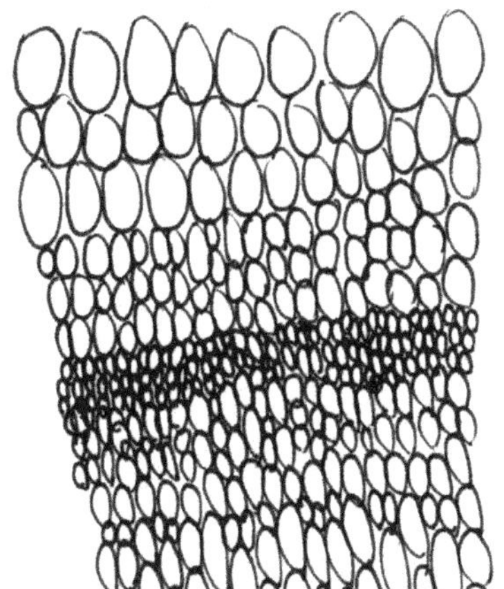

Draw stripes of elongated orbs of various sizes in dense rows to create a textural snakeskin effect. *(©Liv Howard)*

TANGLEATION 4

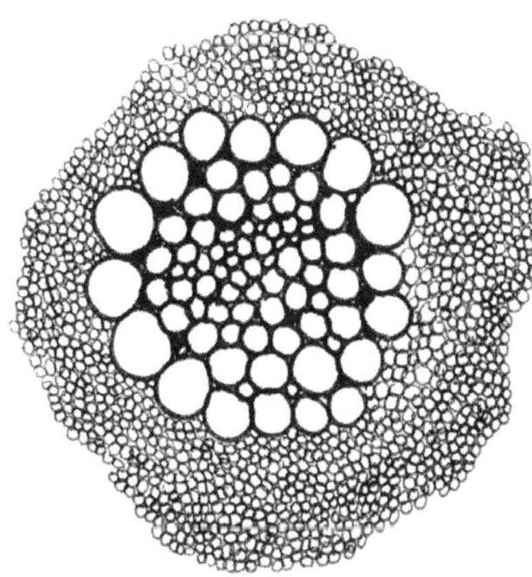

Create teeny, tiny orbs that can be used as shading for dark areas. They can also be used as a filler to add weight and texture.

TANGLEATION 5

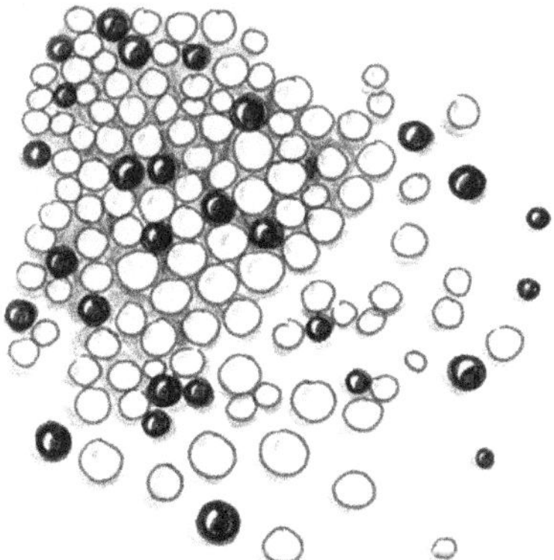

Add interest by clustering light and dark orbs that gradually spread out. Shading and highlights give each orb a 3D appearance.

TANGLEATION 6

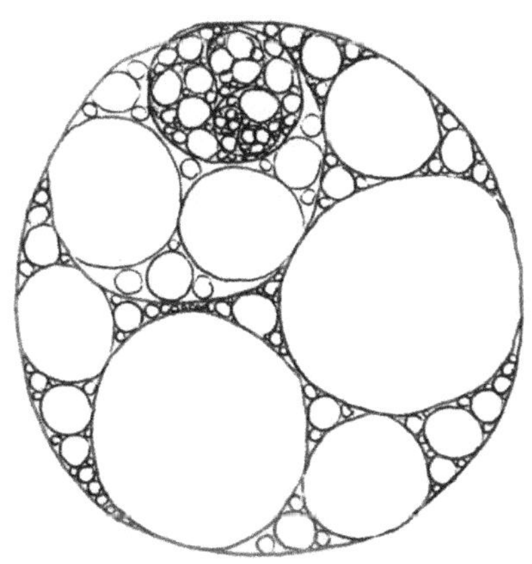

Make the largest orbs fit the space. Then draw the next biggest orbs in between. Repeat with smaller and smaller orbs.

IDEA STARTERS

- Explore layering your orbs, drawing some behind others as you do when drawing HOLLIBAUGH (PAGE 54)
- Draw various size orbs, and tangle inside the largest ones.
- Use tiny TIPPLE as shading for another tangle.
- Space the orbs widely, and draw something in between them. Stripes look nice.

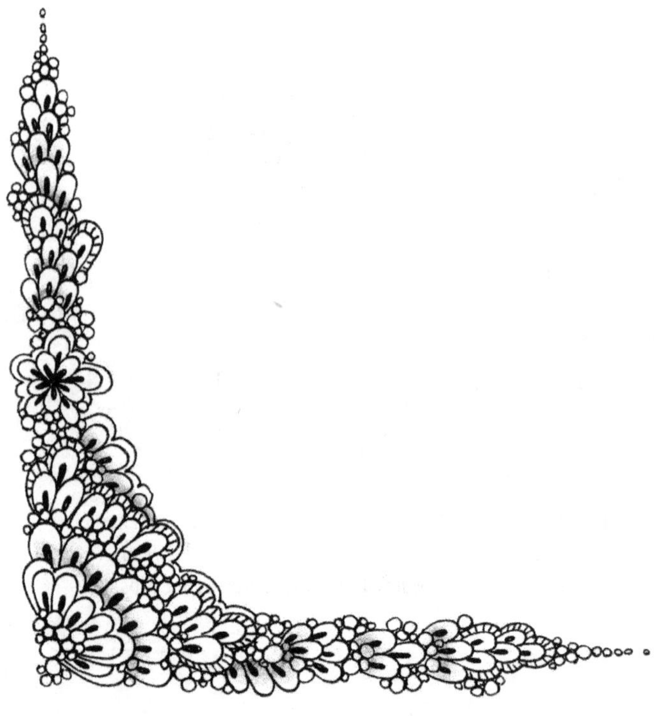

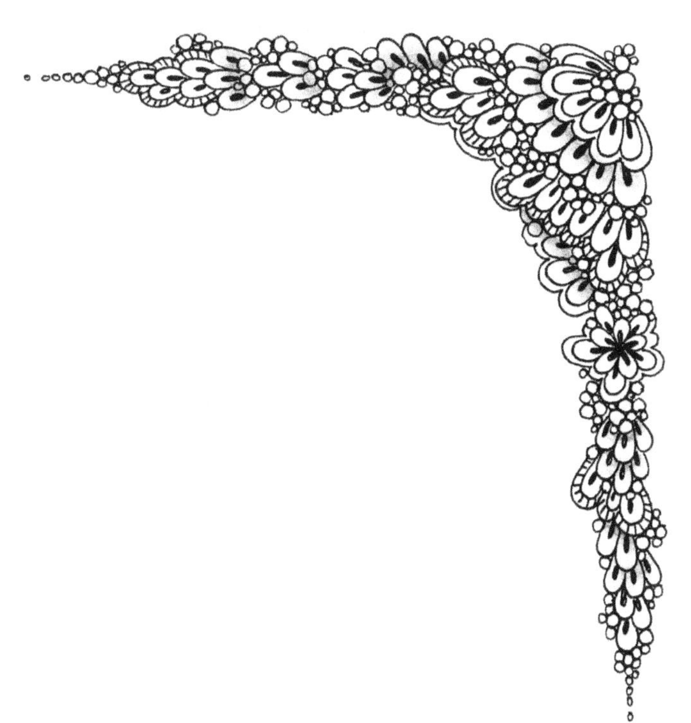

✏ Smile when you tangle. The physical act of smiling will cause your brain to believe you are smiling for a reason, and you will feel happier.

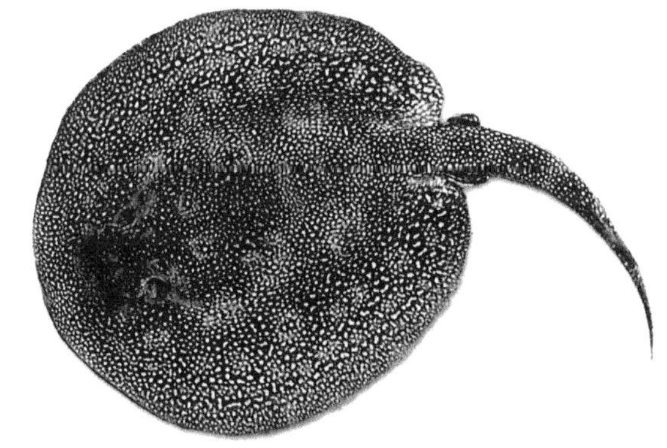

TIPPLE

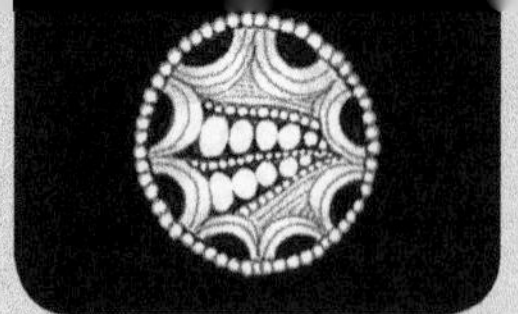

HOLLIBAUGH

by Nick Hollibaugh

Inspired by a pile of scrap wood, Nick Hollibaugh shows how to create a complex-looking result by drawing one stroke at a time, each drawn behind the previous one. This is one of the basic lessons in the Zentangle Method. **HOLLIBAUGH** *is great for dramatically filling large open spaces or for connecting one tangle to another.*

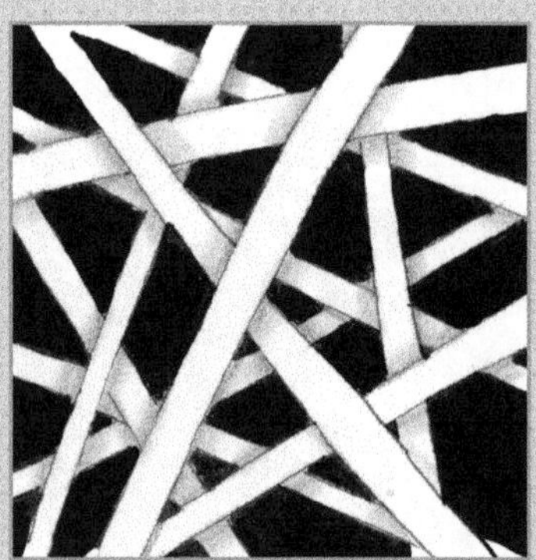

an official Zentangle tangle

To begin, draw two parallel lines creating a "stick." Draw a second stick without crossing the first; pick up your pen, and skip over the first stick, making the second look like it is behind the first. Continue layering your sticks until the space is full. This dimensional effect is enhanced by shading along the outside of each stick to cast a shadow on the ones behind it.

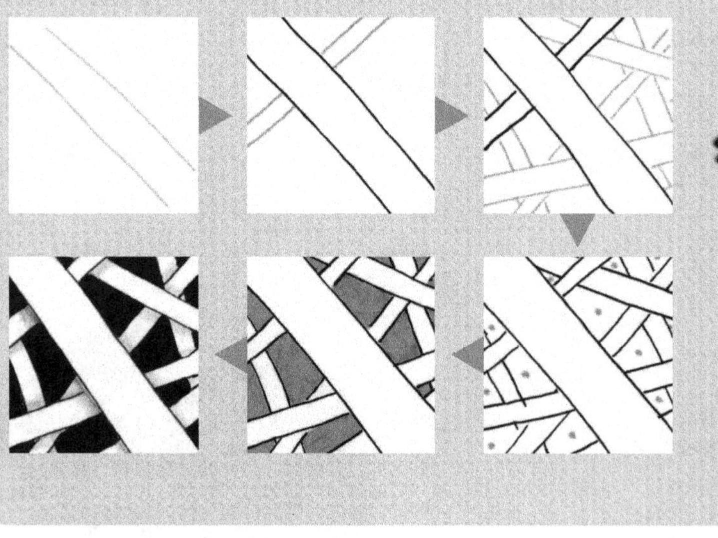

TANGLEATION 1

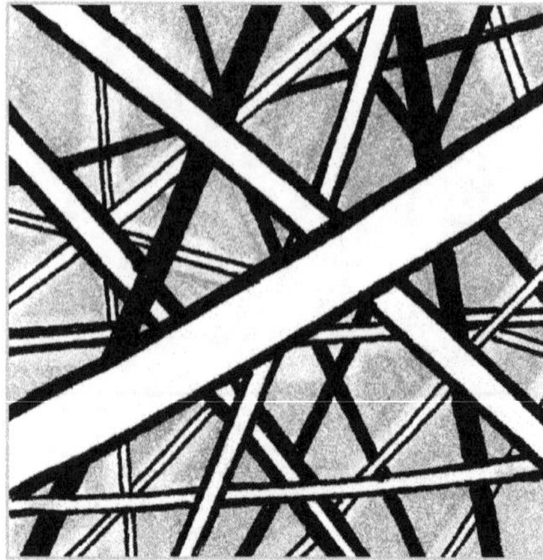

Vary the size and color of your sticks. Here, black and white really pop against the gray background.

TANGLEATION 2

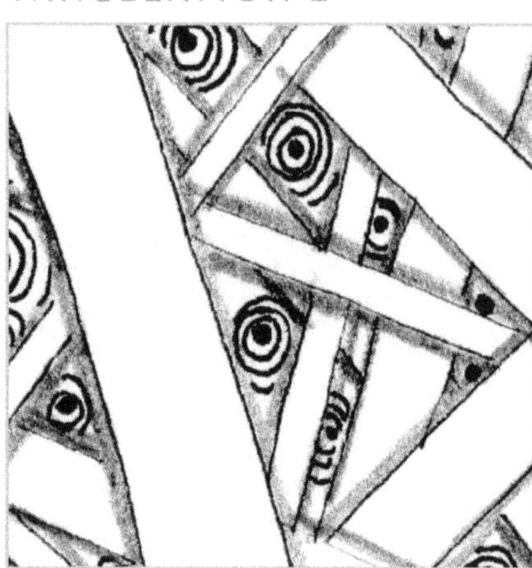

Fill in the background with another tangle. The roundness of **PRINTEMPS** contrasts with the straightness of **HOLLIBAUGH**.

TANGLEATION 3

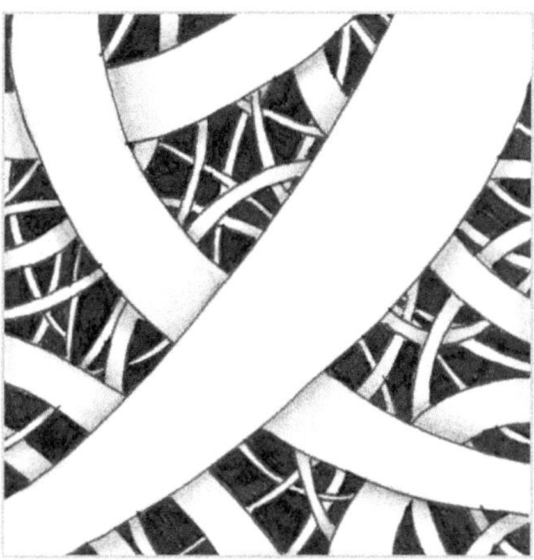

Start with fatter sticks in the foreground. Gradually decrease stick widths as you add more layers to enhance the illusion of depth.

TANGLEATION 4

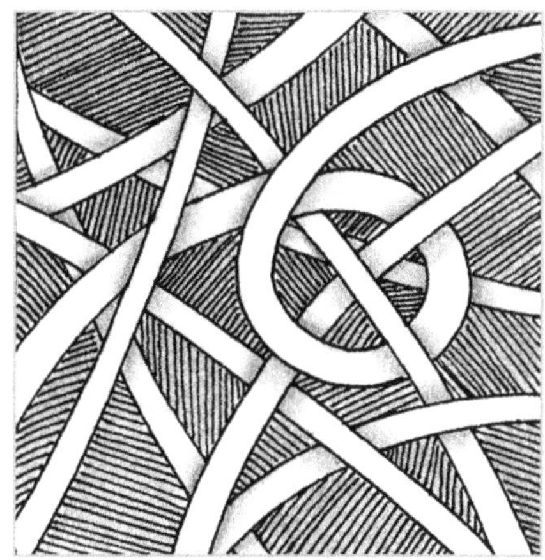

Use curved sticks instead of straight ones. Fill in the background with lines or stripes to accentuate the sticks.

TANGLEATION 5

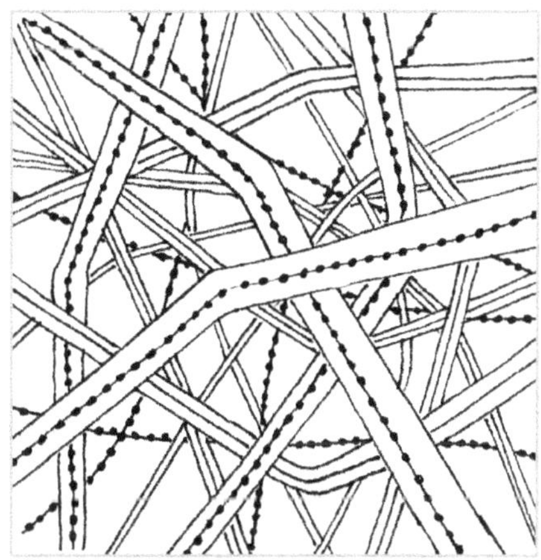

Leave both the sticks and background white for a lighter version. Combine bent sticks with **BEADLINES** for added interest.

TANGLEATION 6

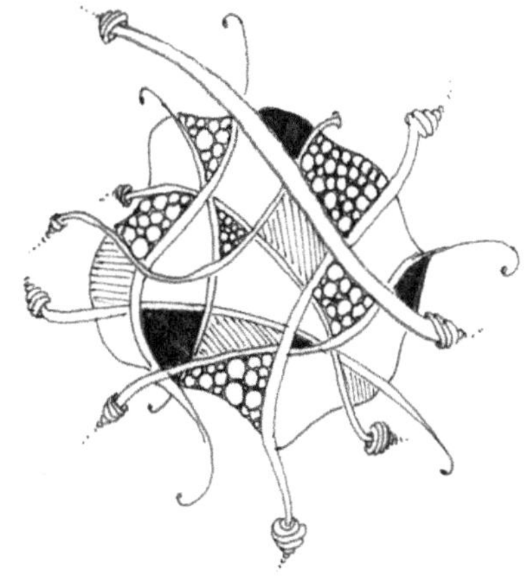

Make **HOLLIBAUGH** a centerpiece by putting **ZINGER** on the end of each stick, and filling the white spaces with other tangles.

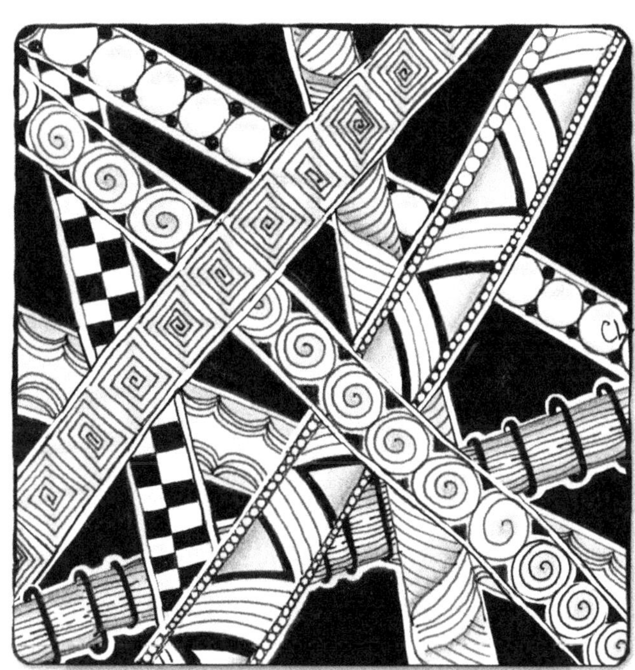

BOTH OF THE ART PIECES FEATURE **HOLLIBAUGH** USED AS A STRING. THE EFFECTS ACHIEVED SHOW THE DRAMATIC IMPACT FILL, SPACE, AND TANGLE CHOICE CAN HAVE.

Tile features: **HOLLIBAUGH, KNIGHTSBRIDGE, CRESCENT MOON, ONOMATO, SHATTUCK, ZANDER, AMBLER,** *and* **SNAILZ.**

IDEA STARTERS

- After completing all of your sticks, add auras.
- Add an aura to each stick as you draw it. See how different it looks than it did adding the auras at the end.
- Draw some curvy sticks, and shade to make them look like a jumble of ribbons.
- Make black sticks on a white background.
- Draw one tangle on the sticks and another in the background.

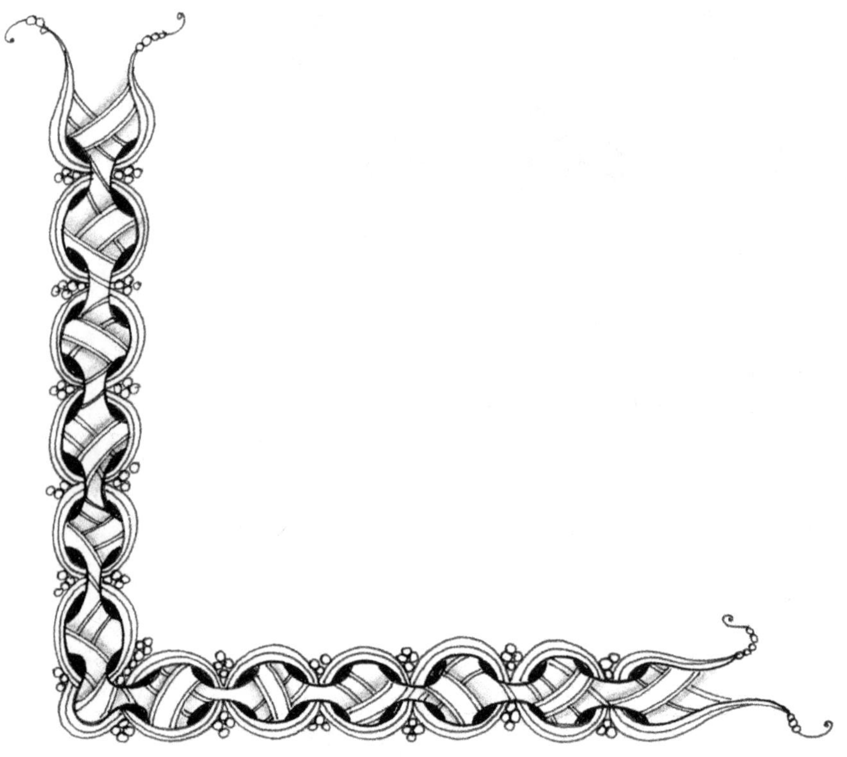

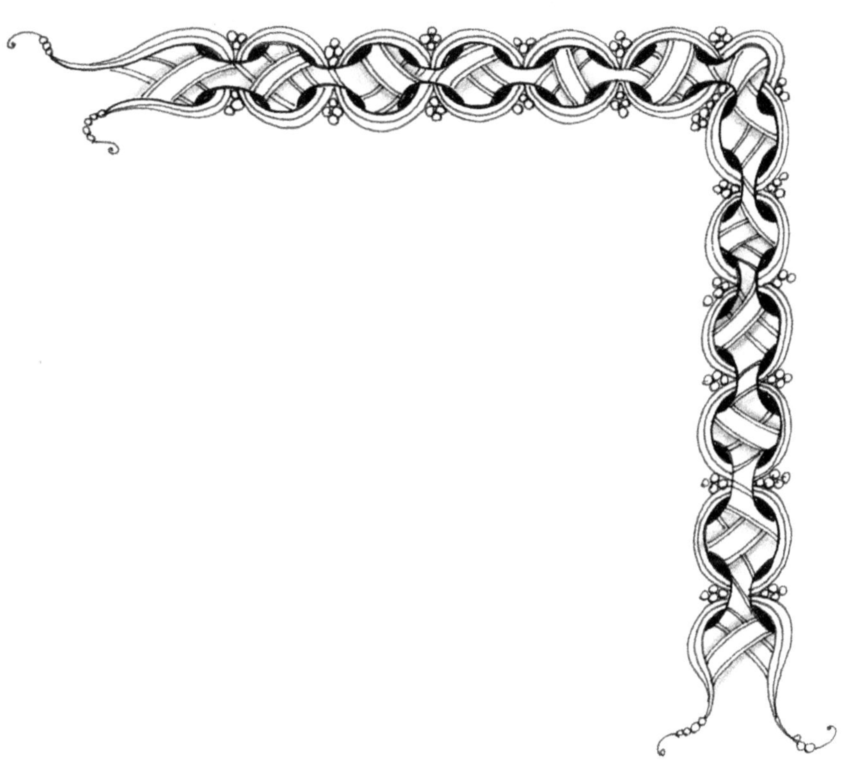

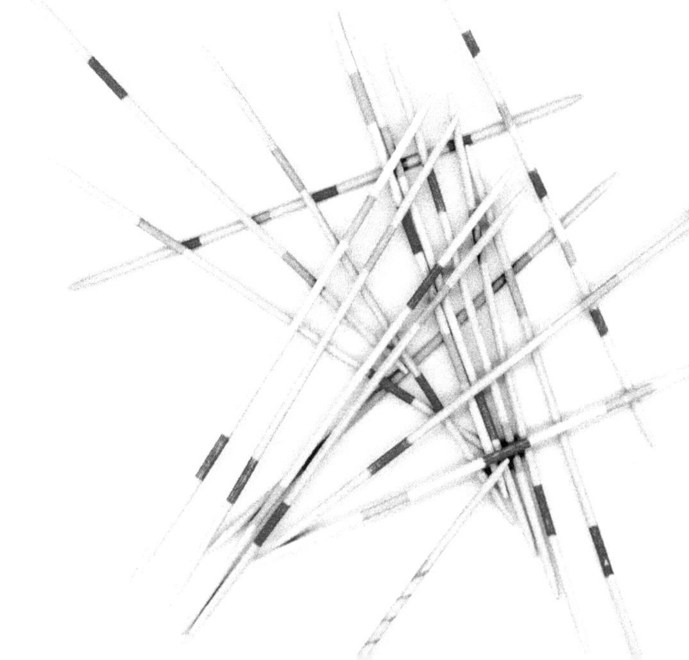

✏ There is no up, down, left, or right in Zentangle art. Always hold your tile (or book) in the direction that feels most comfortable to you.

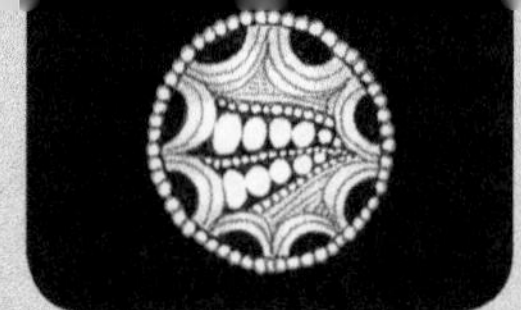

CRESCENT MOON

by Rick Roberts & Maria Thomas

"CRESCENT MOON *is like a gift—a present from Zentangle, as it is so satisfying and versatile. It is also great for keeping you in the moment—the present. You have to really focus on coloring in those half-circles and spacing those auras. It is no wonder it is used in nearly by every CZT in introductory classes. It's a classic." Amy Broady, CZT.*

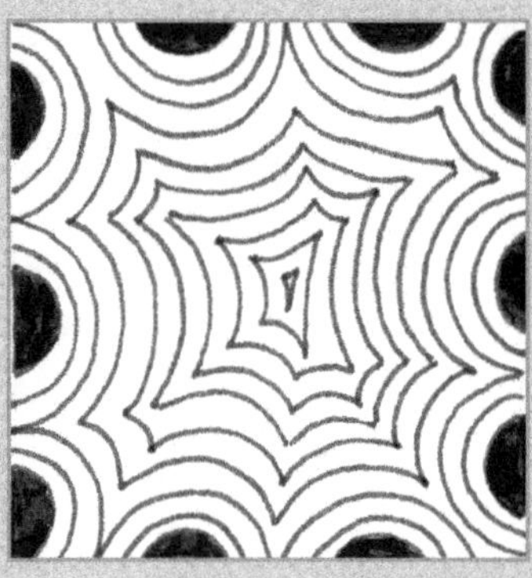

an official Zentangle tangle

Begin by drawing "ladybugs" (arcs) all around your string and coloring them black. Fill the rest of the space with a series of auras. Then decide if you want to add enhancements. Filling auras with dots, lines, shades of gray, orbs, etc. is a great way to personalize them. Just as the moon changes every night, your CRESCENT MOON may also.

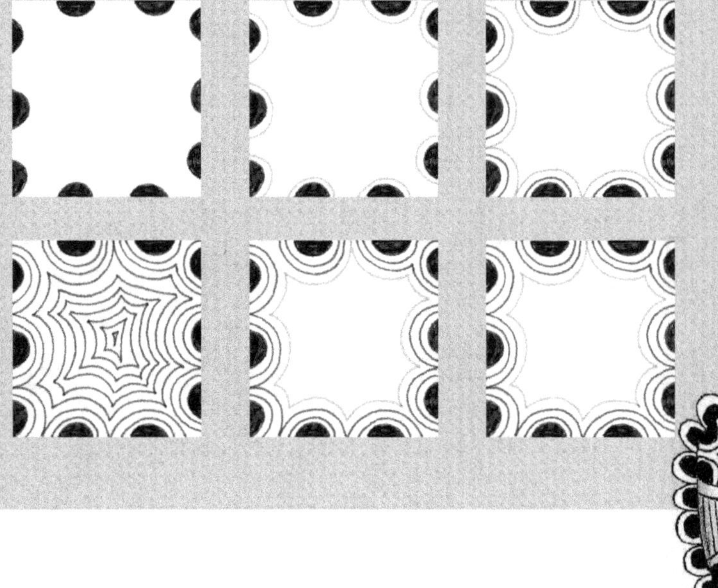

TANGLEATION 1

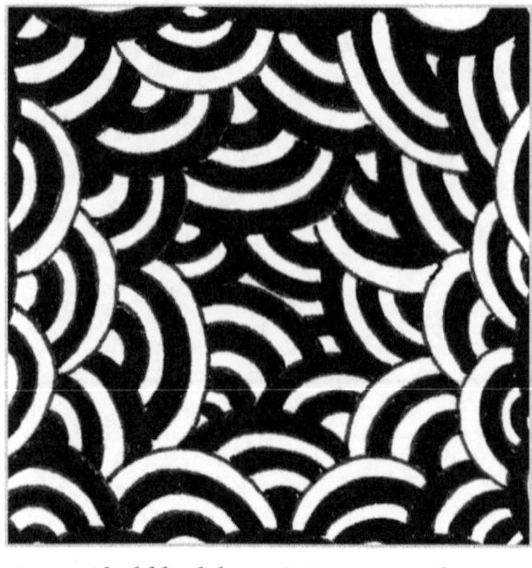

Create a bold look by striping every other aura. Stack the auras from the outside in towards the center to create depth and interest.

TANGLEATION 2

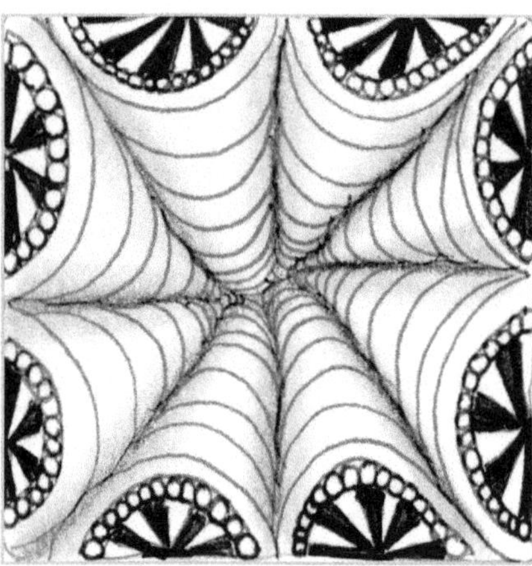

Dress the ladybugs with festive pinwheels. To add dimension, make the auras fat and wide closest to the ladybugs; draw them progressively narrower as they near the center.

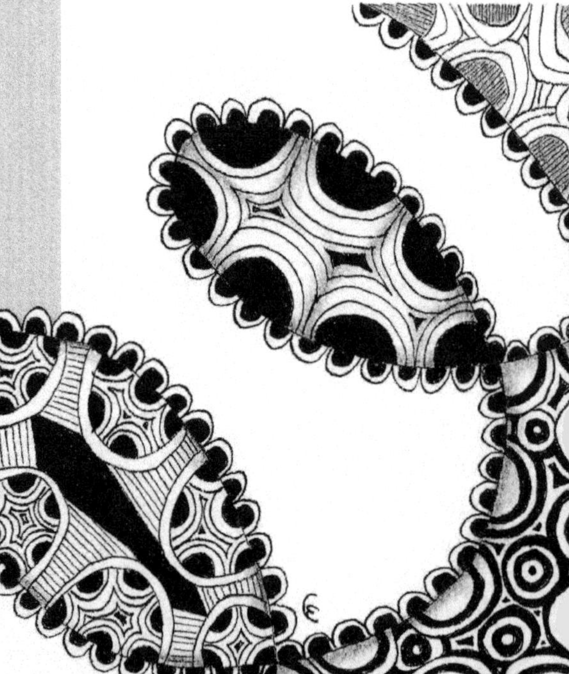

TANGLEATION 3

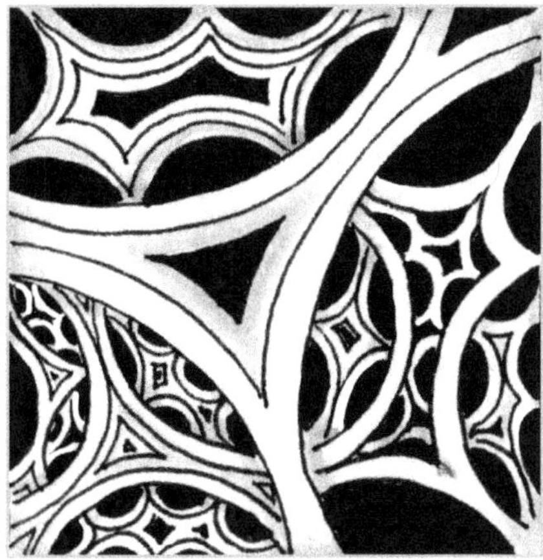

Use CRESCENT MOON as the initial string. Then fill inside each ladybug with smaller CRESCENT MOONS for a complex look.

TANGLEATION 4

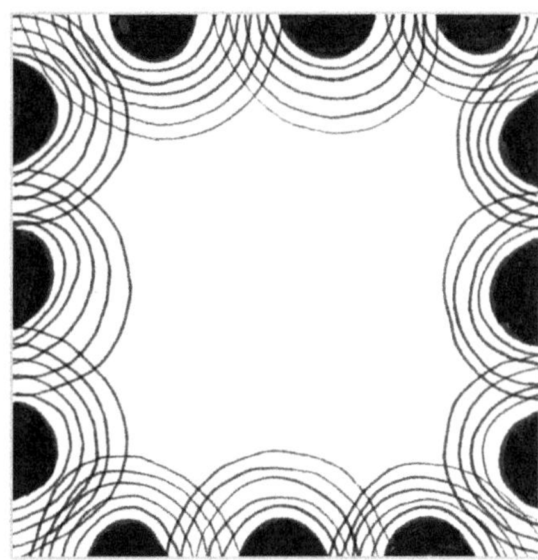

Overlap auras to create interesting texture at the intersections. (A beginning student labeled this a mistake. We disagree!)

TANGLEATION 5

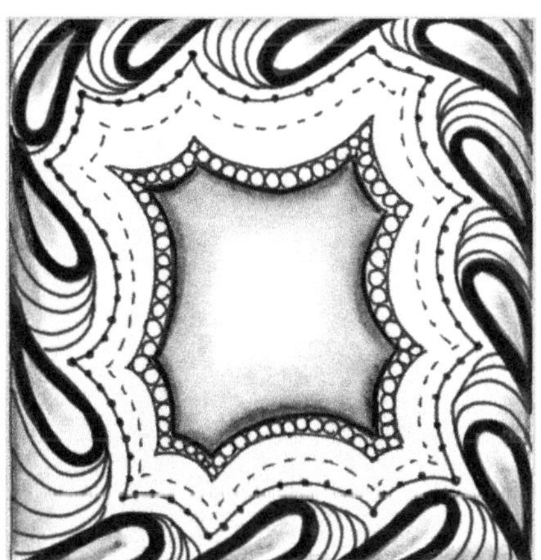

Begin with teardrop shapes instead of ladybugs. Decorative auras and careful shading create this elegant tangleation.

TANGLEATION 6

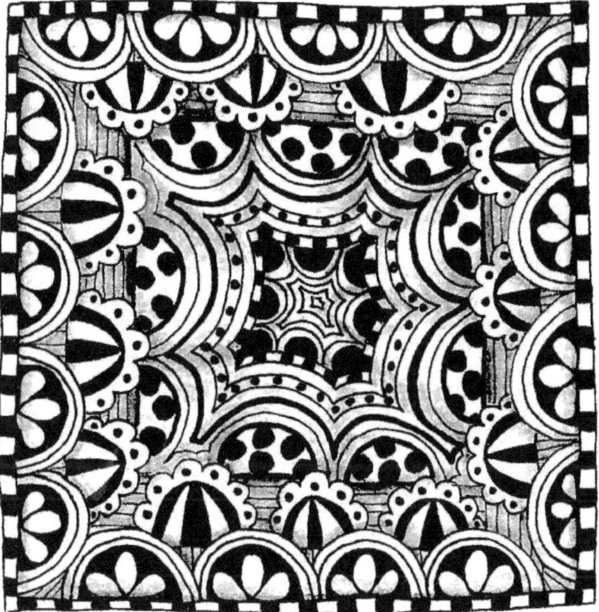

Fill ladybugs and auras with stripes, petals, dots, and lace to produce elaborate results. *(©Adele Bruno)*

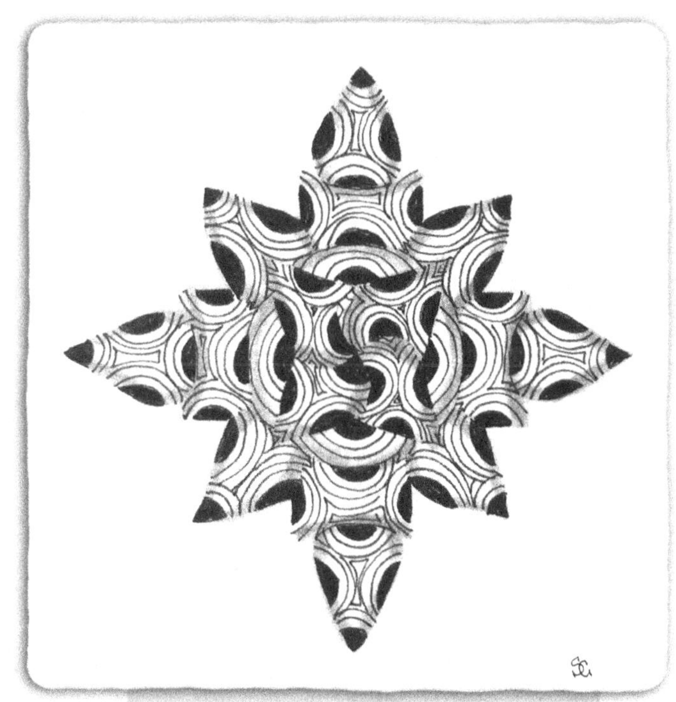

SUE CLARK CREATED AN INTRICATE FOCAL POINT BY LAYERING CRESCENT MOON. SHADING HELPS DEFINE THE LAYERS AND ADD INTEREST.

Template: ©The Bright Owl

IDEA STARTERS

- Start your ladybugs on either side of the same line, back to back.
- Add highlights (***sparkles***) or patterns to your ladybugs.
- Play with different ways to join your auras, such as overlapping them.
- Use tangles or designs to decorate between the auras.
- Instead of starting at the string and working inwards, start at the center of a section and work toward the edge.

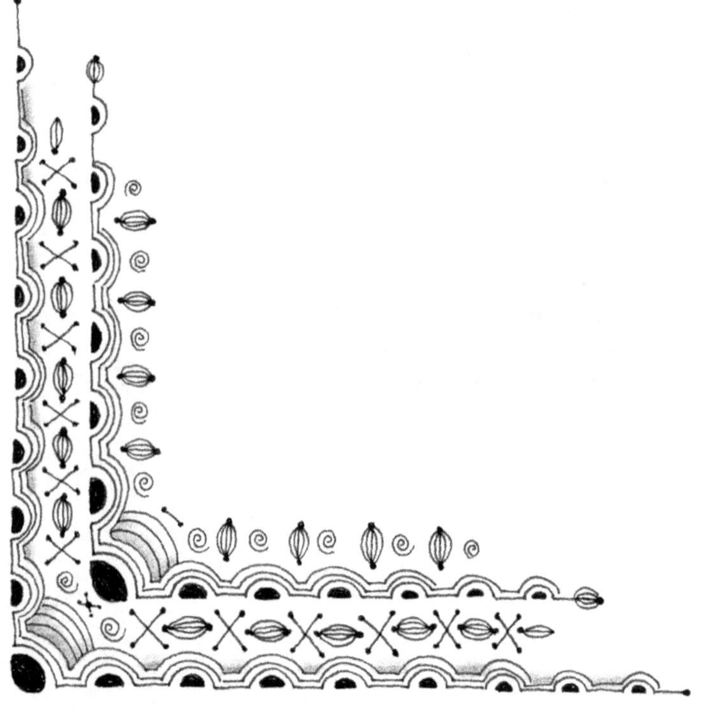

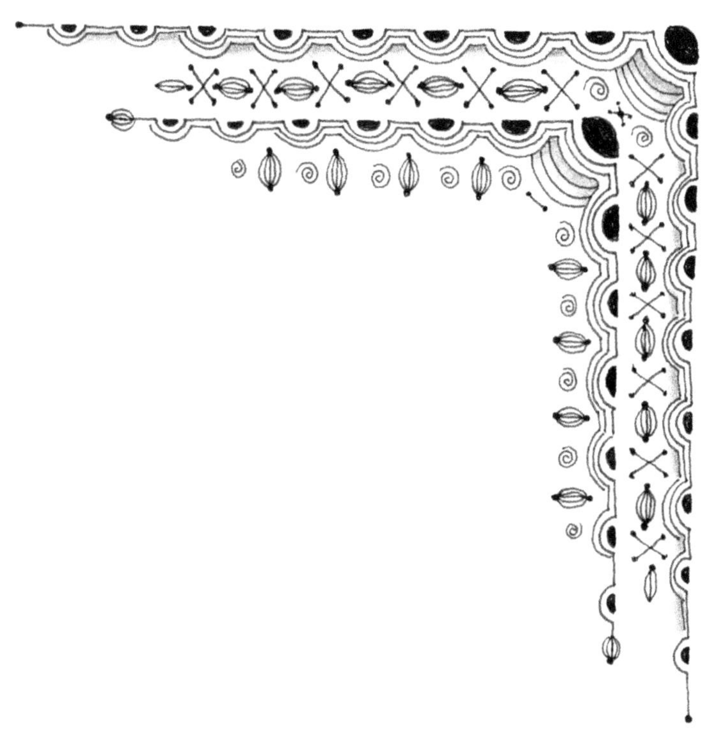

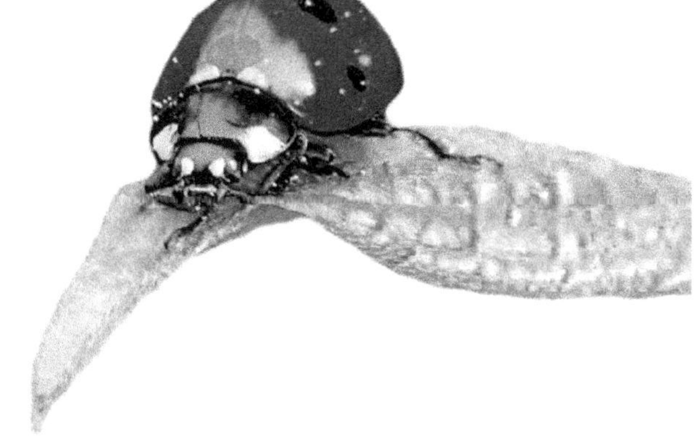

✏ Focus only on the stroke you are making. As you make each mark, allow yourself to experience the pen gliding across the paper. Notice the beauty of the ink as it flows onto the paper.

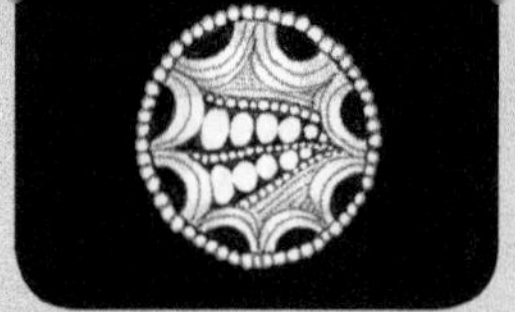

SETON

by Alexa Letourneau

SETON *was inspired by the frosted glass windows at our church, Seton Parish. I have admired the pattern for years but could not figure out how to turn it into a tangle. Thankfully, my daughter came to the rescue, deconstructing the pattern into six simple steps. I love how many of the tangleations resemble beautiful quilts. ~ Cris*

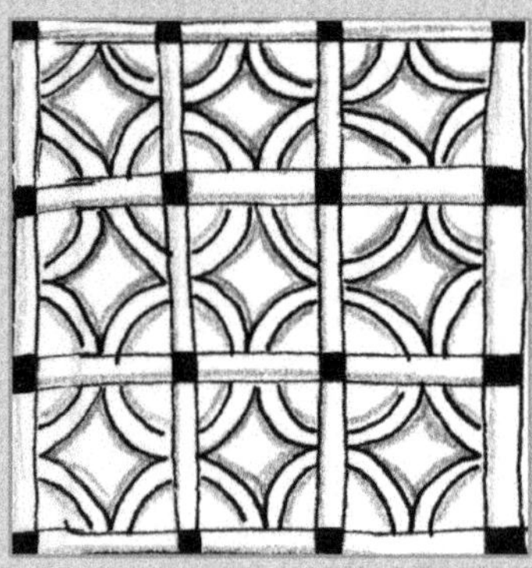

While SETON looks like circles behind a lattice, you do not need to *try* to draw circles. In the third step, draw four arcs, one from the center of each square to the center of the adjacent square. When you add an aura in the fourth step, the circles appear as if by magic.

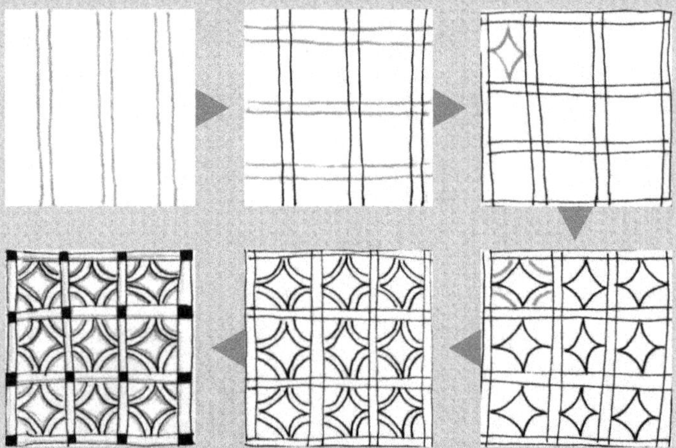

TANGLEATION 1

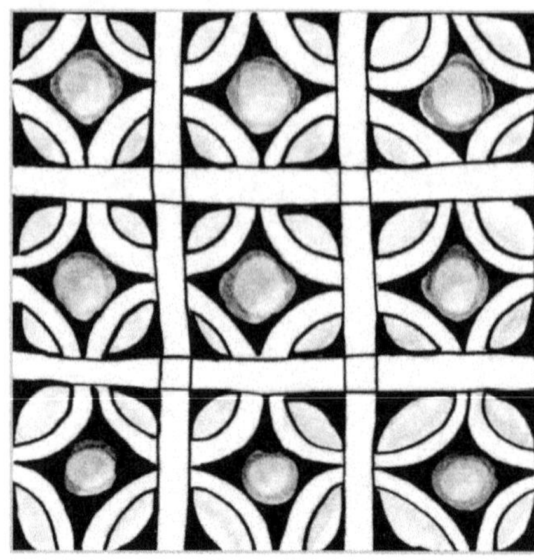

Use rounding to create orbs in the center and petal shapes at each intersection. Shade to give depth.

TANGLEATION 2

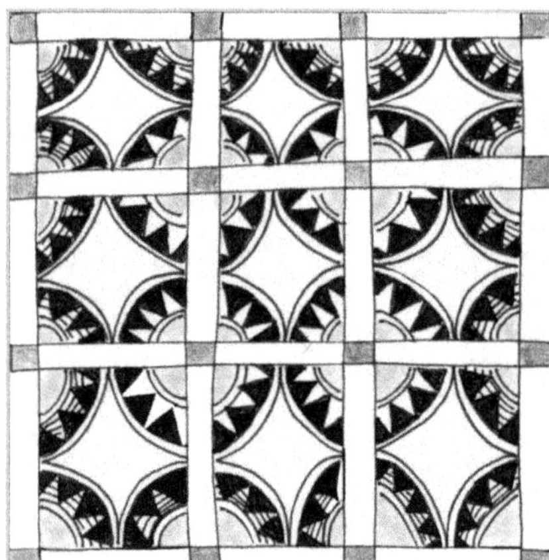

Create a quilt-like appeal to the circles in the background with a sawtooth pattern and dramatic shading.

TANGLEATION 3

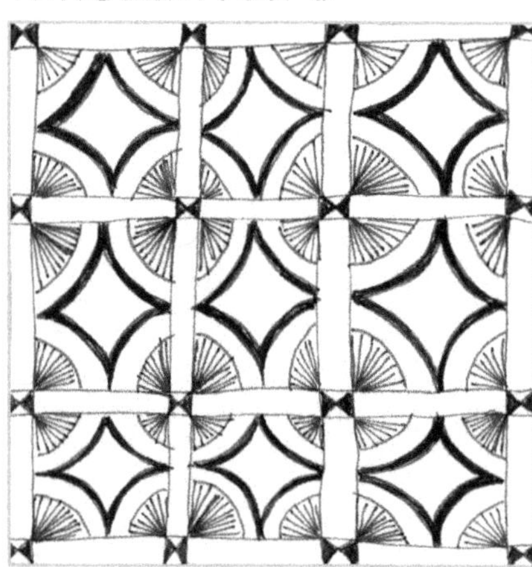

Draw an X in each small box, and color the opposite sides to create mini bow ties. Add lines that fan out and thick auras in the center.

TANGLEATION 4

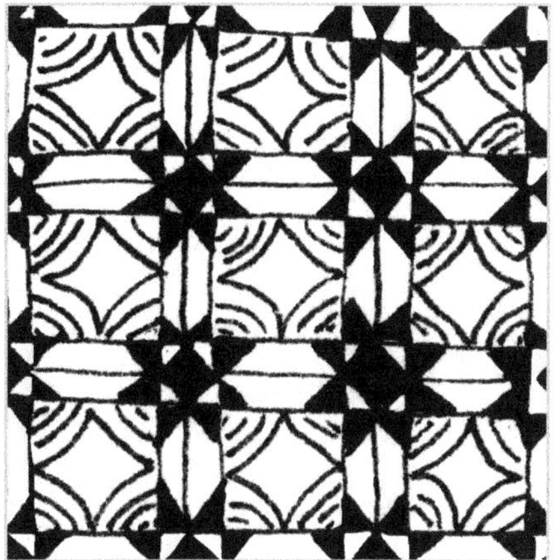

Divide the lattice in half. Draw a V shape outside each intersection. Add a diamond in the center. Aura the inside of each arc.

TANGLEATION 5

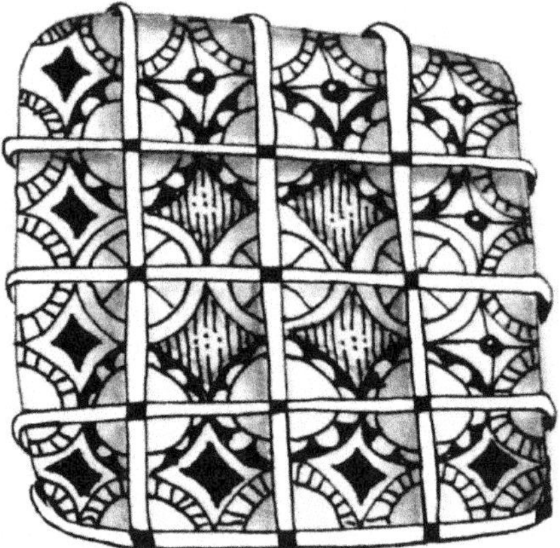

Curve the ends of the lattice around the edge. Use dramatic shading to make it pop off a highly decorated background. *(©Marty Deckel)*

TANGLEATION 6

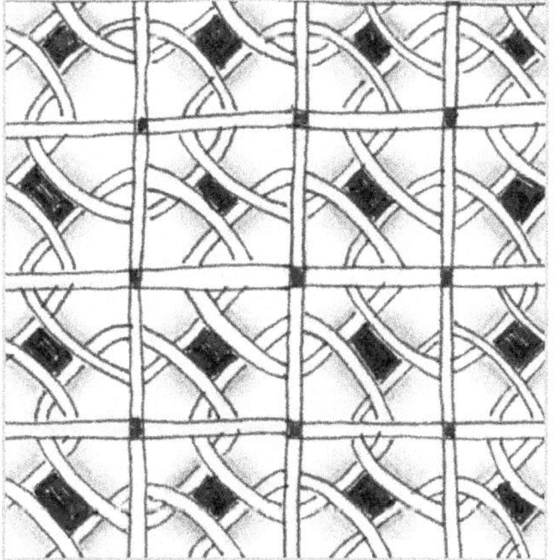

Interlock the background shapes like Olympic rings. Fill in some of the blank spaces with black, and shade for drama.

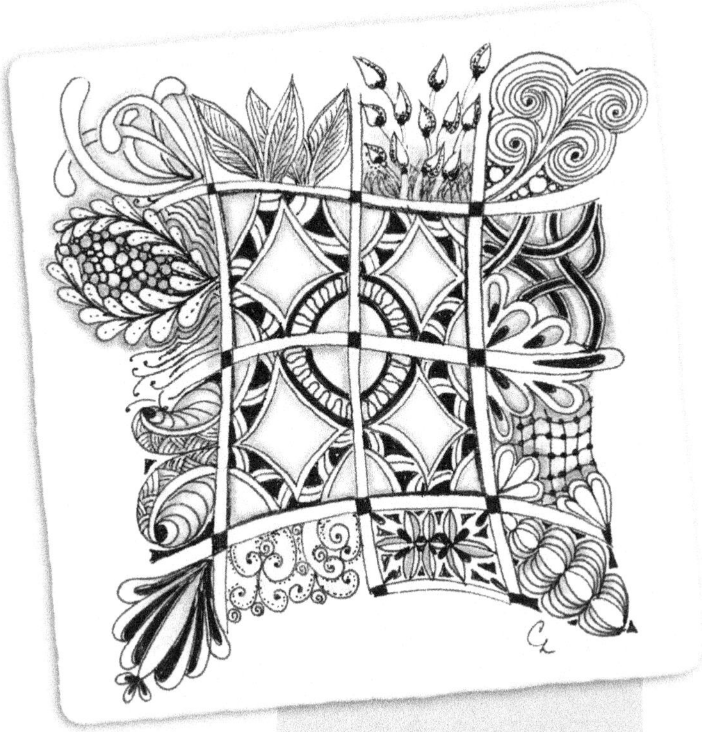

SETON IS THE BASE OF THIS SAMPLER-STYLE TILE. AN OPEN LATTICE AT THE SIDES ALLOWS THE TANGLES TO FLOW OUT.

Tile features: SHATTUCK, POKE LEAF, FESCU, FLUX, FLOORZ, HOLLIBAUGH, MOOKA, OPUS, *and* TIPPLE.

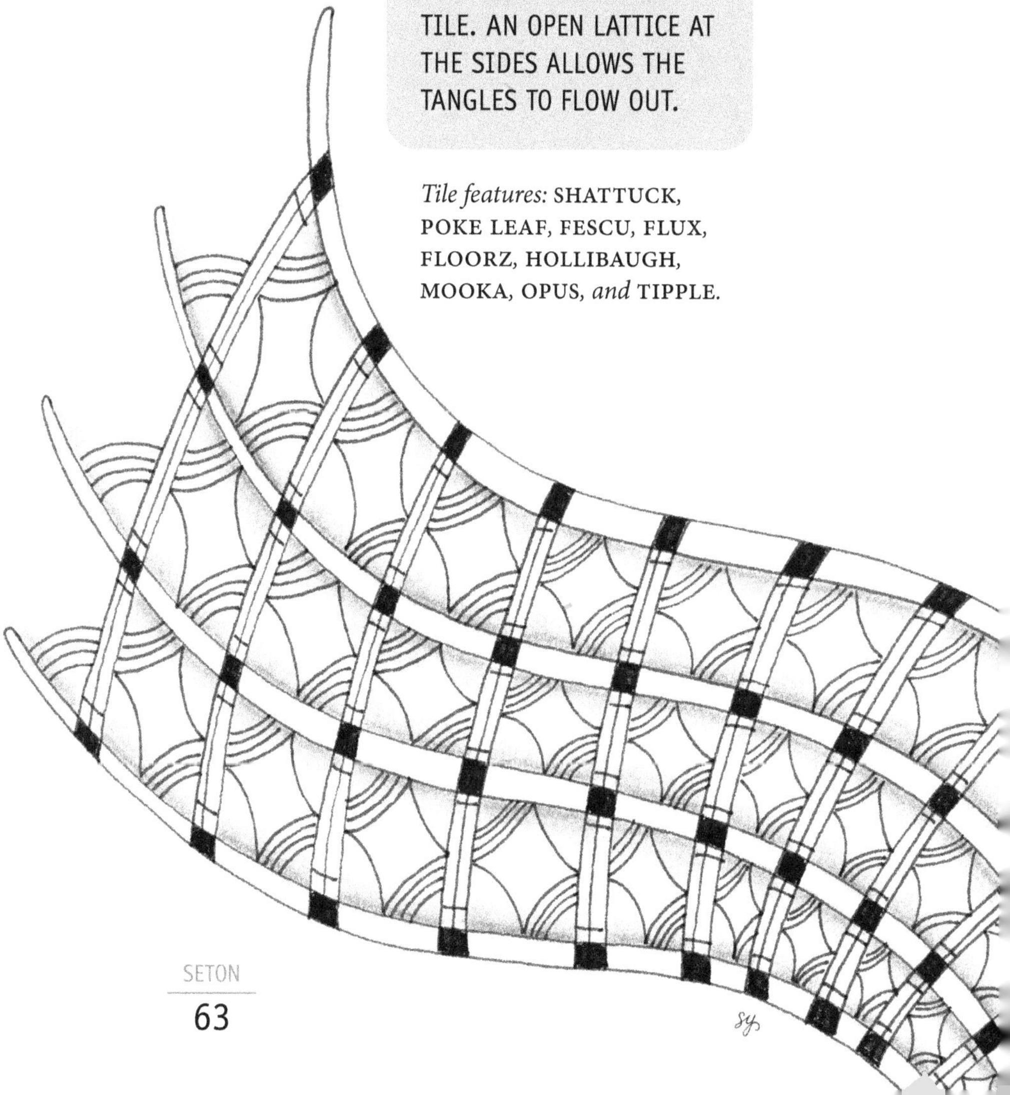

IDEA STARTERS

- Explore different patterns to fill the circles and auras.
- Vary your grid. See Unlock the grid (PAGE 41).
- Draw straight lines instead of curved arcs for diamonds instead of orbs.
- Tangle in the space between the lattice and orbs.
- Add additional auras.

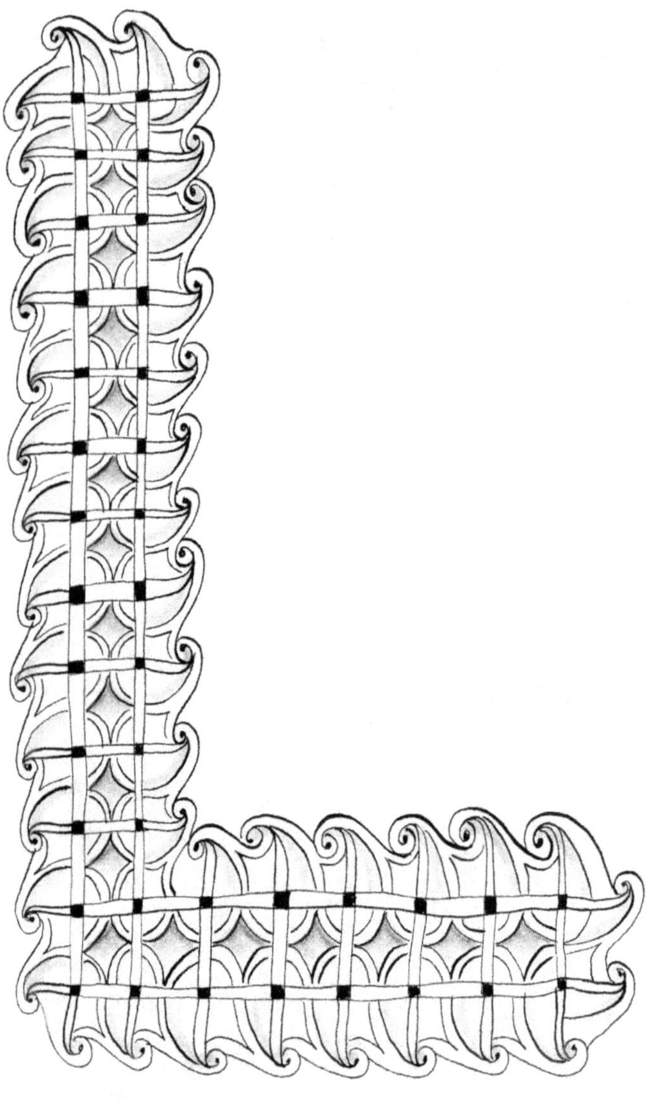

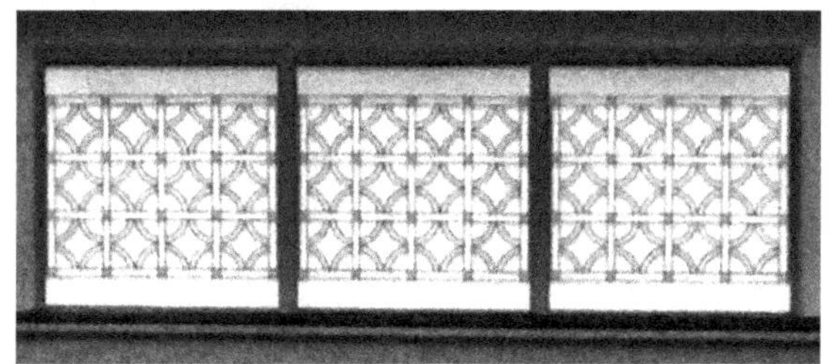

✏ Do not forget to breathe. Do not hold your breath while you draw because if you do not get enough oxygen, you begin to feel sluggish instead of "zenergized."

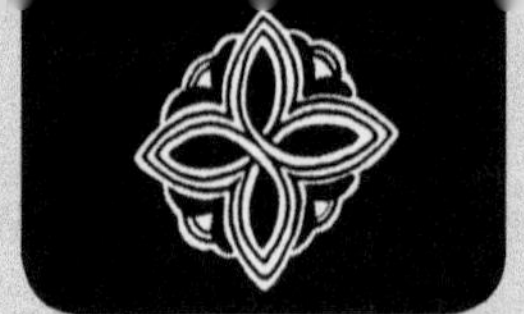

PAISLEY BOA

by Amy Broady, CZT

Inspired by her love of paisley, Amy developed this flowing arrangement of paisley shapes on a ski trip while watching her family gracefully glide back and forth down the slopes. Can you see their tracks in the initial stroke? This flowing tangle adds a touch of beauty and softness to any Zentangle artwork.

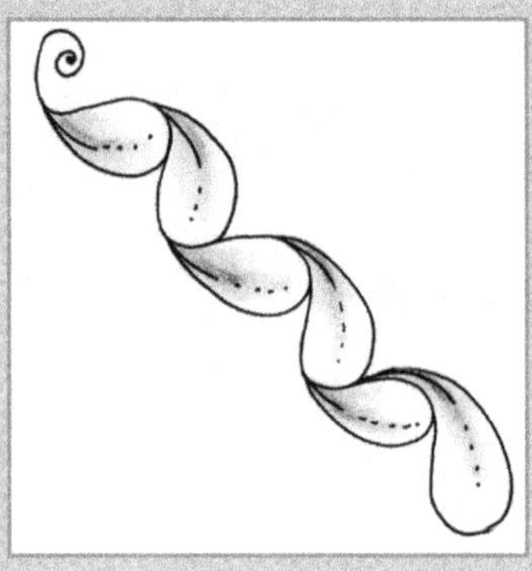

A paisley shape is a C shape wrapped around the outside of an S shape. Start with a line of continuous waves (or connected S's). Then connect the top and bottom of each S shape with a C curve. Turn the tangle over, and repeat on the other side. Add dramatic shading to create a dimensional ribbon effect.

(See alternate step-outs on p. 69)

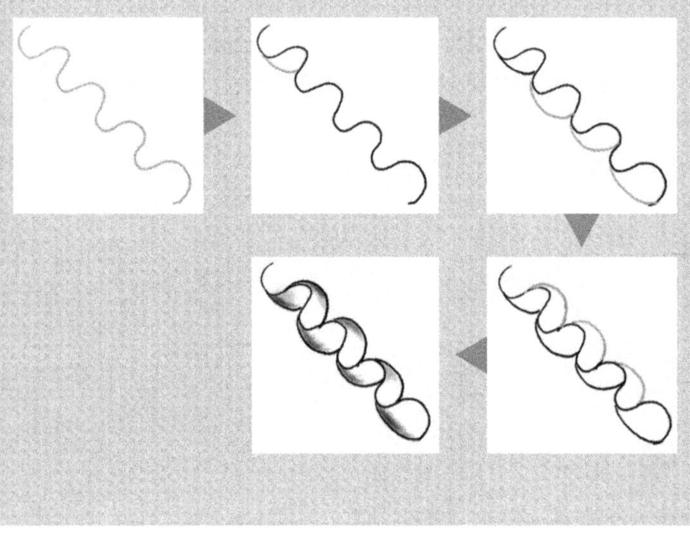

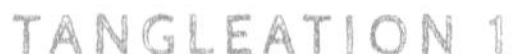

TANGLEATION 1

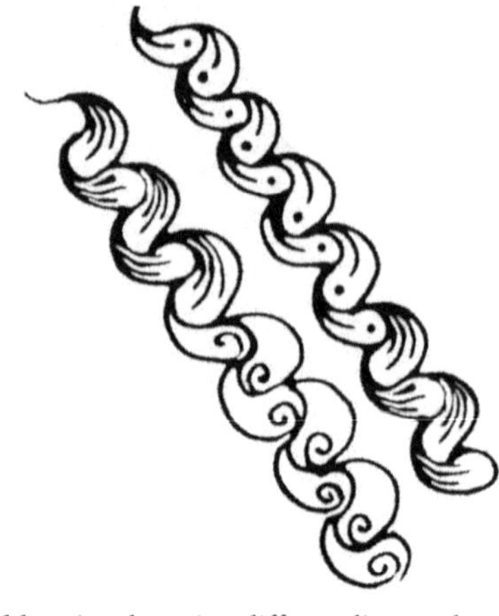

Add variety by using different line work to fill the paisley shapes. Feel free to use more than one in the same line! *(©Amy Broady)*

TANGLEATION 2

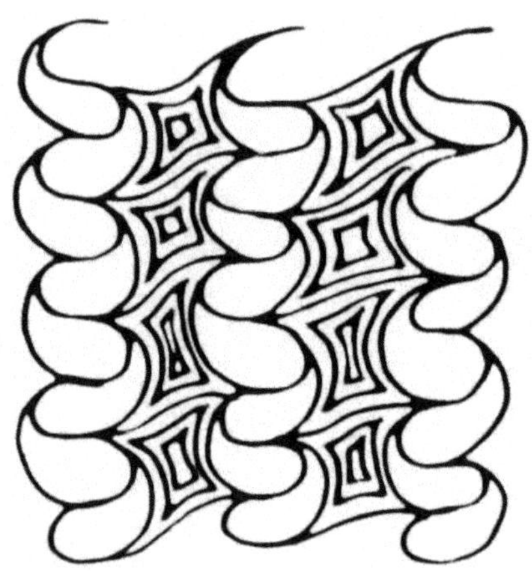

Connect rows of **PAISLEY BOAS**, and use auras, like the layers of irregular diamonds above, to fill a larger space. *(©Amy Broady)*

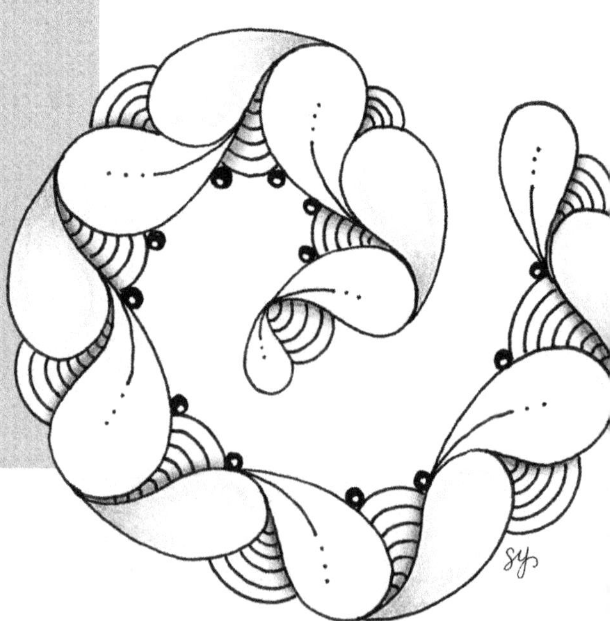

TANGLEATION 3

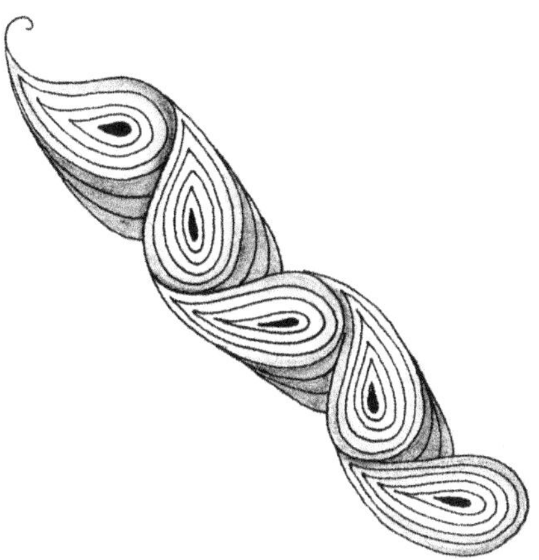

Fill each paisley shape with auras. Then add auras to the outside of each paisley to give depth and dimension.

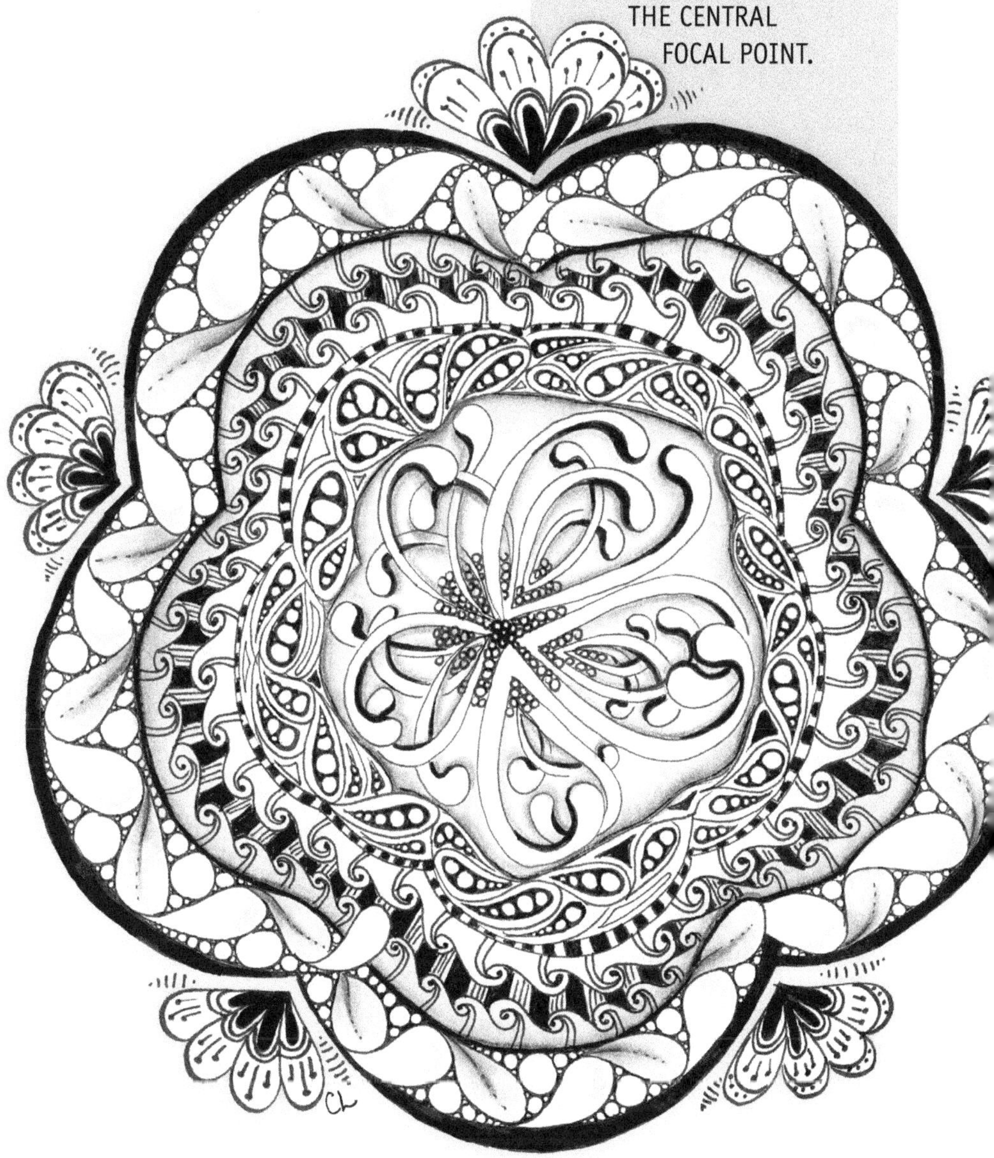

TANGLEATION 4

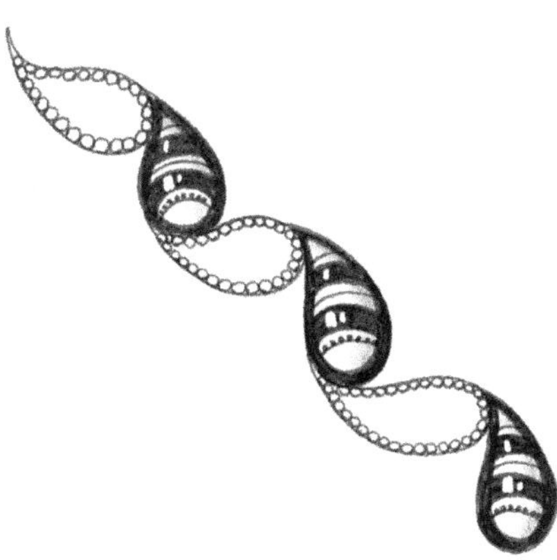

Achieve this Yin Yang look by using delicate line work on one half, and contrasting it with something dark on the opposite.

TANGLEATION 5

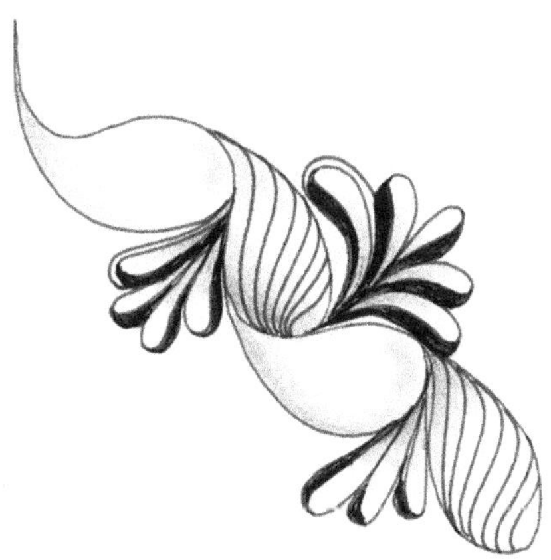

Ink **FLUX** sprouting from intersections to add flair. Draw curved stripes in alternating paisleys to create a twisting ribbon effect.

TANGLEATION 6

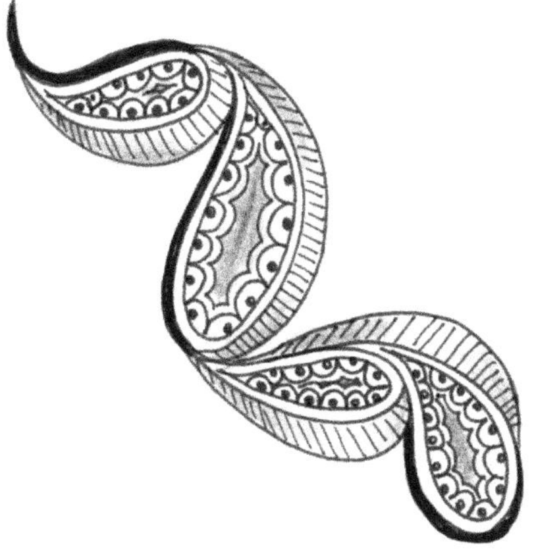

Draw auras and other tangles inside larger paisleys. Striping, shading, and thicker lines add weight and interest.

PAISLEY BOA CAN BE USED TO CREATE BOTH SUBTLE AND DRAMATIC EFFECTS. ON THE OUTER LAYER, ITS LIGHTNESS ADDS AIRINESS. BY CONTRAST, IT IS RICH AND DARK ON THE INNER LAYER, HELPING FORM THE CENTRAL FOCAL POINT.

IDEA STARTERS

- Fill large paisley shapes with a flowing tangle like PAUSHALÖV (PAGE 106).
- Divide your paisley in half, and decorate or shade each side differently.
- Turn your paisley shapes into leaves by adding veins.
- Play with both of the step-outs provided to see the different effects you get.

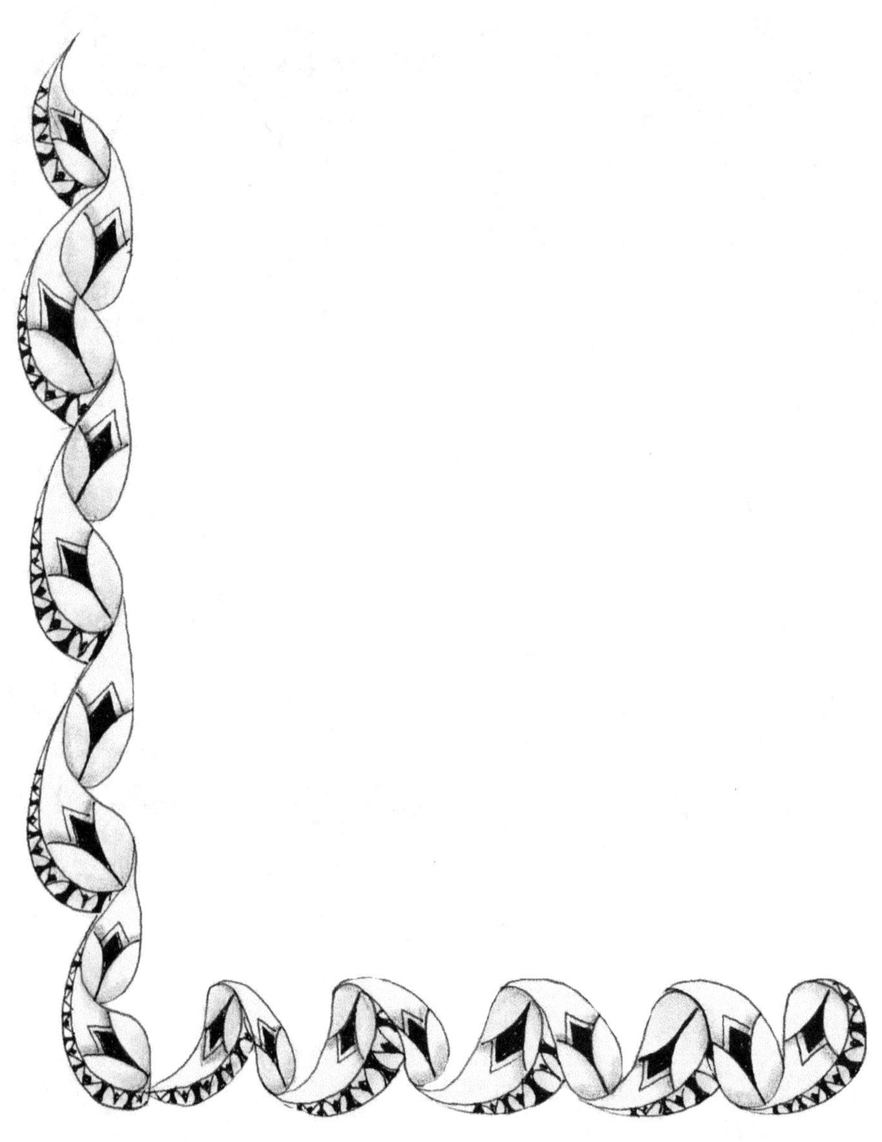

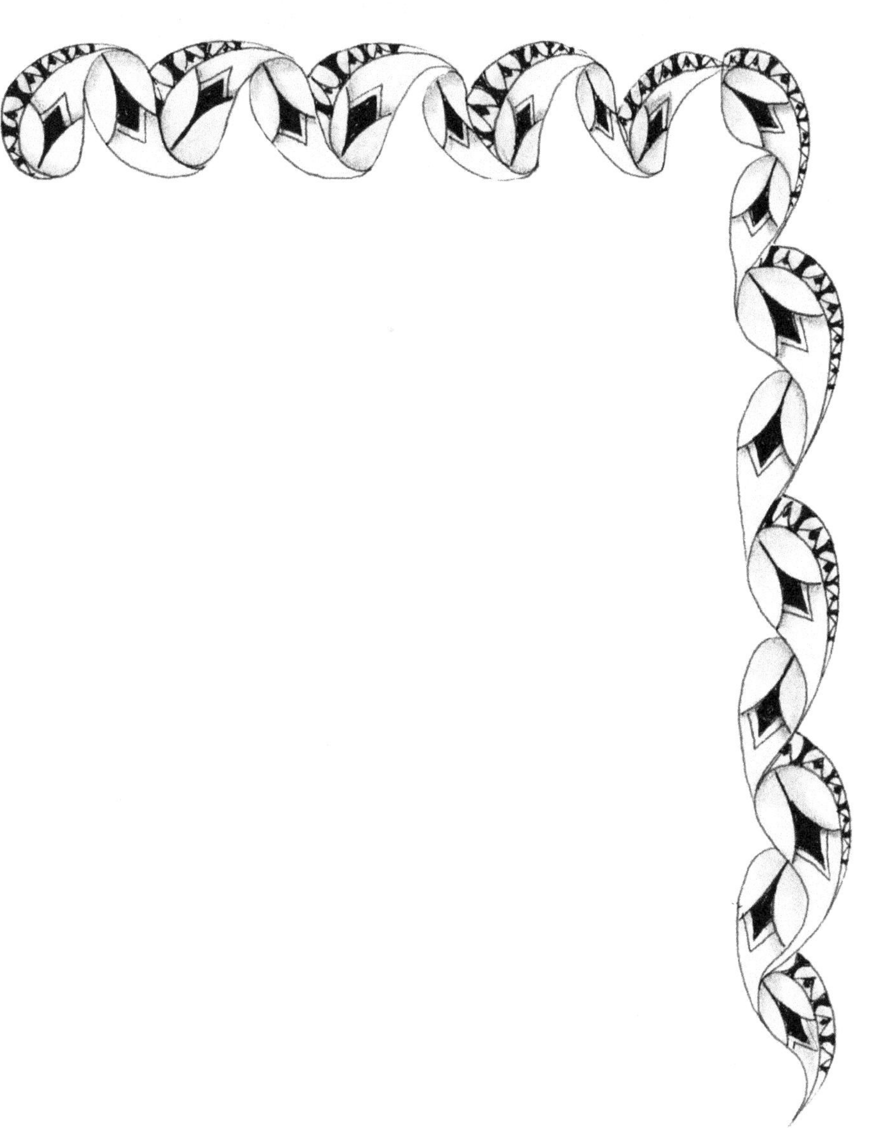

ALTERNATE STEP-OUTS

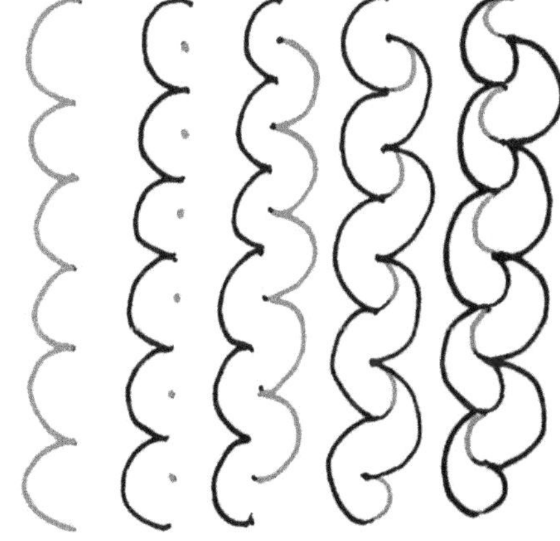

✏ Hold your pen lightly to avoid cramps. It may help to think of it as a paint brush and imagine that you do not want to bend the bristles as you paint.

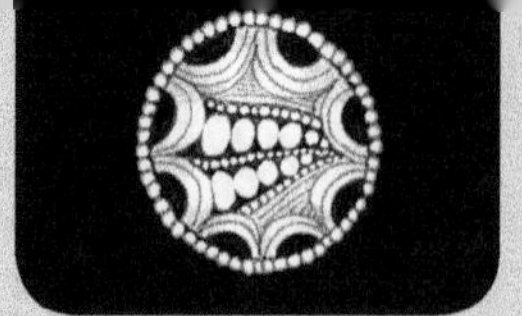

PARADOX

by Rick Roberts

Also known as **RICK'S PARADOX**, *this tangle requires a bit more focus than some. The paradox is that this curvy, complex design is drawn with only simple straight lines, beginning with a triangle. It may take a few tries before you truly make this tangle yours, but it is worth the effort.*

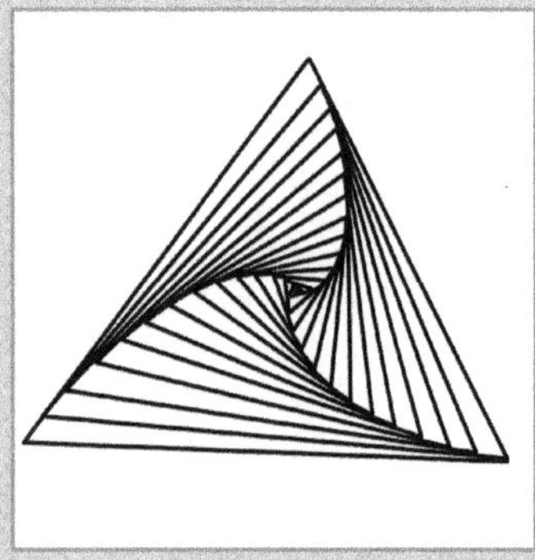

an official Zentangle tangle

The key to **PARADOX** is turning your tile after each stroke. Draw a large triangle. Each time you add a new line, a smaller triangle is created with a skinny and fat end. Begin at the fat end, and draw a line toward the point, or the reverse. Whichever you choose, be consistent. A simple mantra may be helpful to repeat aloud as you tangle: "fat to thin... turn... fat to thin... turn..."

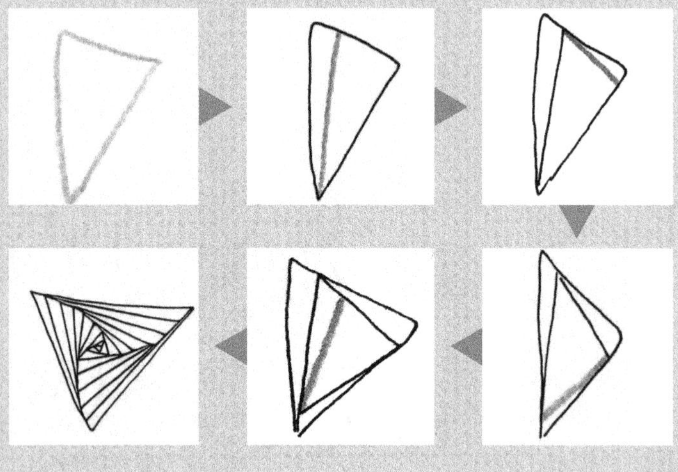

TANGLEATION 1

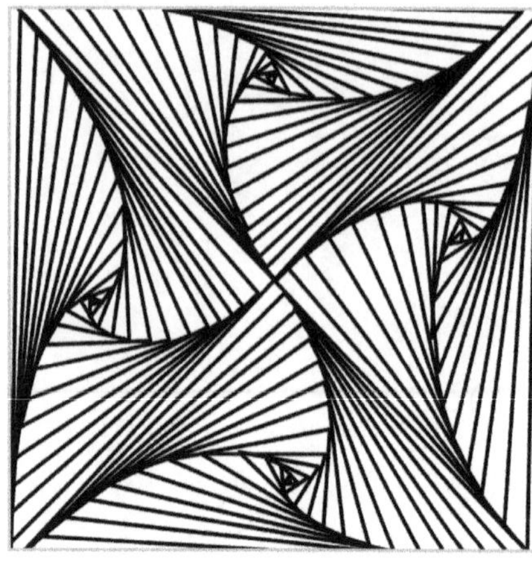

Draw lines from corner to corner to create an X. Ink **PARADOX** in one space, rotate, and repeat in each space *in the same direction.*

TANGLEATION 2

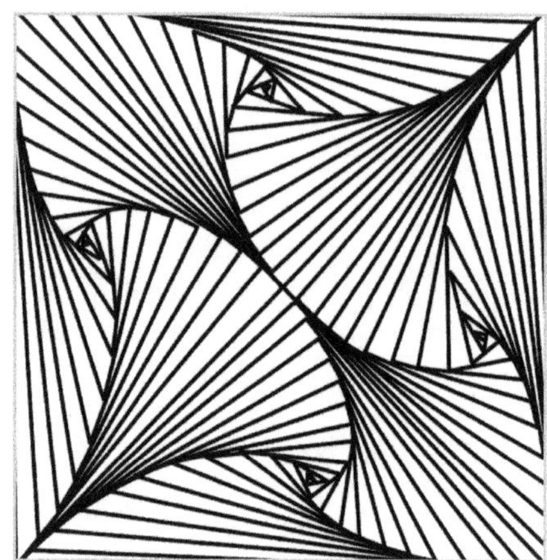

Start as you did in tangleation 1, but as you fill each quadrant with **PARADOX**, change directions.

TANGLEATION 3

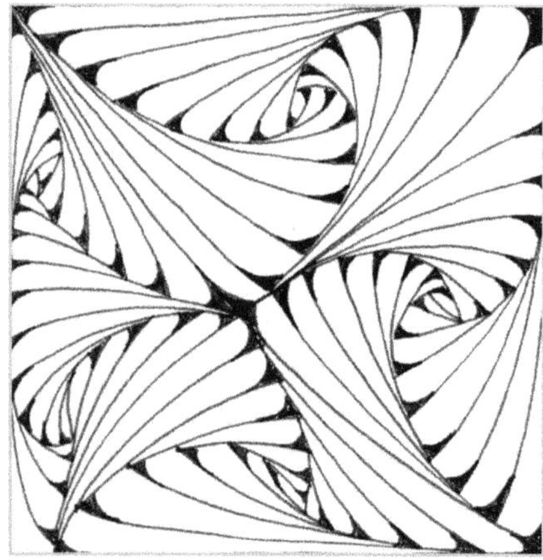

Add rounding on the fat edge of each triangle for a more organic, flowery feel.

TANGLEATION 4

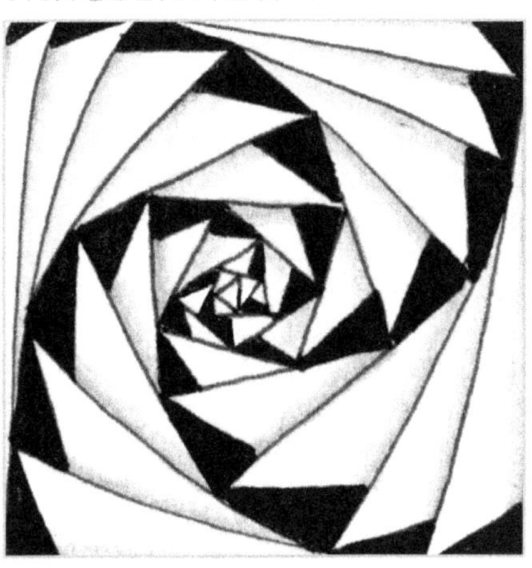

Draw your lines further apart. At the fat end of each triangle, draw another smaller triangle, and fill with black.

TANGLEATION 5

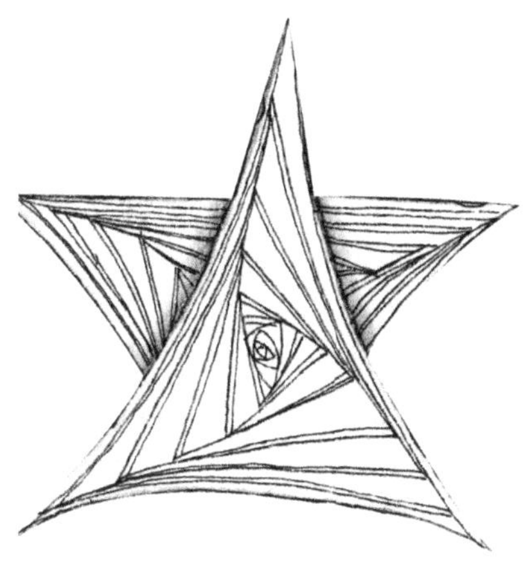

Use a double line instead of a single stroke to achieve a new look. By keeping the lines further apart, it looks less curvy.

TANGLEATION 6

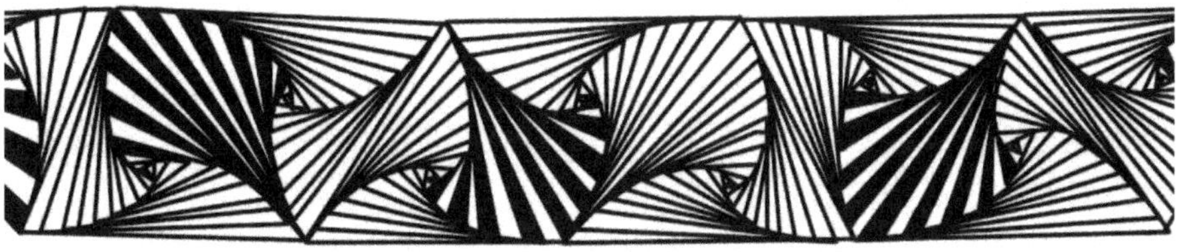

Make a stunning border with **PARADOX**. This beauty alternates between clockwise and counter-clockwise variations. The addition of black to some of the stripes highlights certain fan shapes creating great eye movement.

THIS INTRICATE ZENDALA IS A MONOTANGLE OF **PARADOX**. THE EYE MOVES FROM SHAPE TO SHAPE, LIKE A SPINNING TOP, WHIRLING IN WONDER.

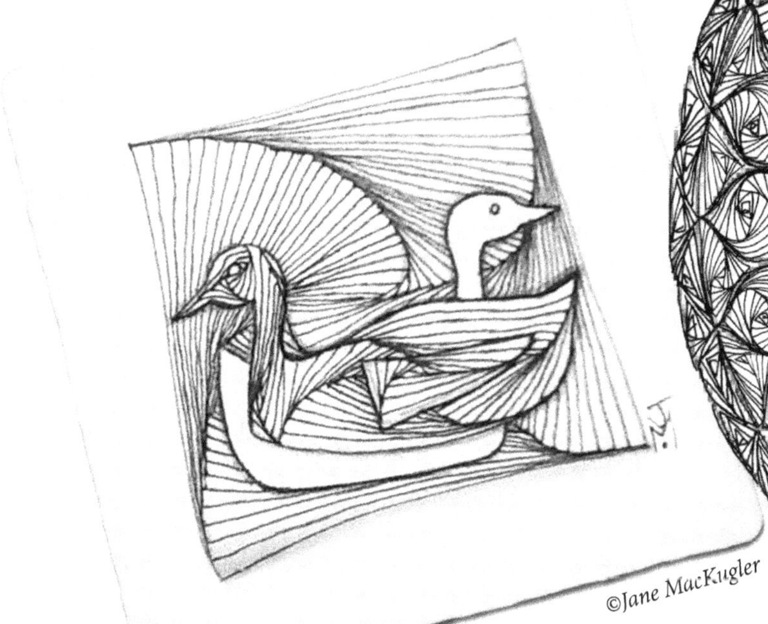

©Jane MacKugler

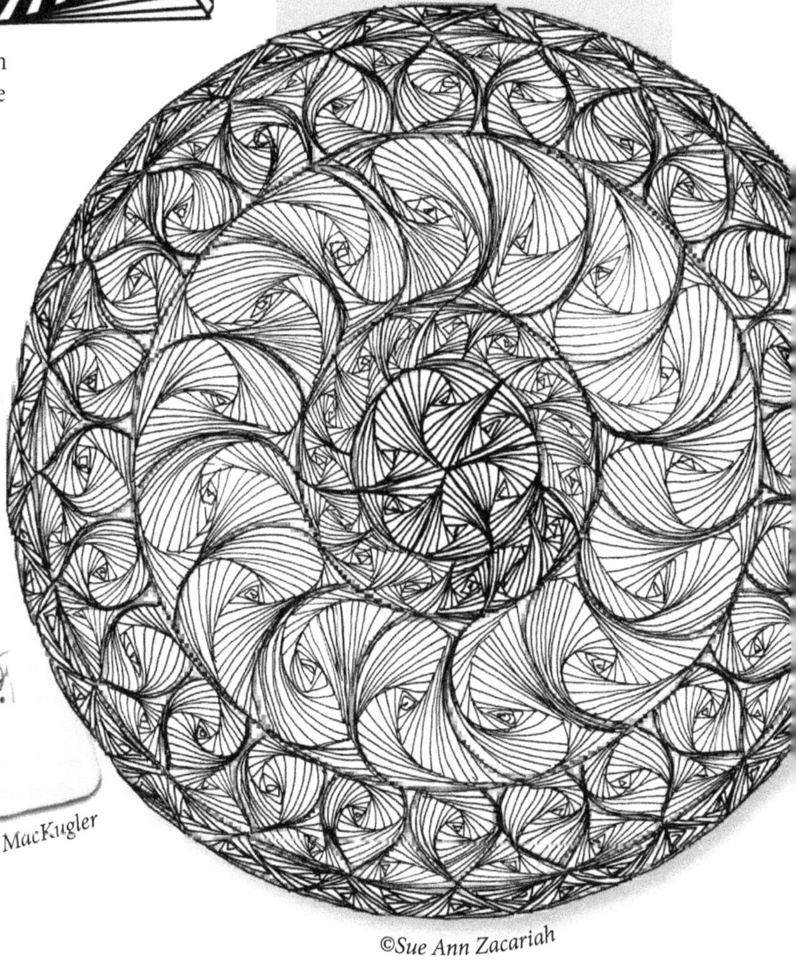

©Sue Ann Zacariah

IDEA STARTERS

- Draw a spiral, and divide it into triangles. Fill each triangle (or every other one) with PARADOX.
- Draw a large PARADOX with wide spaces, and tangle in each or every other space. Why not use BRAZELET (PAGE 122)?
- Divide an orb into wedges. Fill each wedge with PARADOX.
- Vary your line weight when drawing PARADOX. Use delicate lines, double lines, thick lines, etc.

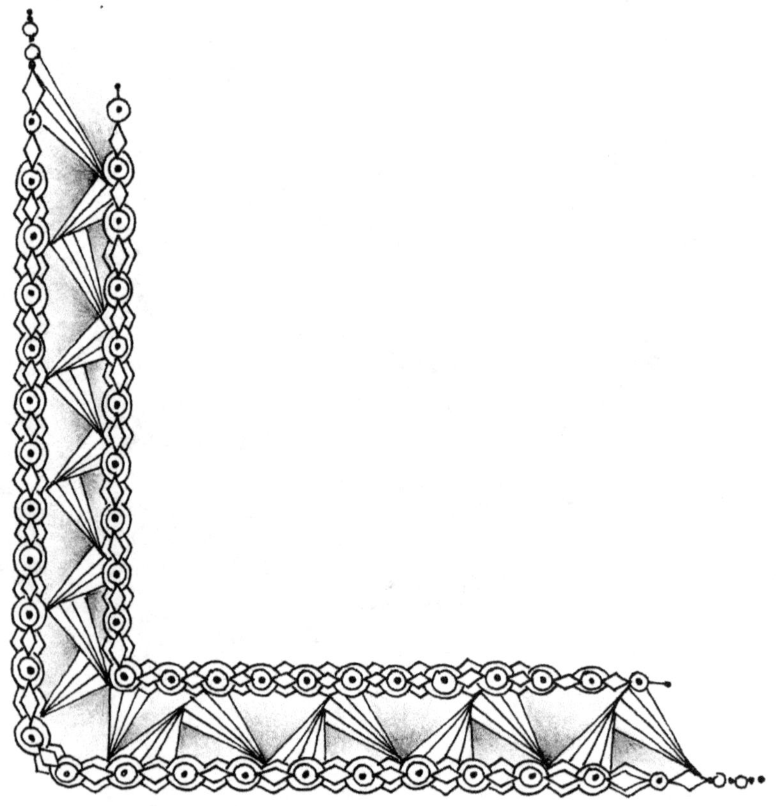

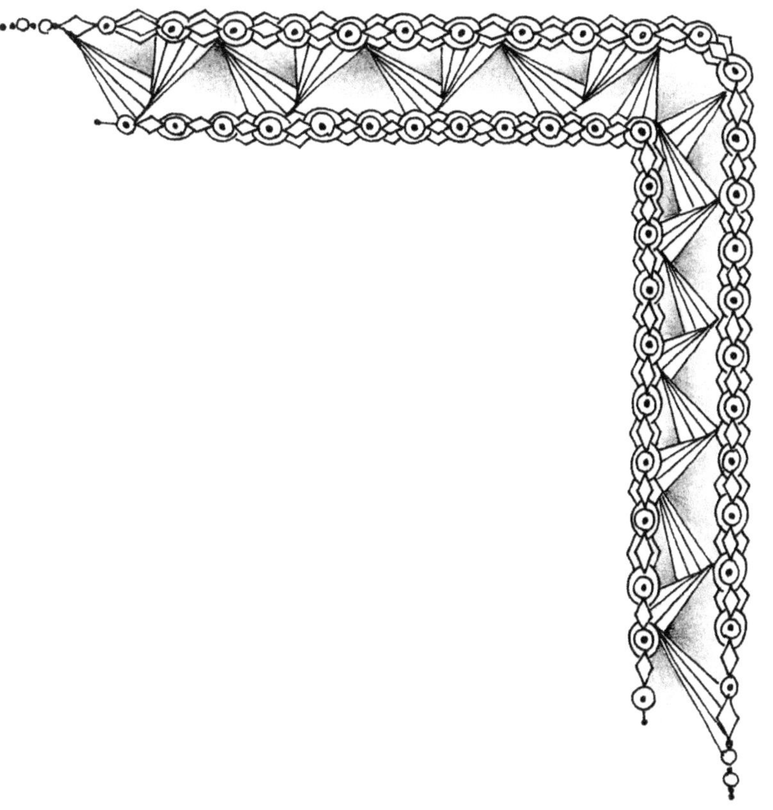

✏ Learn to accept your "mistakes," and relabel them "tangleations." Did your line not go where you intended it to? Not a problem. Think of it as an opportunity to go off in an unexpected direction.

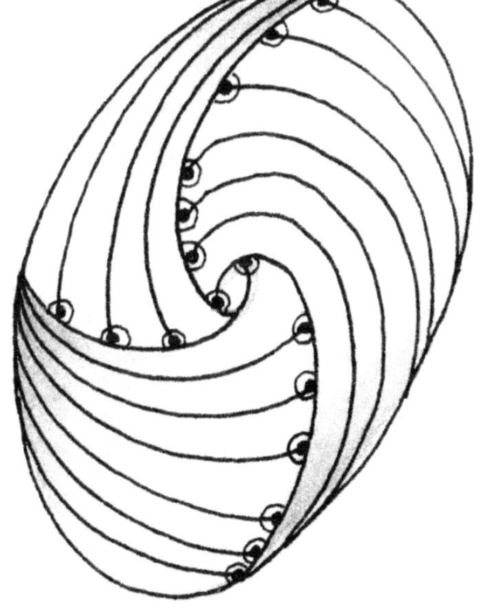

PARADOX

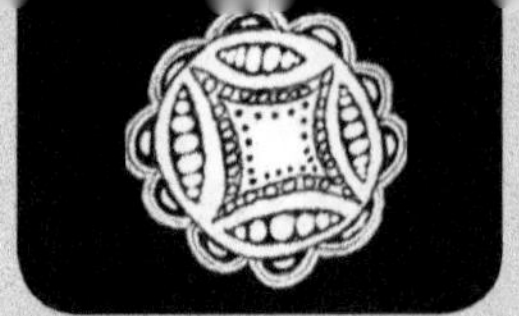

GÜRTEL

by Cris Letourneau, CZT

GÜRTEL *takes root from the German word* gürtelschnalle, *meaning buckle. A beautiful Gothic pewter buckle on eBay was the inspiration for this tangle.* **GÜRTEL** *is curvy, graphic, and round without being frilly. Its versatility as a medallion, fill, or grid makes it a fun tangle to play with.*

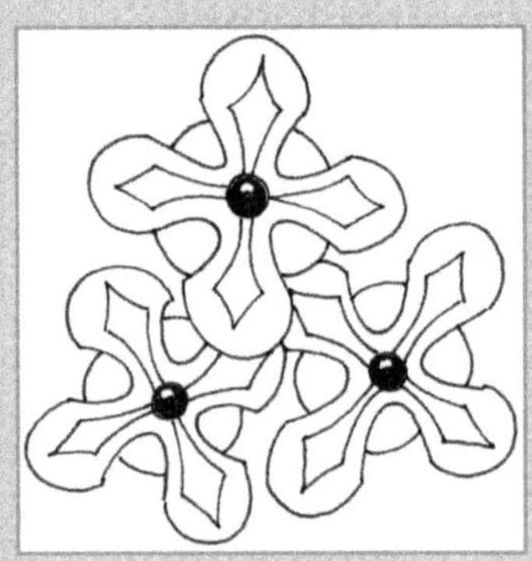

While it may look complex, **GÜRTEL** exemplifies the definition of a tangle. It is easily deconstructed into a series of steps and is made up of the simplest of strokes. Orbs, V shapes, U shapes, and arcs are put together to create versatile medallions.

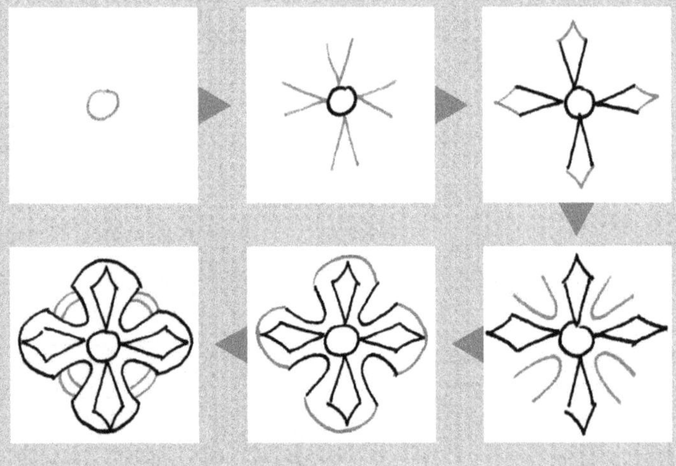

TANGLEATION 1

Add extra circles and auras to create a variety of beautiful medallions reminiscent of a cross pattée or Maltese Cross.

TANGLEATION 2

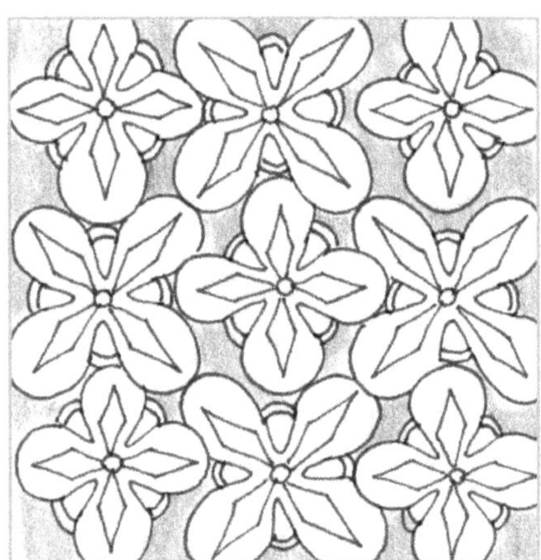

Draw large **GÜRTELS** on a grid, with only the tips touching. Add smaller **GÜRTELS** in the blank spaces, rotating them 45°.

TANGLEATION 3

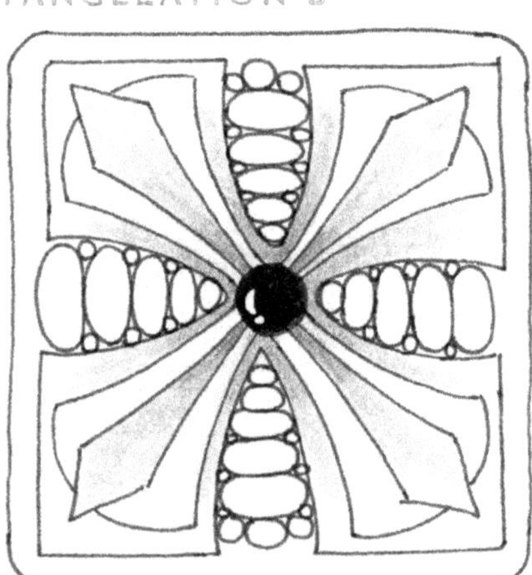

Put **GÜRTEL** in a square. Change the shape of the auras around the points. Add orbs to the spaces in between to fill in the space.

TANGLEATION 4

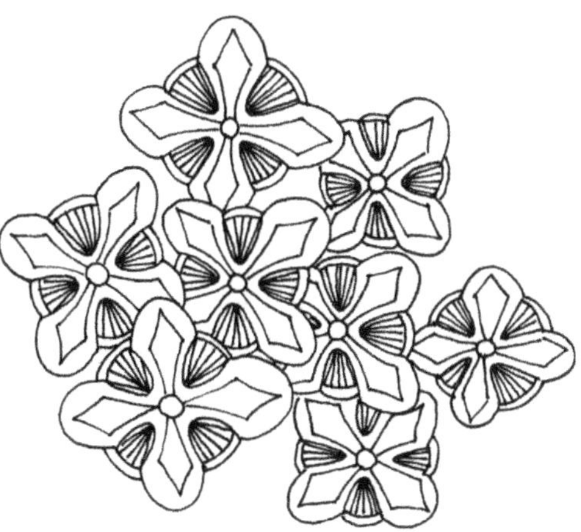

Layer **GÜRTEL** in a free-form style. Draw one in the foreground. Then add partial ones, each behind the next, creating depth.

TANGLEATION 5

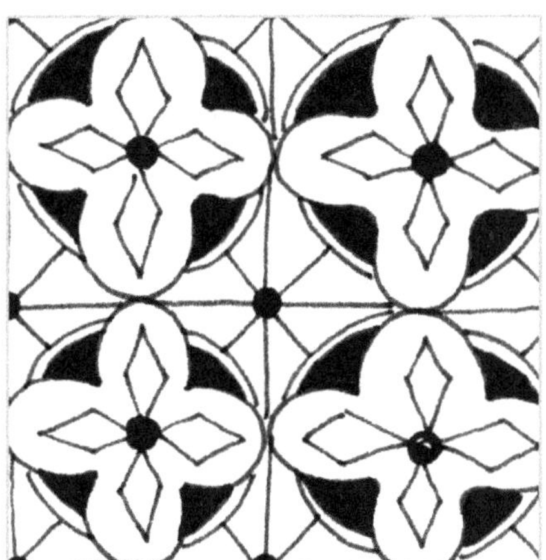

Place **GÜRTEL** on a grid. Complete the medallions first. Then add the connectors in between for a stained glass look.

TANGLEATION 6

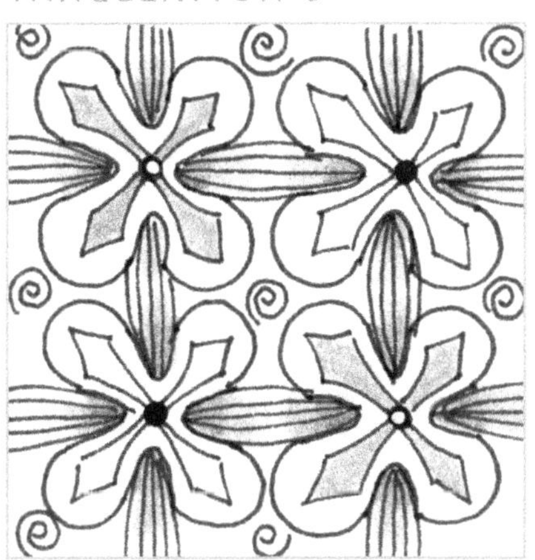

Draw ribbon-like connectors between the **GÜRTEL** shapes. Add spirals and shading for a strong resemblance to **KEMBLE**.

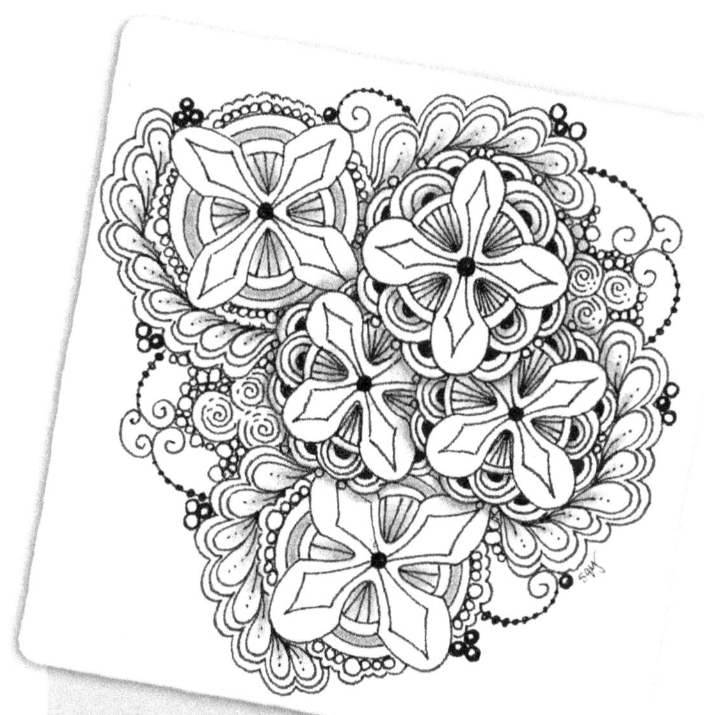

LAYERS OF FREE-FORM GÜRTELS CREATE A BEAUTIFUL ENSEMBLE. DELIBERATE SHADING ENHANCES THE LAYERING EFFECT CREATING DEPTH AND INTEREST.

Tile features: **GÜRTEL**, **FLUX**, **CRESCENT MOON**, **TIPPLE**, *and* **PRINTEMPS**.

IDEA STARTERS

- Change the number of V's you draw around your orb. Instead of 4, use 6 or maybe even 8.
- There are a lot of elements that make up this tangle. Leave one or two out and see what happens.
- For a touch of elegance, add pearls to the ends of the diamonds.
- Change the scale of different elements. For instance, make the center orb larger and the diamonds shorter.
- Add auras or patterns to the background orbs.

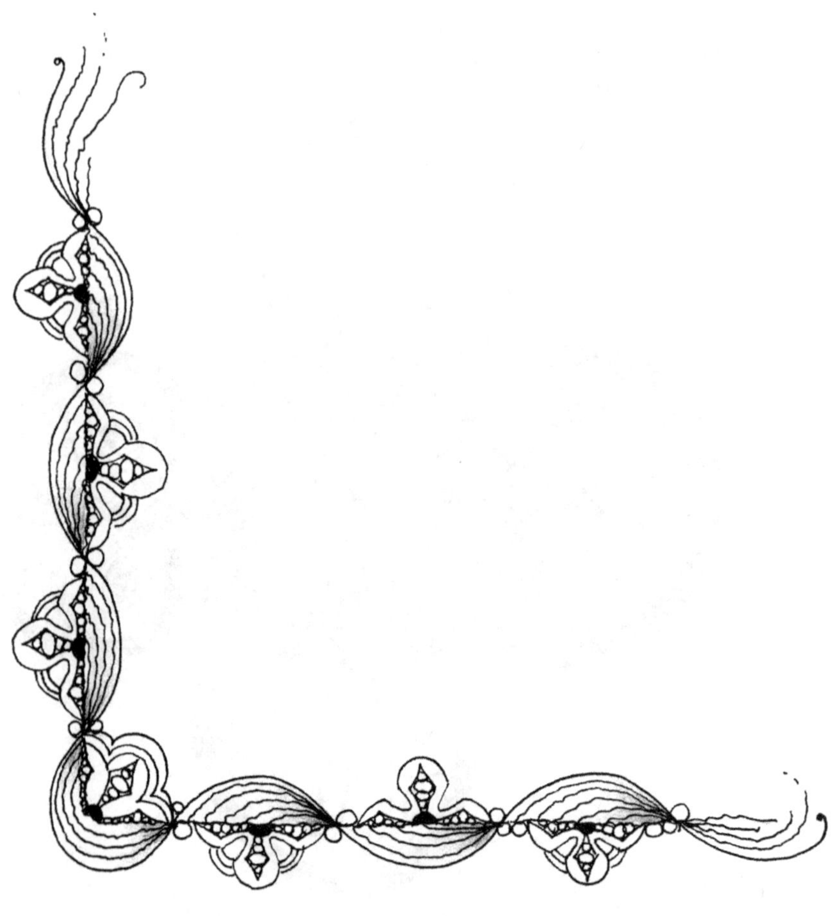

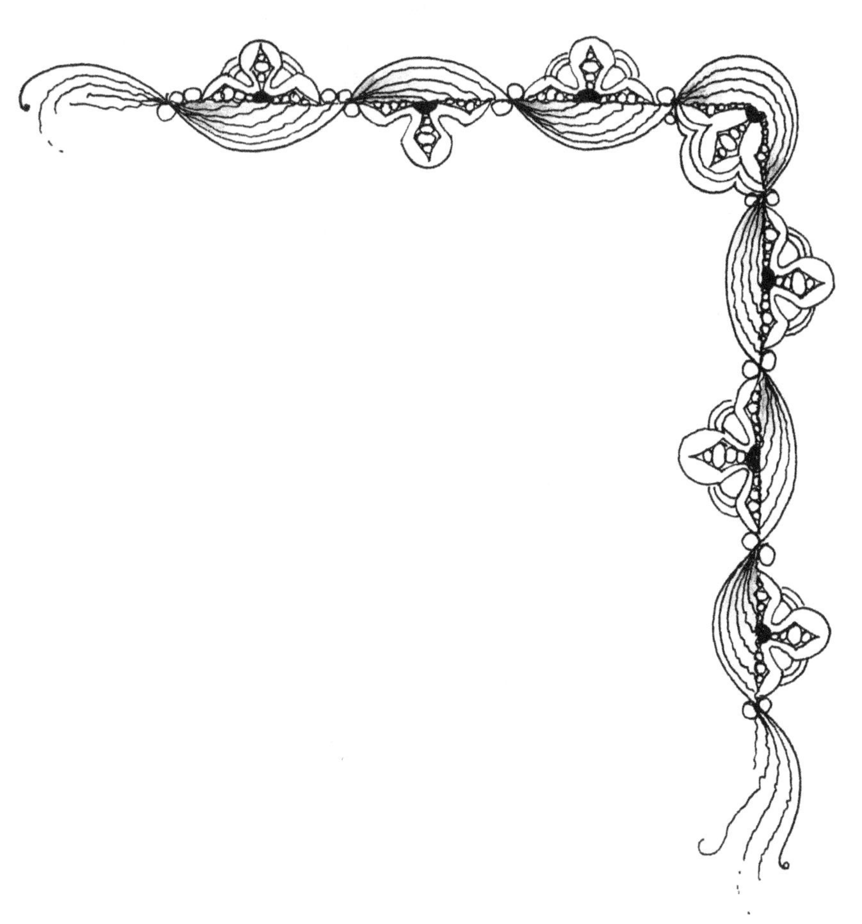

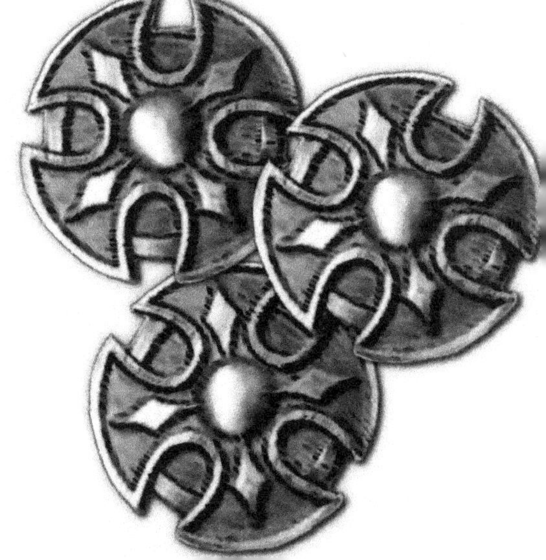

✏ Make each tangle your own. Keep reminding yourself that if you make an identical copy of someone else's work, yours will be redundant.

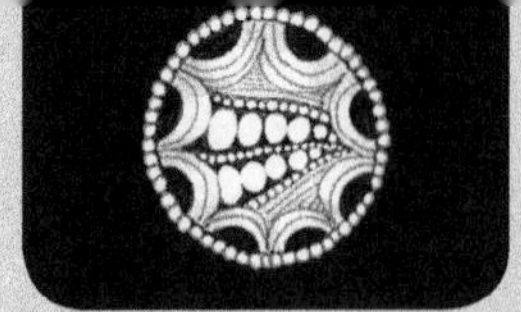

TAGH

by Rick Roberts & Maria Thomas

Simple and organic, TAGH *is an excellent fill tangle, easily adapted to cover any size or shaped space. Its versatility is a result of its simple forms: easily recognizable "petals" with "seed" accents. You can also use it as a tool to subtly guide the viewer's eye in any direction you choose.*

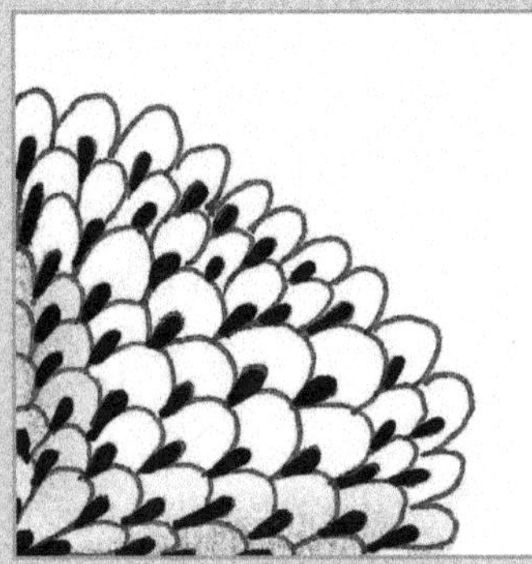

an official Zentangle tangle

Draw the first petal shape in one corner. Add layer after layer of additional petals fanning out from behind the first. This creates a rhythmic, directional pattern. Seed shapes complete the look.

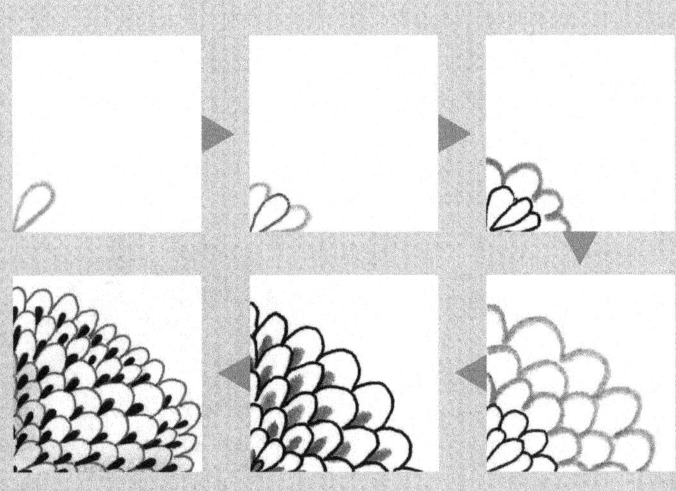

TANGLEATION 1

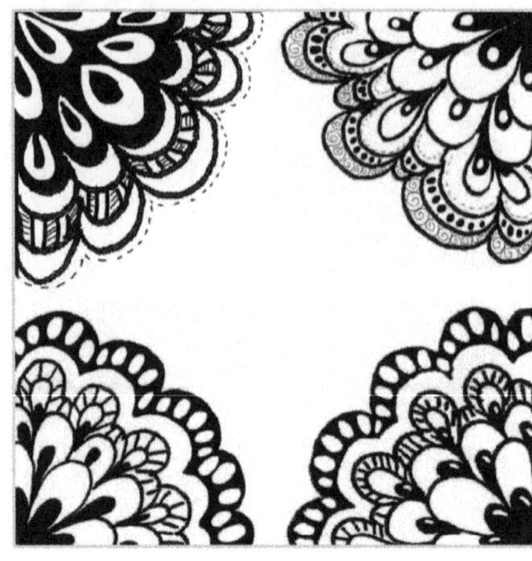

Draw **TAGH** from multiple corners to guide the viewer's eye to the middle. Fill the auras to create even more interest.

TANGLEATION 2

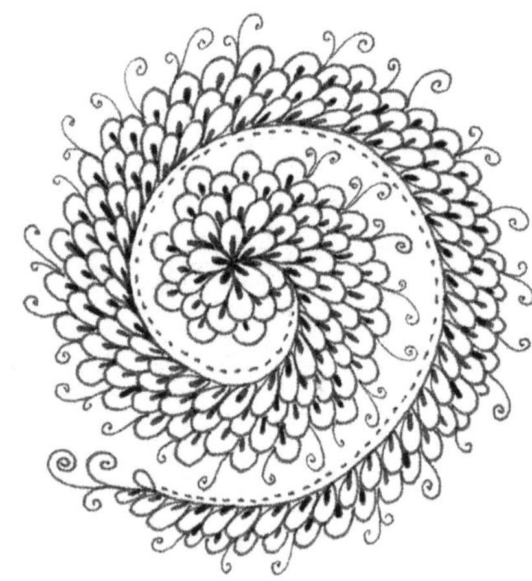

Put **TAGH** into a spiral pattern with flourishes and stitching to create a lovely focal point.

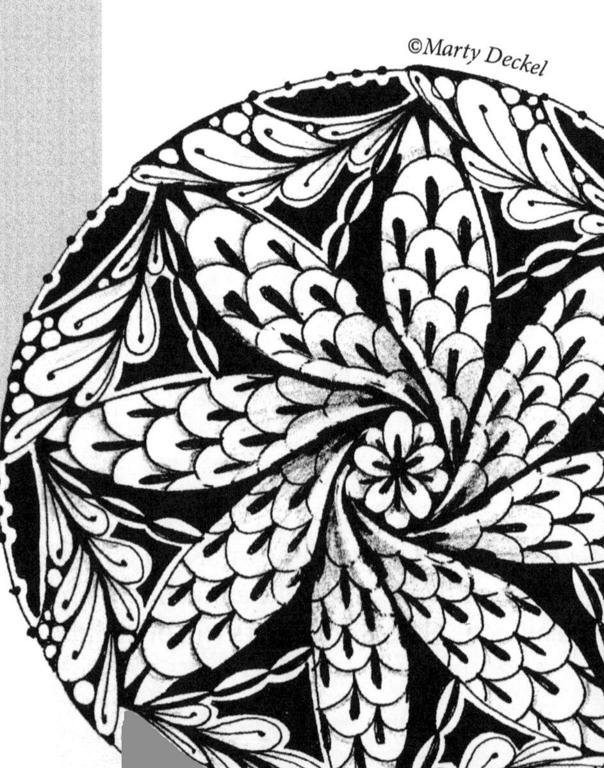

©Marty Deckel

TANGLEATION 3

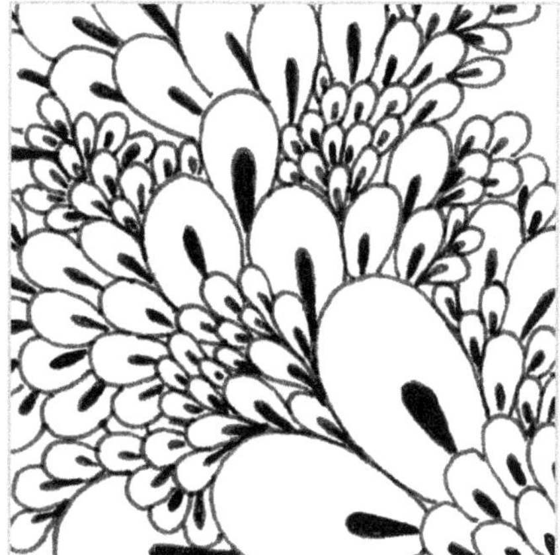

Vary the size of the petals, and create clusters of similar sized petals for a completely new look bursting with energy.

TANGLEATION 4

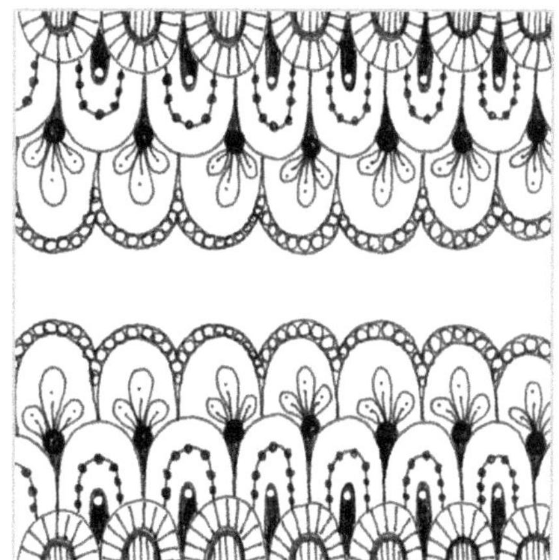

Use **TAGH** as a layered border. Draw the bottoms of the seeds square instead of pointed to give a more geometric feel.

TAGH CAN ALSO BE USED AS A STRING WITH BEAUTIFUL RESULTS. HERE EACH PETAL HAS BEEN FILLED WITH A DIFFERENT TANGLE; EVEN THE SEEDS HAVE BEEN TANGLED. THE LAYERS ADD DIMENSION TO THE DESIGN.

Tile features: FLUX, CADENT, SEZ, PARADOX, *and* CRESCENT MOON.

TANGLEATION 5

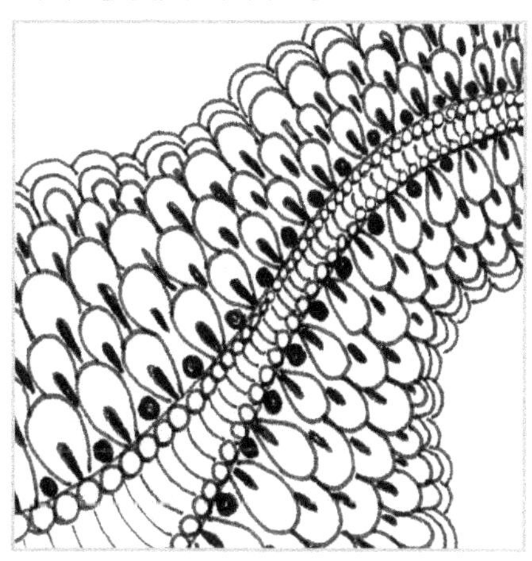

Ink **TAGH** along a curved line. Use black pearls to fill the spaces along the central line, and use auras to accent the final row.

TANGLEATION 6

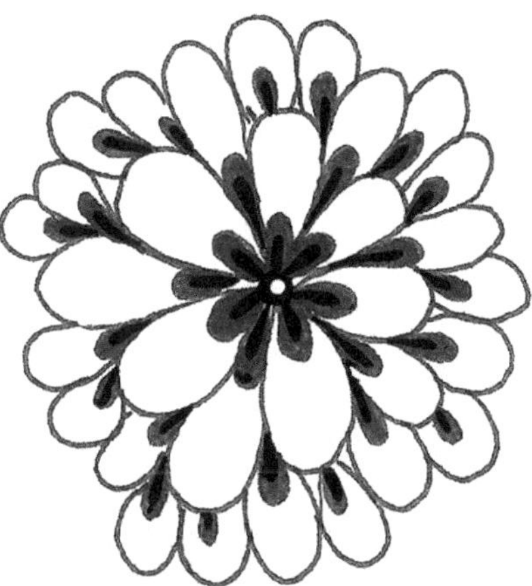

Radiate petals from the center to create a flower-like focal point on your tile.

IDEA STARTERS

- Vary the size and shape of the seeds inside the petals.
- Fill the seed with one pattern and the rest of the petal with another.
- Draw multiple auras around the seeds, and decorate them.
- Change the shape of your petals. Why not try ovals, orbs, or pill shapes?
- Add an aura (or two) to each petal as you draw it. Decorate them if you wish.

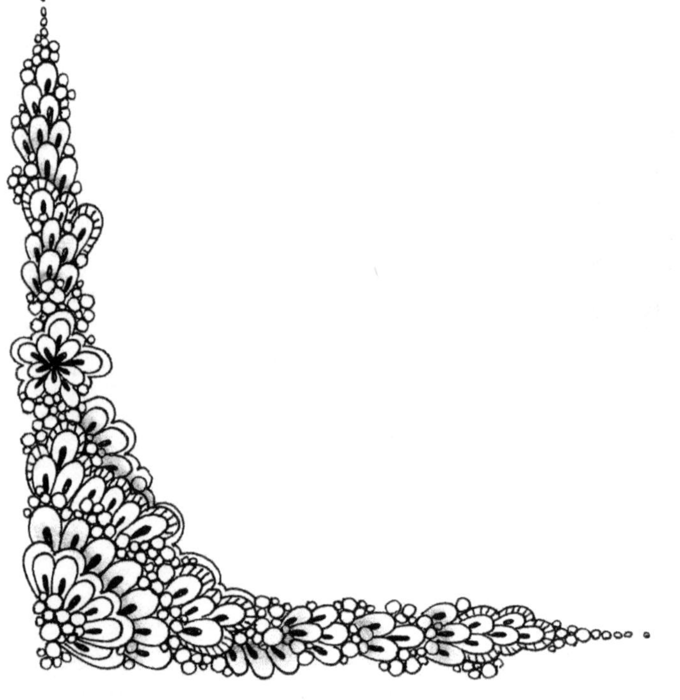

✏ Do not put the cap on the back of the pen while you are tangling. This makes your pen heavier and more off-balance in your hand. Less muscle fatigue = increased enjoyment.

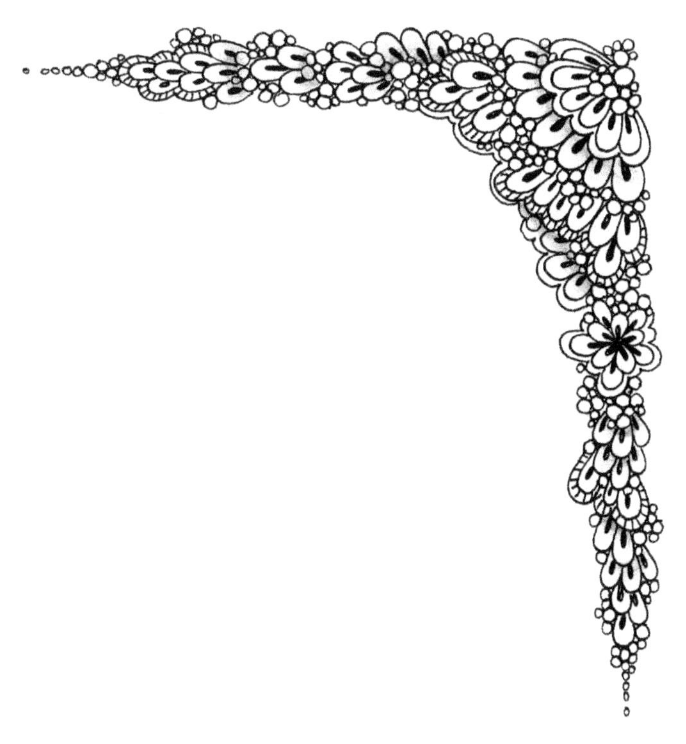

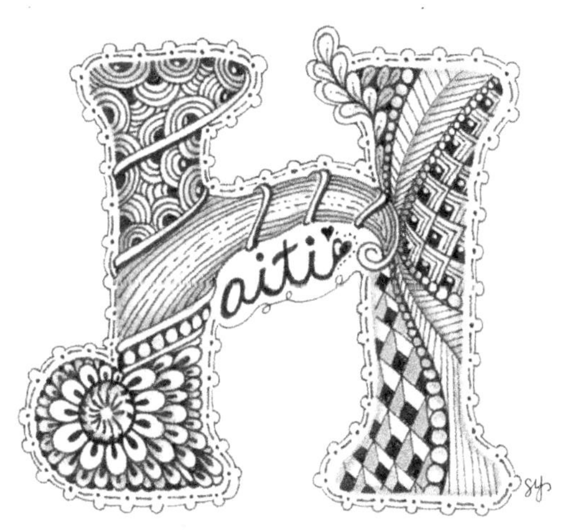
aiti

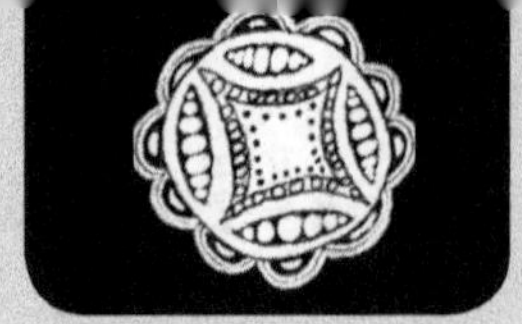

KEMBLE

by Sonya Yencer

While thumbing through a popular home decor magazine, Sonya stumbled across some inspiring upholstery fabric from which KEMBLE *emerged. This versatile grid-based pattern is a harmonious blend of geometric and organic elements. However you personalize it,* KEMBLE *will add a unique flair as a fill for your Zentangle art.*

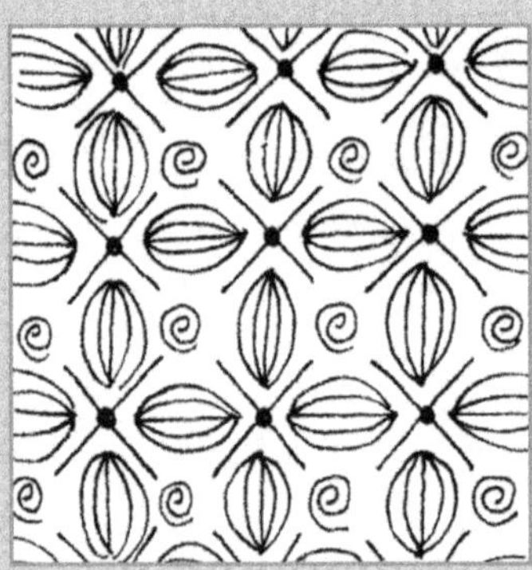

The key to KEMBLE is the start. When creating your dot grid, be sure to allow enough space in between the dots to add all of the elements that anchor to the grid. Tight spacing makes it more challenging, but creates beautiful results as well. *(See alternate step-outs on p. 85.)*

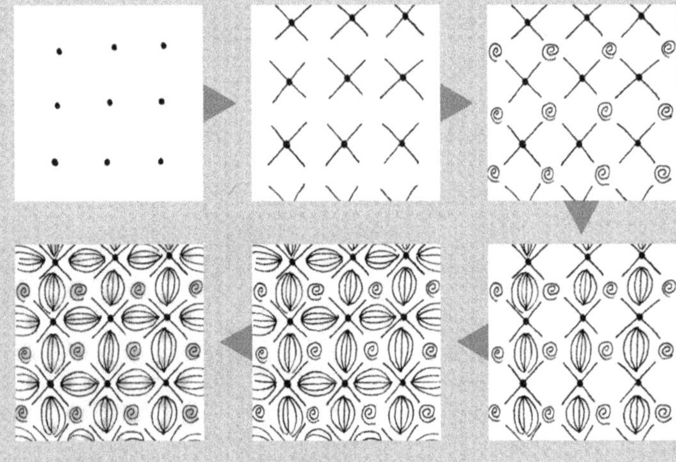

TANGLEATION 1

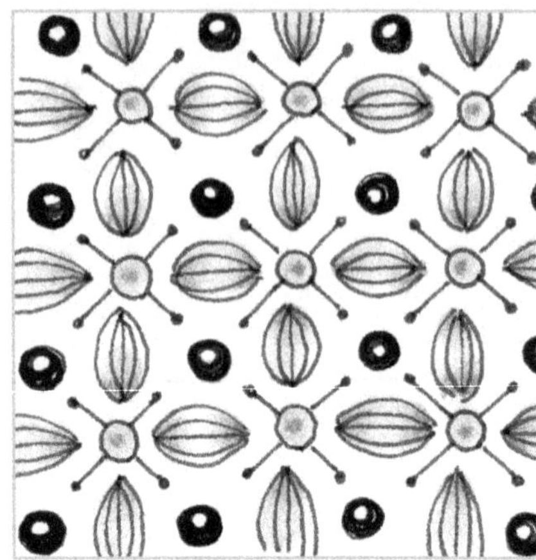

Replace dots and spirals with large white and black pearls if a darker, heavier fill is desired.

TANGLEATION 2

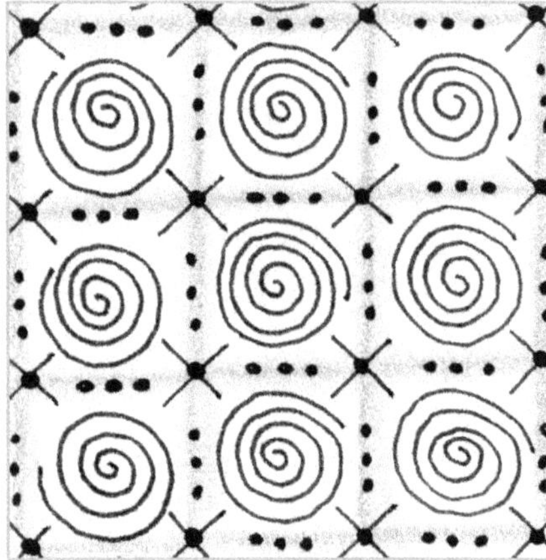

Vary the scale of the elements. Here, the spirals are enlarged and the Xs reduced. Shading the grid completely changes the look.

TANGLEATION 3

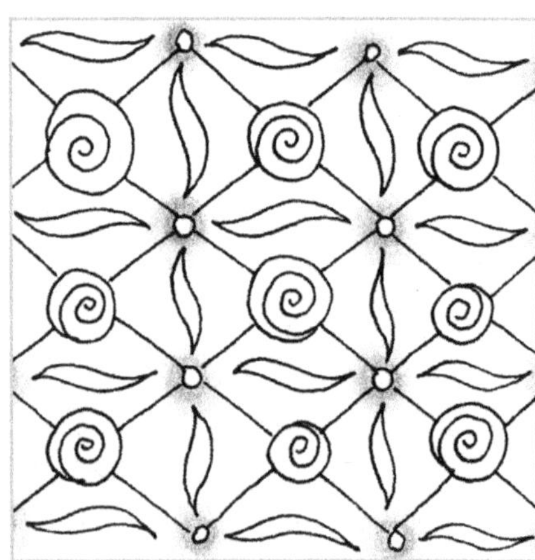

Connect the Xs and the spirals. Simplify the petals to a single wavy line to create a pattern reminiscent of a flowered lattice.

TANGLEATION 4

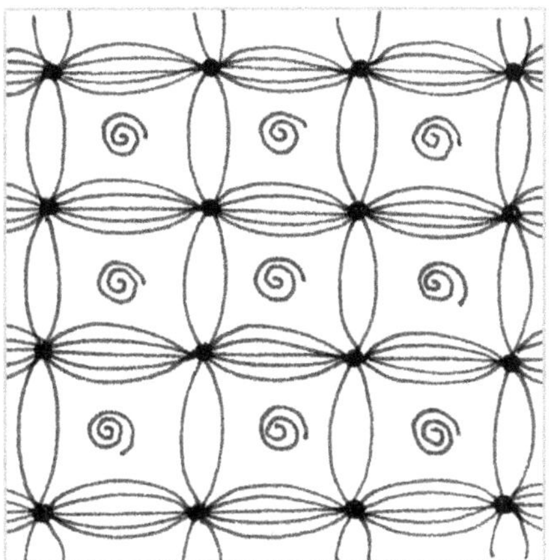

Connect the petal shapes to emphasize the grid Leave off the 'X' shape and fill the horizontal petals with lines.

TANGLEATION 5

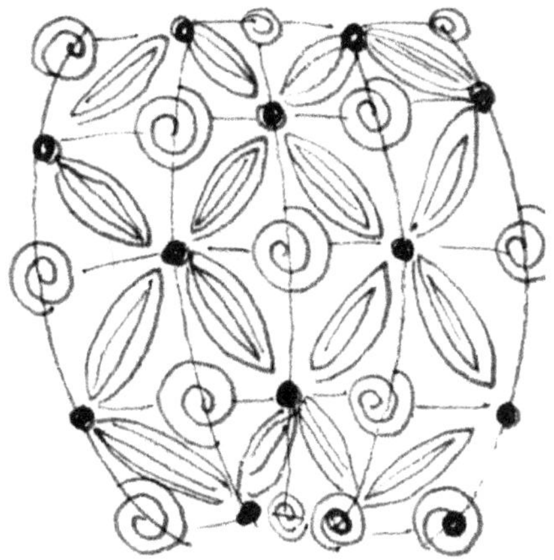

Draw **KEMBLE** on a curved grid taking inspiration from longitude and latitude lines. Give it a global twist!

TANGLEATION 6

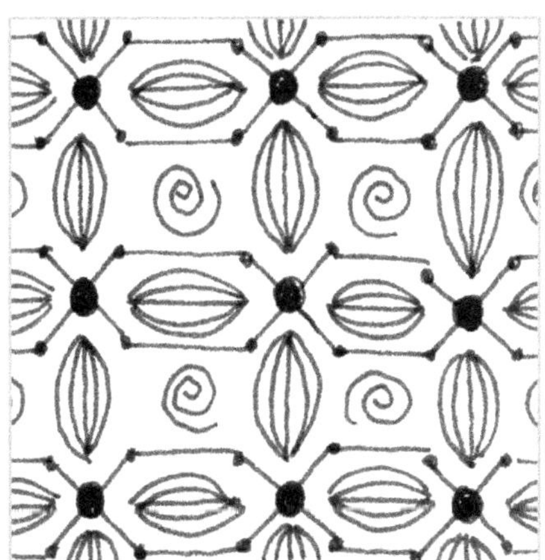

Create a more geometric look by connecting the dots. Use horizontal or vertical lines. Feeling adventurous? Do both!

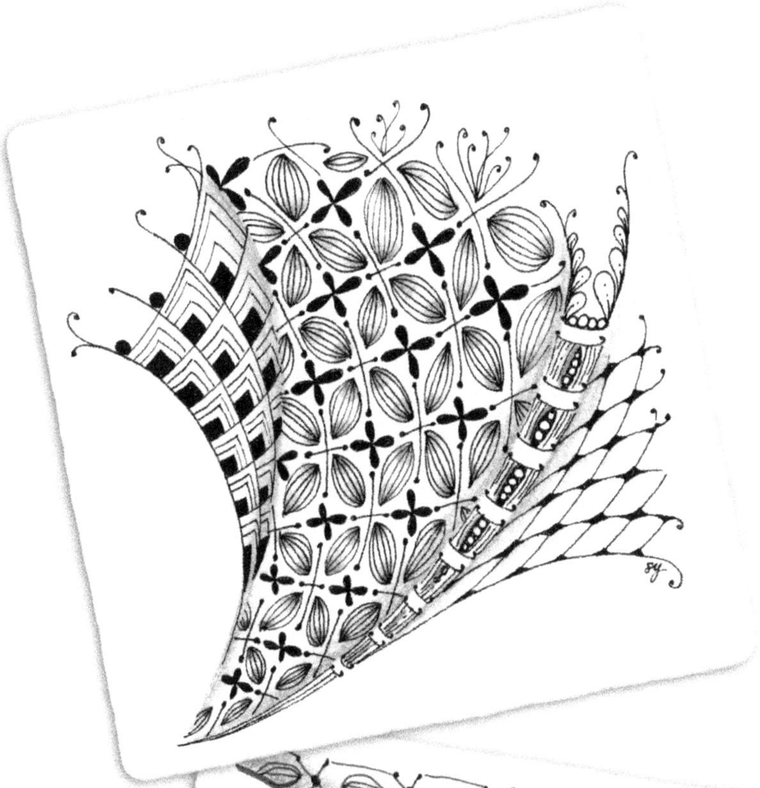

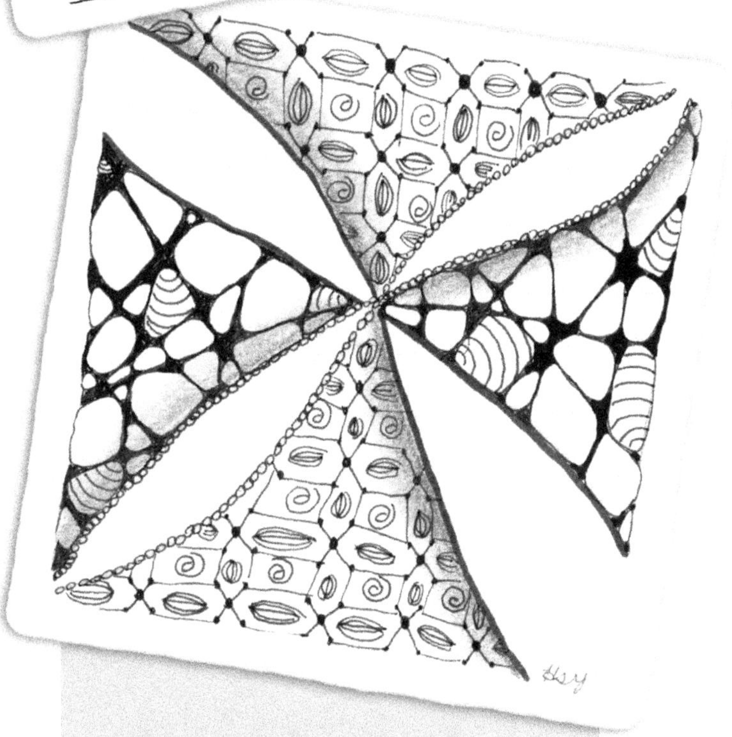

AS DEMONSTRATED ABOVE, KEMBLE PLAYS WELL WITH OTHER TANGLES. HERE A MOTHER / DAUGHTER PAIR SHOW THEIR INDIVIDUALITY USING KEMBLE WITH VERY DIFFERENT RESULTS.

(top) Tile by Sonya Yencer features: KEMBLE, FLUKES, ZANDER, FLUX, *and* FLOORZ. *(bottom) Tile by Hana Yencer features:* KEMBLE *and* 'NZEPPEL.

IDEA STARTERS

- Substitute different shapes for the spirals in your design.
- Instead of putting your X's in straight lines, curve them into a rainbow.
- Shade the individual elements, leaving the background white.
- Shade only the background.
- Draw larger orbs or pearls at the end of each X instead of tiny dots.

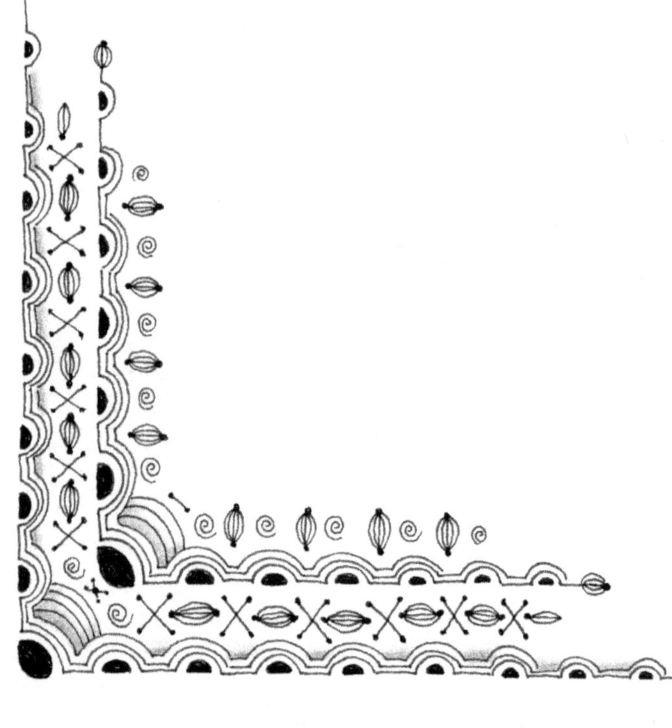

✏ Let go of judgment. After you finish each stroke, let it go. How can you judge something that is incomplete? To quote the Beatles, “Let it be.”

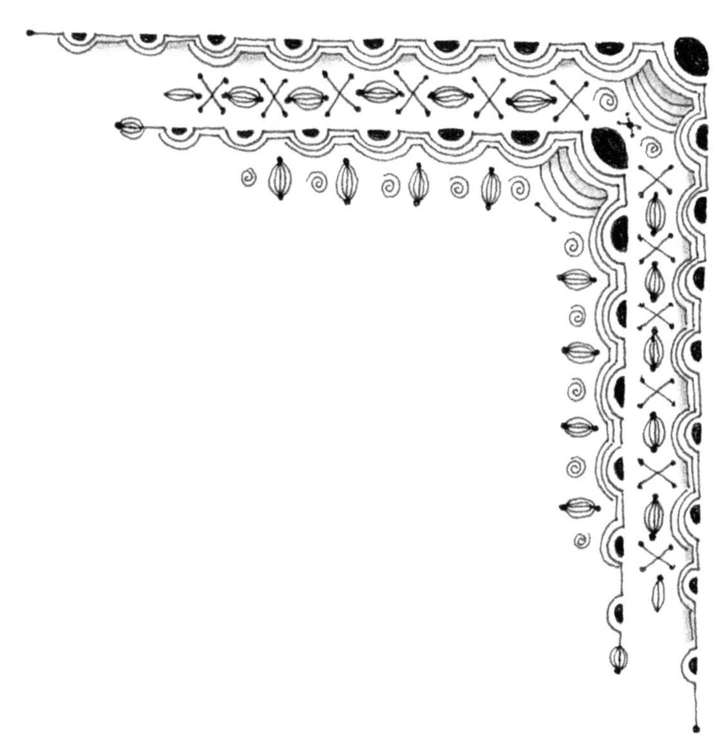

ALTERNATE STEP-OUTS

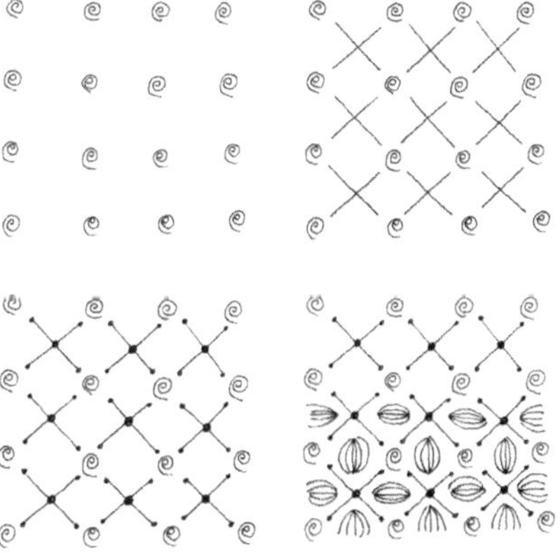

DRAGONAIR

by Norma Burnell

Want to add some magic to your Zentangle art? Look no further than DRAGONAIR. *Born of the artist's love of fairy tale creatures, this tangleation of* CADENT *is a flowing design that creates great eye-movement in whatever direction you choose. Let your imagination run wild as you draw the graceful curves of* DRAGONAIR.

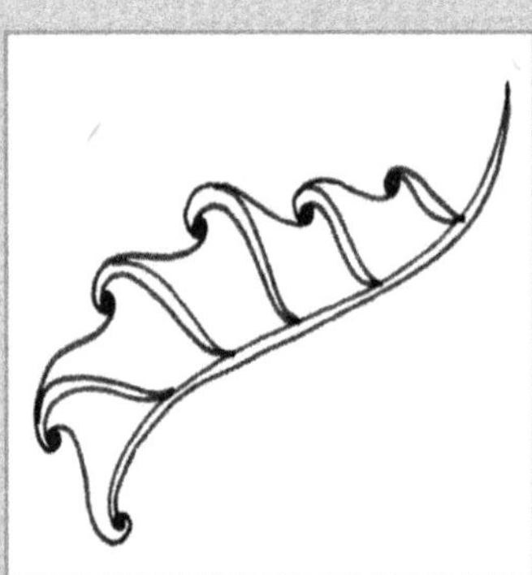

Like waves on an ocean, the curves of DRAGONAIR rise and fall, accentuating the shape of the initial line to which all other lines are anchored. Draw your anchor line in whatever shape you desire. Add curved lines with small black dots on the ends fanning out from the anchor line. Connect the dots with S shapes to create the outside edge. Voila!

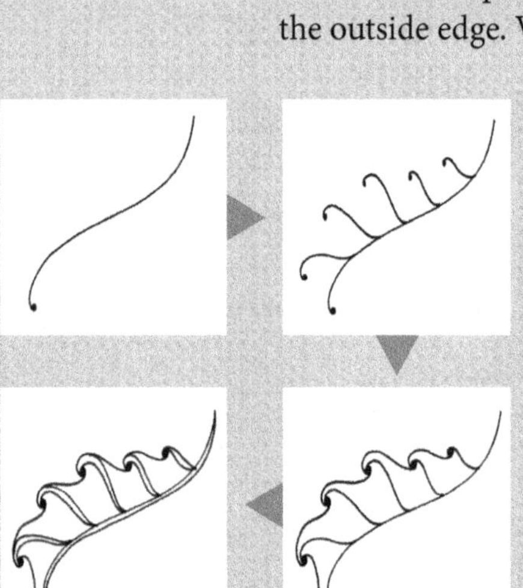

TANGLEATION 1

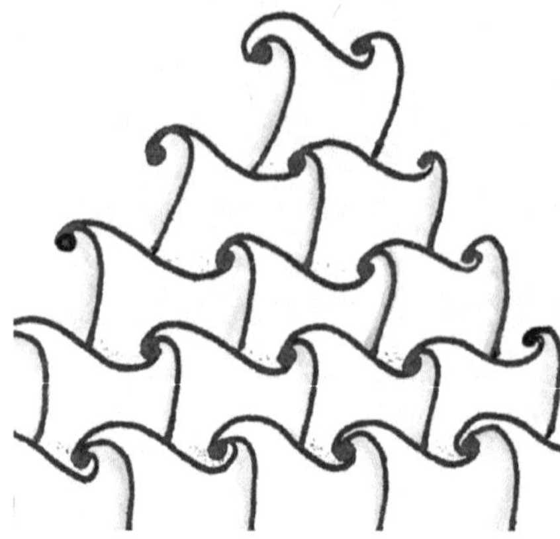

Stack the curvy shapes to fill a space with life and energy. Add shadows to emphasize the layered effect.

TANGLEATION 2

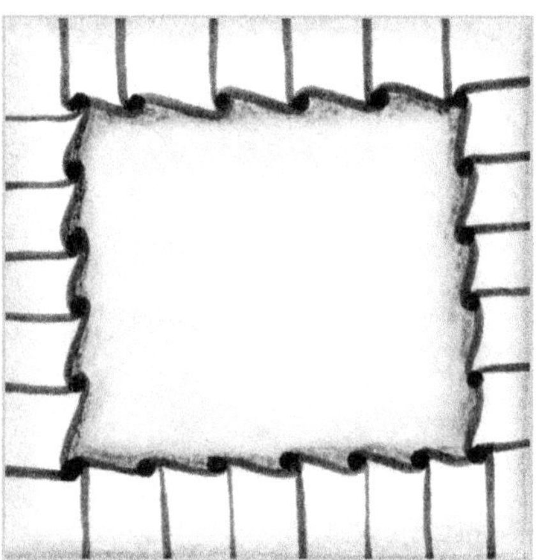

Draw your lines military style: standing up straight and spaced out evenly. This gives the impression of a nice ruffled edge.

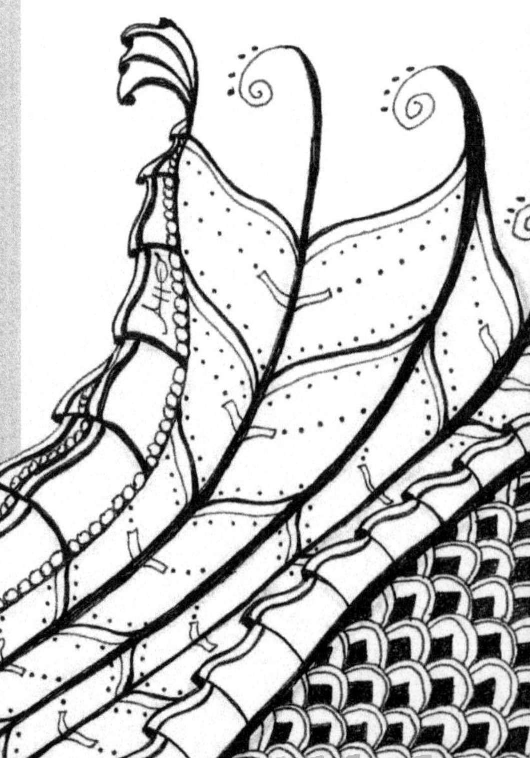

©Alice Hendon

TANGLEATION 3

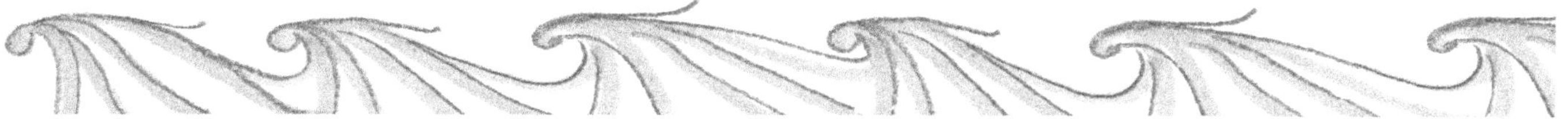

Begin with widely spaced curves to create a wavelike look. Connect the curves by a series of divergent lines and shade. Surf's up!

TANGLEATION 4

Start with curved lines: some short; some tall. Make the connecting stroke extra wavy to exaggerate the scrolled look.

TANGLEATION 5

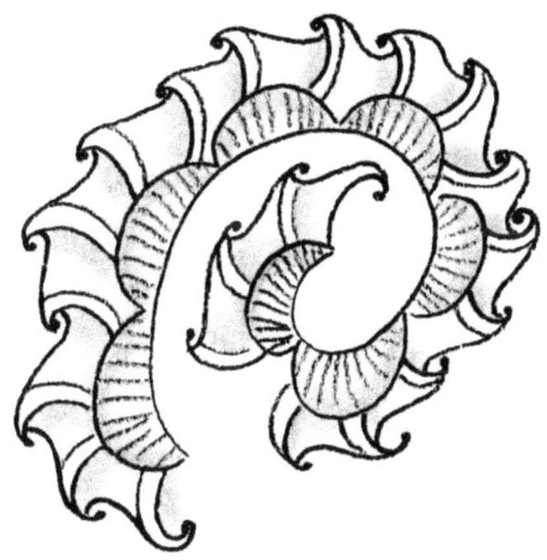

Draw **DRAGONAIR** in a spiral atop **FIRCLE**, decreasing the size from the outside toward the inside.

TANGLEATION 6

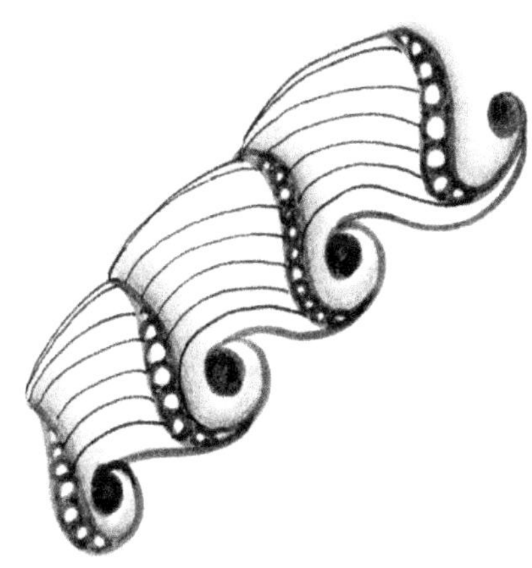

Add stripes and orbs to create art reminiscent of a musical staff. Shadows create dimension and pull the eye across.

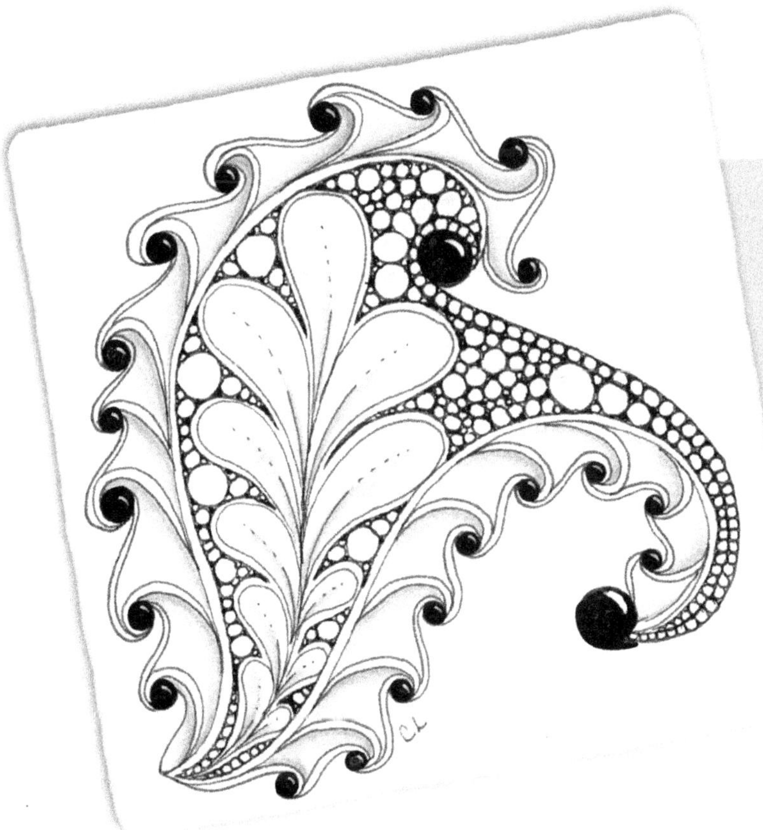

DRAGONAIR GIVES ORGANIC FLAIR TO THIS TILE, ACTING AS BOTH THE STRING AND THE LACY BORDER. IT SETS A GRACEFUL FRAMEWORK FOR THE OTHER TANGLES.

Tile features: FLUX, DRAGONAIR, *and* TIPPLE.

IDEA STARTERS

- Add auras to the S shape across the top.
- Draw two rows of DRAGONAIR facing each other. Tangle the space between them.
- Add horizontal or vertical stripes.
- Vary the size, spacing, and amount of curve in your initial lines.

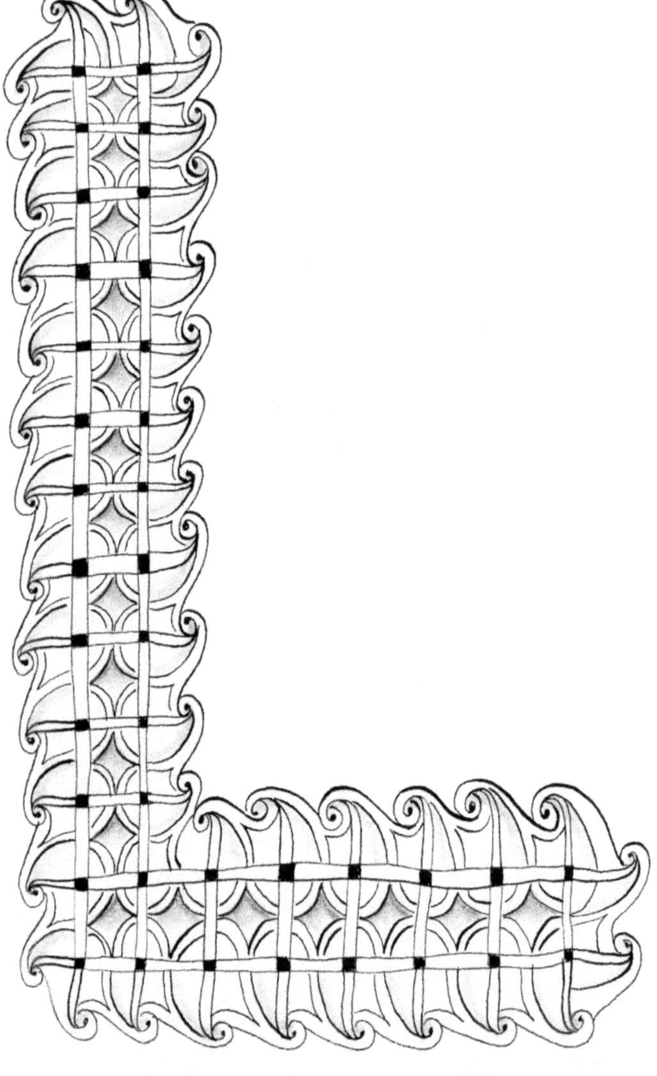

✏ Do not let internal or external criticism of a wobbly line rob you of the joy of creating.

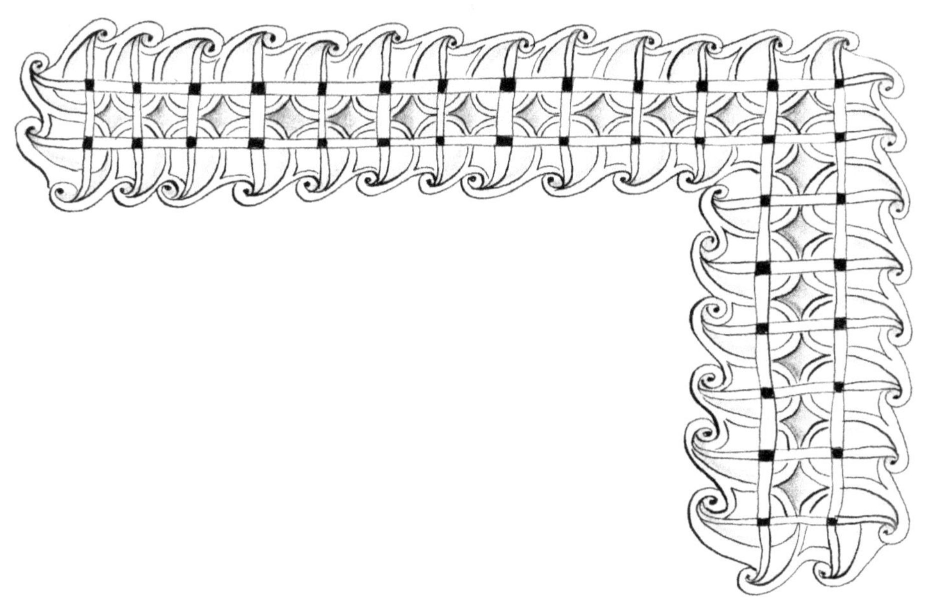

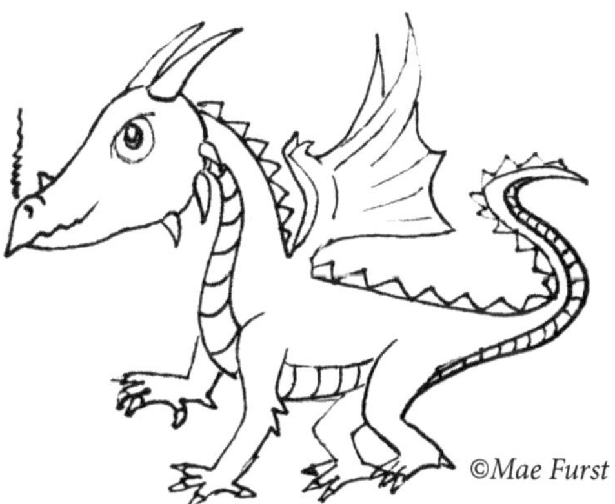
©Mae Furst

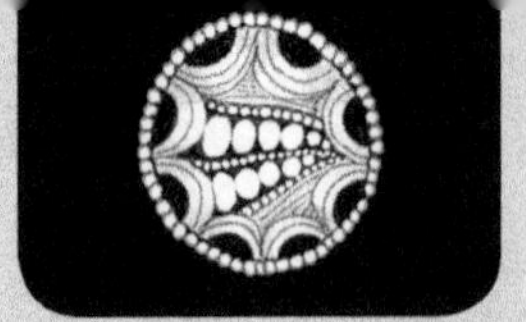

VERDIGOGH

by Rick Roberts & Maria Thomas

Inspired by the beauty of a simple pine branch, **VERDIGOGH** *adds an organic and natural touch to any tile. As with many tangles, it contains very few elements that when repeated again and again in a layered formation, create a complex-looking pattern.* **VERDIGOGH** *is actually very easy to draw and personalize.*

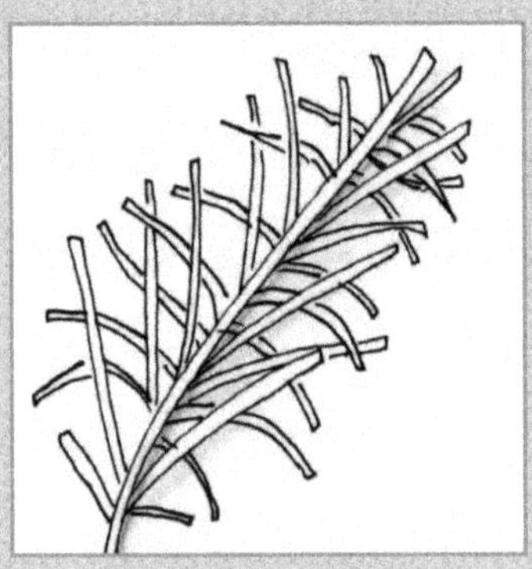

an official Zentangle tangle

Ink a "stem" of any length and direction. "Needles" are added incrementally on both sides of the stem. The first few needles will appear in the foreground. The next layer of needles goes behind the first, the next layer behind that, and so on, changing the angle of the needles with each layer. This creates the illusion of depth and complexity.

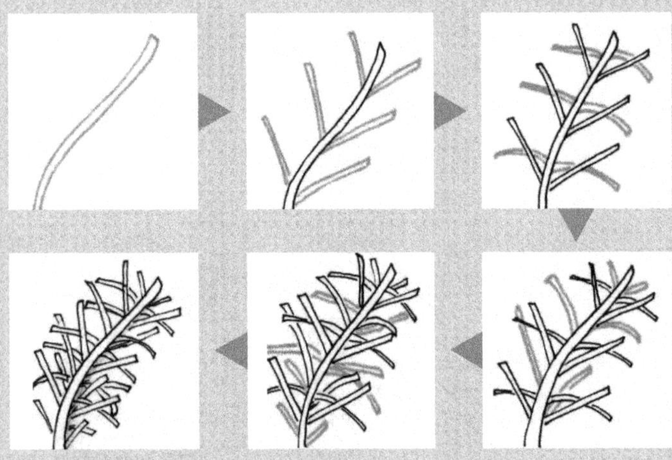

TANGLEATION 1

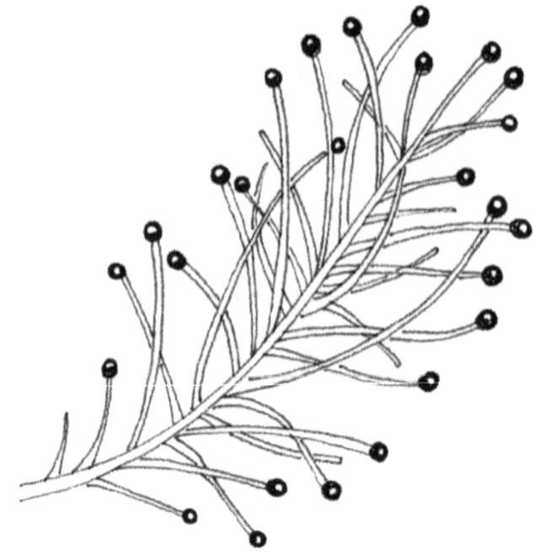

Curve slender needles for a flowing affect. Black pearls at the end of each needle serve as elegant jewelry for **VERDIGOGH**.

TANGLEATION 2

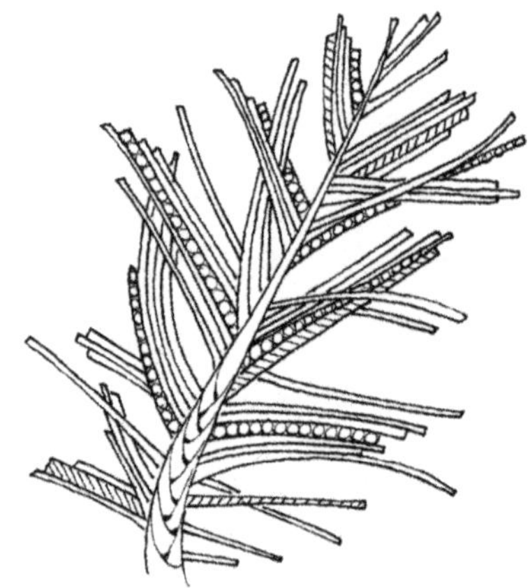

Draw clusters of square-tipped needles filled with orbs and stripes for an unusual look. Tangle the stem to add even more interest.

TANGLEATION 3

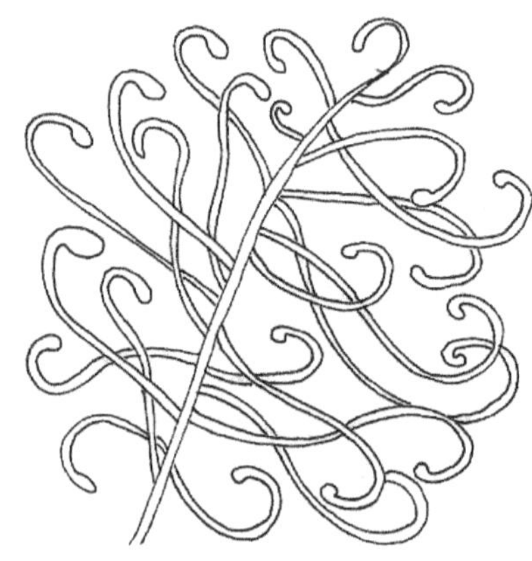

Use curvy tendrils with rounded spiral tips similar to **MOOKA** for a softer look. *(©Emily Classon)*

TANGLEATION 4

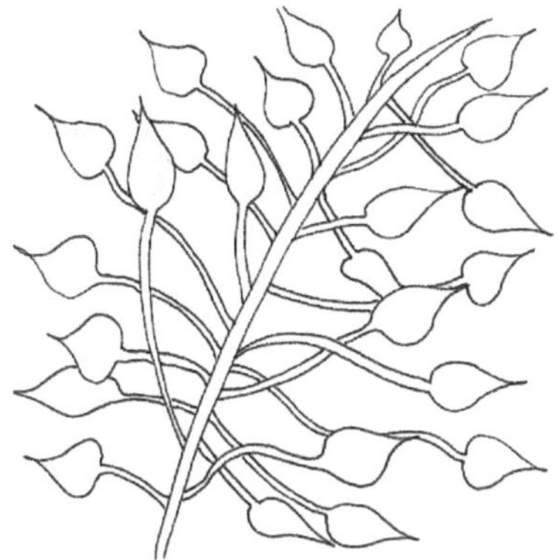

Add spade or diamond shapes to the end of each needle. Cross the needles back and forth over one another to add depth. *(©Emily Classon)*

TANGLEATION 5

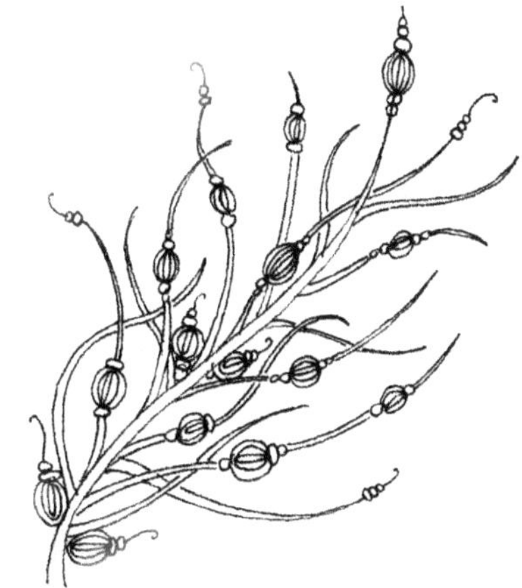

Exaggerate the waviness and curve of both the stem and needles. Embellish the needles midway with different shapes.

TANGLEATION 6

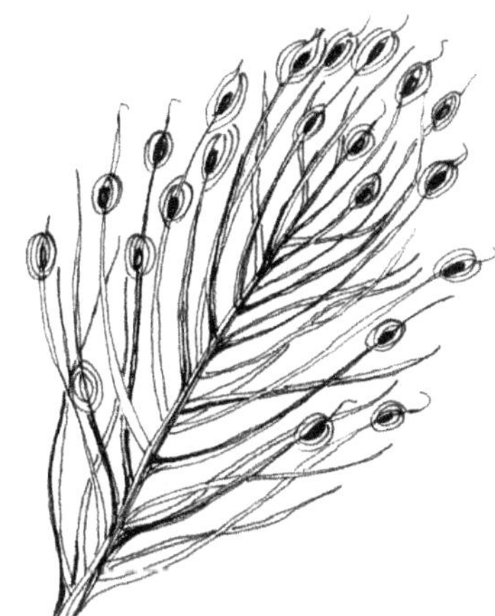

Add dark-eyed layered embellishments toward the end of each needle, giving a nod to peacock feathers.

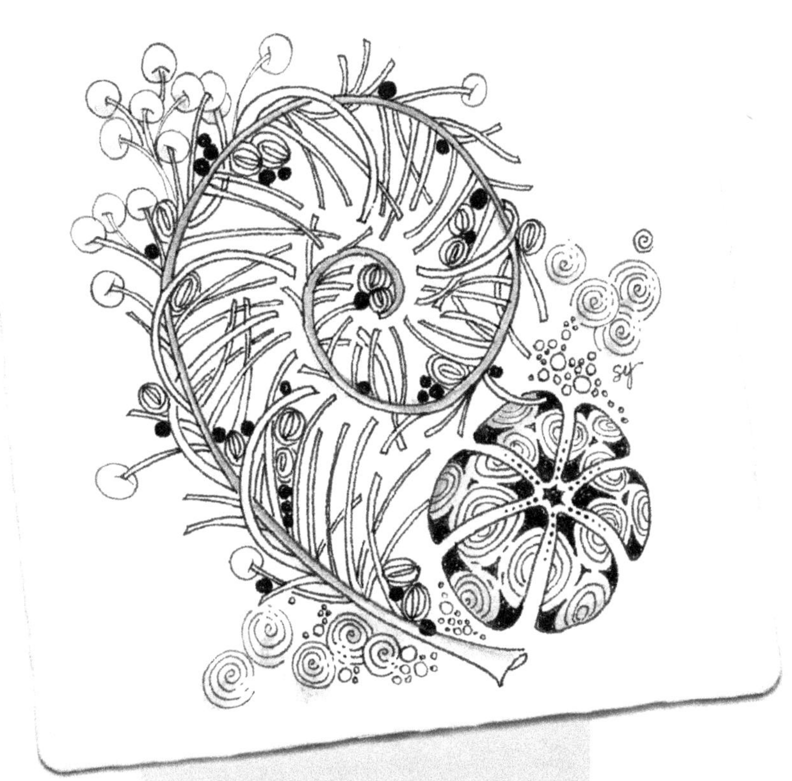

REMINISCENT OF A DELICATE FERN FROND UNCURLING, FORMING VERDIGOGH INTO A TIGHT SPIRAL CREATES DELICIOUS VISUAL EXCITEMENT IN THIS TILE.

Tile features: VERDIGOGH, TRIPOLI, PRINTEMPS, *and* POKEROOT. *Shell features:* VERDIGOGH, BLACK PEARLZ, *and* BTL JOOS.

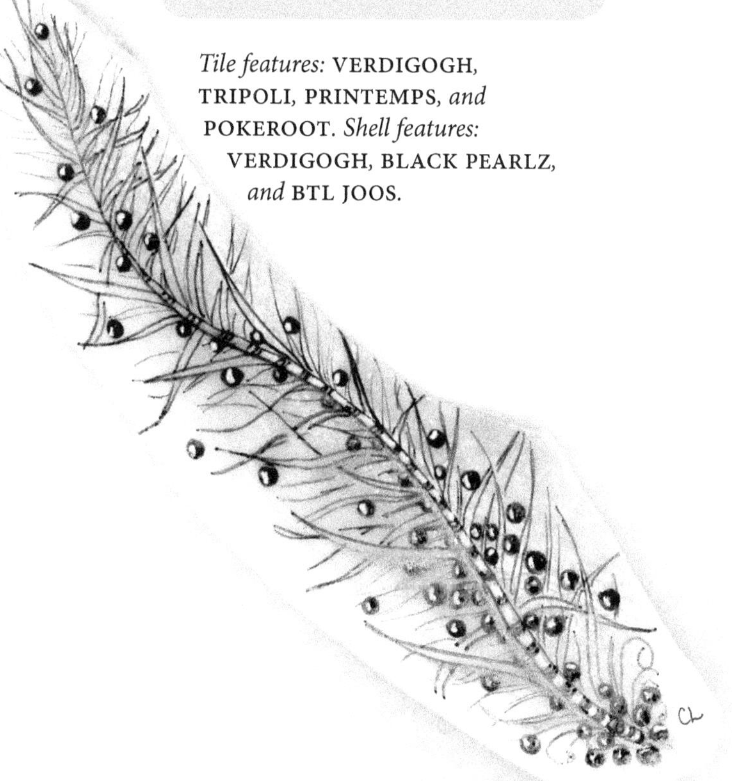

IDEA STARTERS

- Draw auras around everything: the stem, needles, and any embellishments you add.
- Add leaves to convert your evergreen into a deciduous tree branch.
- Draw the needles on just one side of the stem.
- Vary the length and thickness of both your stem and needles.
- Fill or shade inside some of your needles.

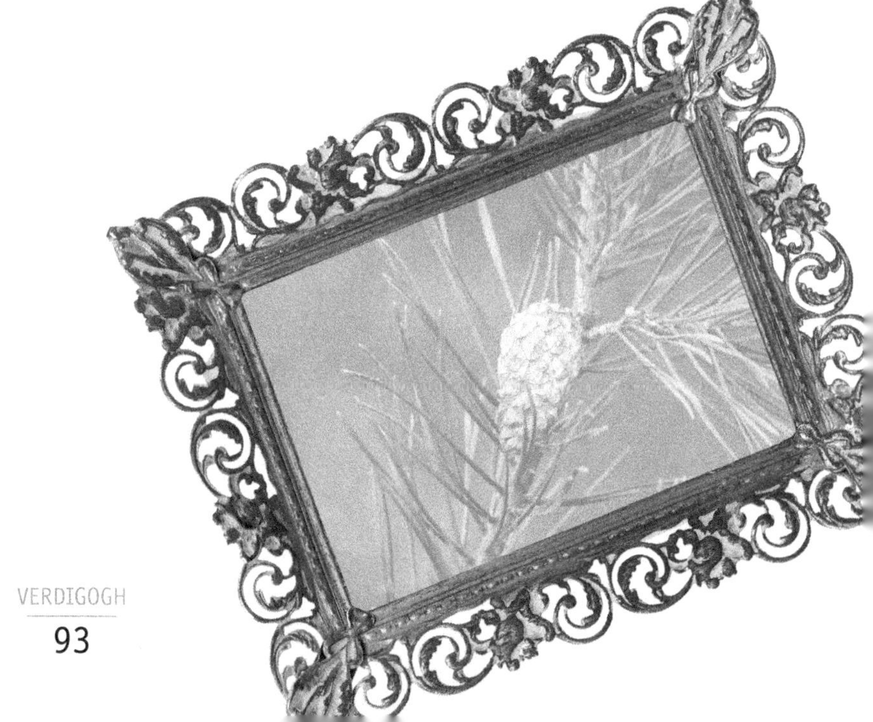

✏ "Be not afraid of going slow, be afraid of standing still." ~ Chinese proverb. Practice being deliberate. Use Zentangle as a tool to help you intentionally slow down.

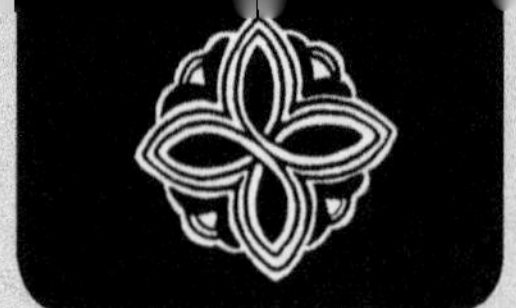

MI²

by Mimi Lempart

This uniquely woven tangle has quickly become a favorite. Lush with basket weave curves that flow in and out creating an illusion of depth and complexity, MI²'s large empty spaces are ripe for personalization. Auras, pearls, leaves, flowers, and dramatic shading are just a few of the ways you can make this tangle your own.

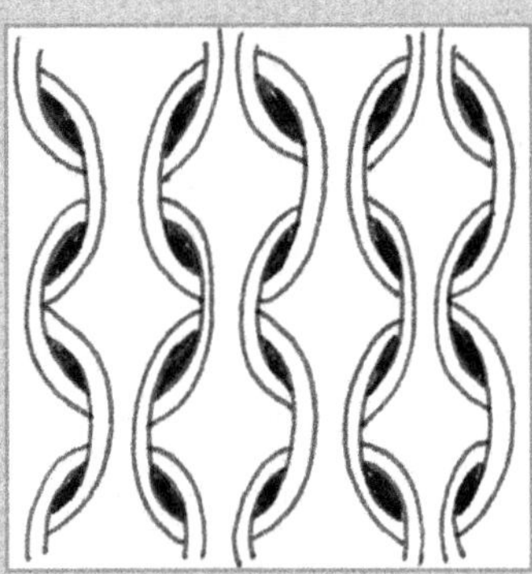

Surprisingly, MI² is a grid-based tangle. After completing a dot grid, draw horizontal rows of alternating arcs connecting pairs of dots. Shift down a row into the empty spaces and follow the same pattern until everything is connected. Fill in all of the seed shaped connection points. Finally, add auras to each line to emphasize the woven affect.

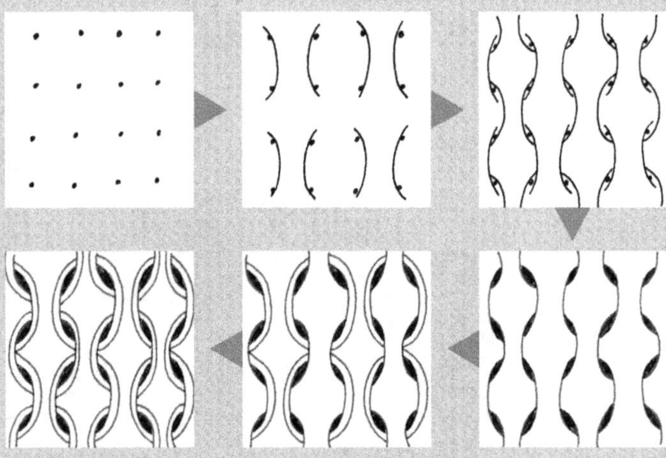

TANGLEATION 1

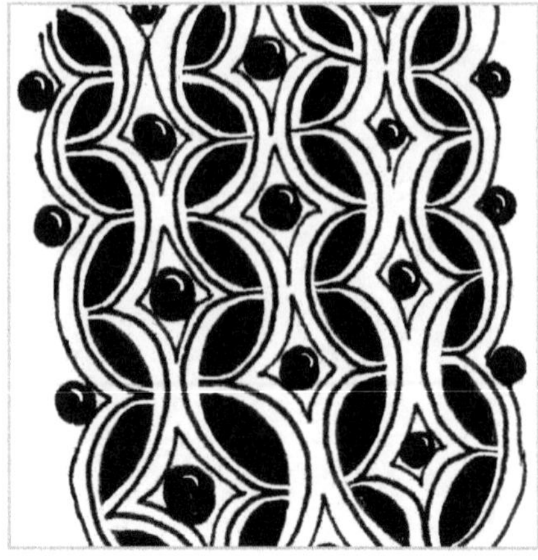

Create a tight grid with large seed shapes and multiple auras to achieve a bold look. Add black pearls for emphasis.

TANGLEATION 2

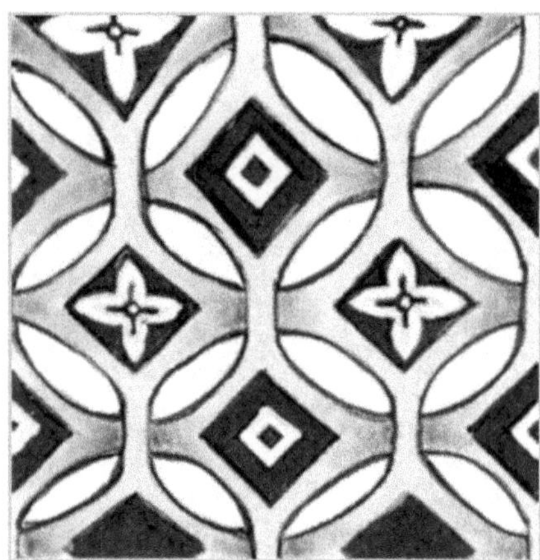

Draw your grid lightly in pencil. Elongate the arcs connecting the dots. Keep the seed shapes white. Add diamonds in the centers. *(©Maria Vennekens)*

TANGLEATION 3

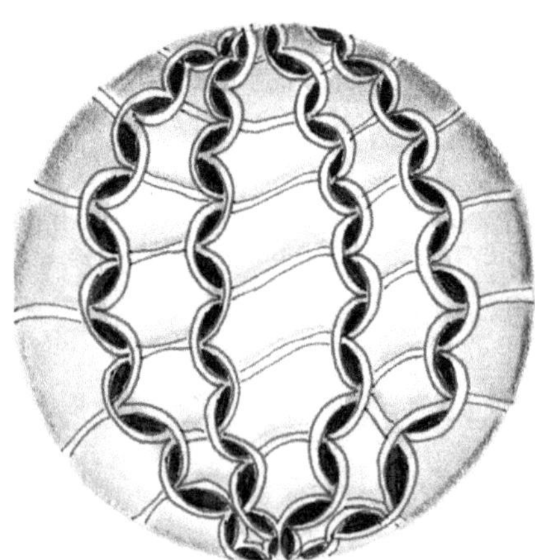

Weave MI² around an orb. Begin with a dot grid based on latitude and longitude lines. Make long, flowing connection lines.

TANGLEATION 4

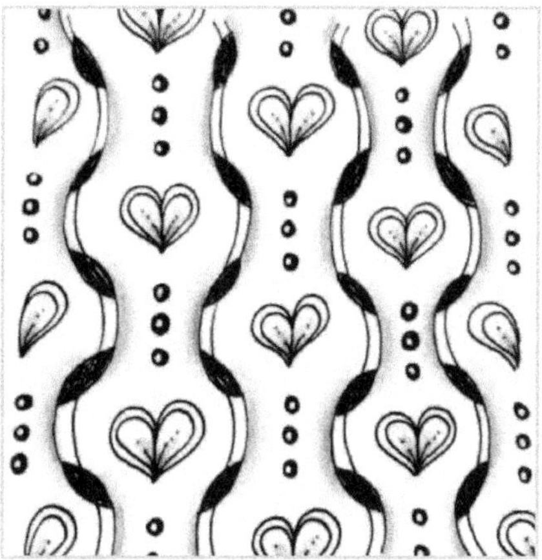

Begin with a wide dot grid. Draw a double line connecting the seeds shapes to create a vertical striping effect.

TANGLEATION 5

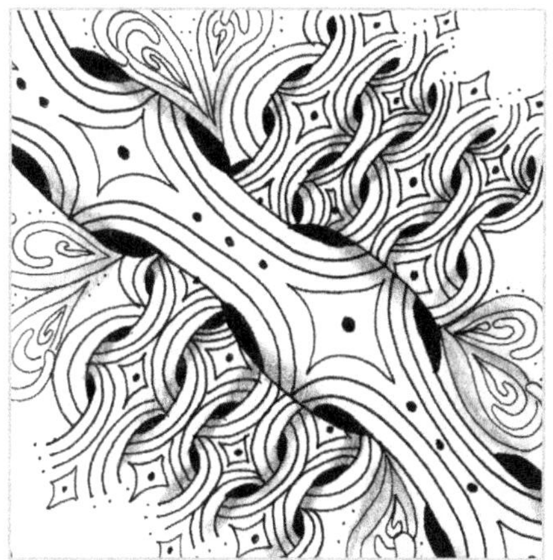

Use multiple sizes of MI^{2} in the same space. Leave the ends of the design open; embellish them with diamonds and MOOKA. *(©Sue Clark)*

TANGLEATION 6

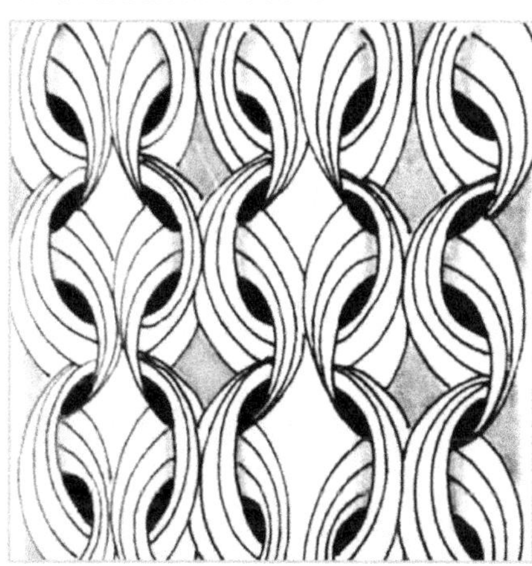

Fan each set of auras out around each arc. Draw the aura narrow at one end, making it thicker as you progress to the opposite end.

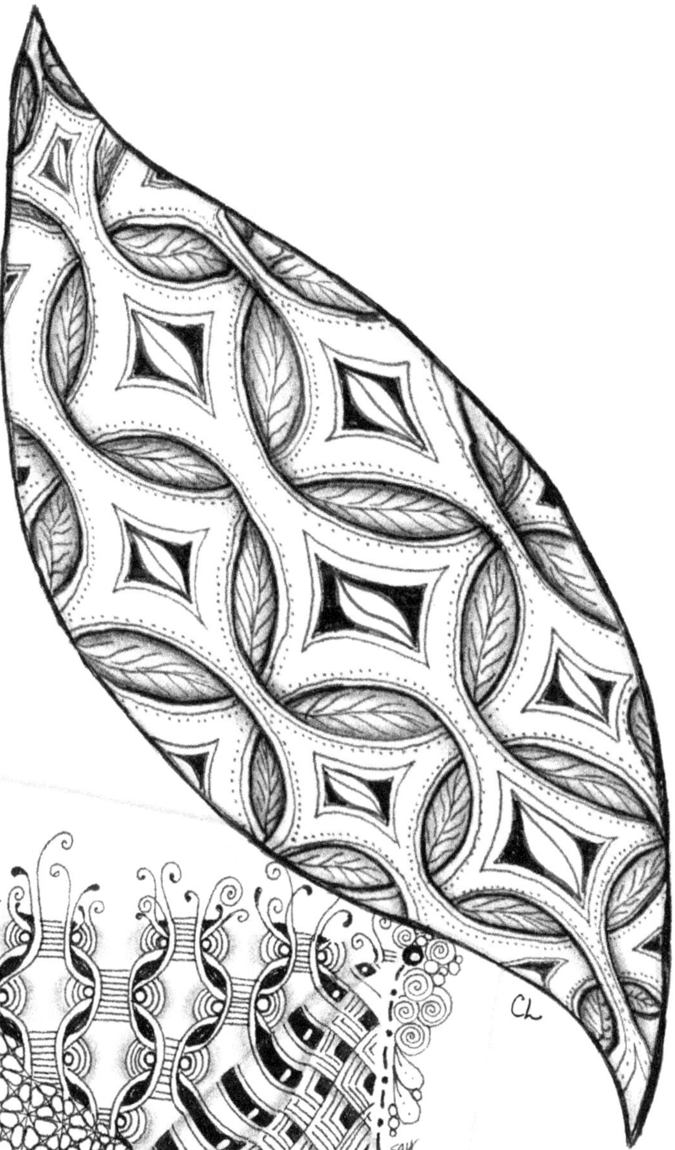

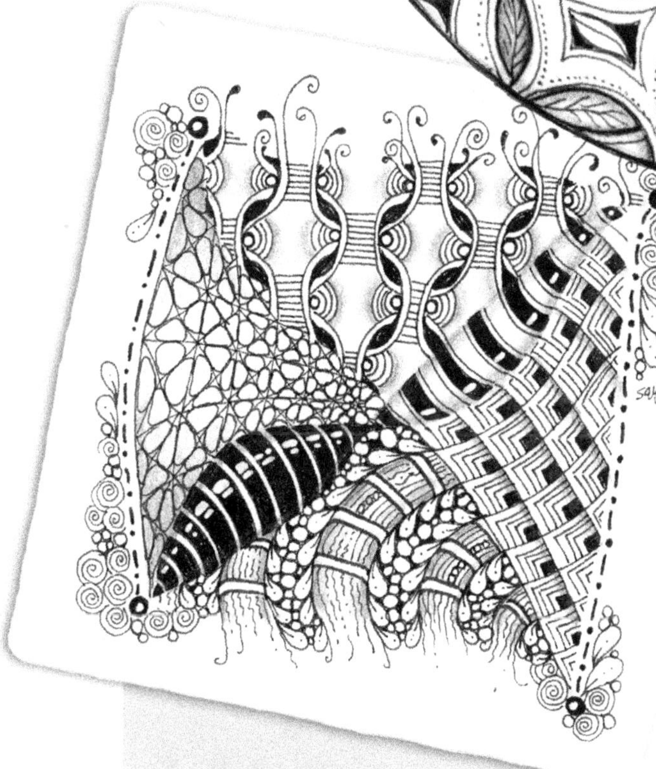

CL

say

VISUAL EXCITEMENT RIPPLES THROUGH THIS TILE FEATURING AN EXPLOSION OF MI^{2}.

Tile features: MI^{2}, 'NZEPPEL, STRIPING, FLUX, FLUKES, *and* ZANDER.

IDEA STARTERS

- Exaggerate any single element of MI² and see what results.
- Tangle between every other "strip" of MI² as Marty Deckel did on the facing page.
- Substitute BEADLINES for the auras.
- Like other grid based tangles, change the shape of your grid; use a fan shape or a curved grid. Or how about a wavy grid?

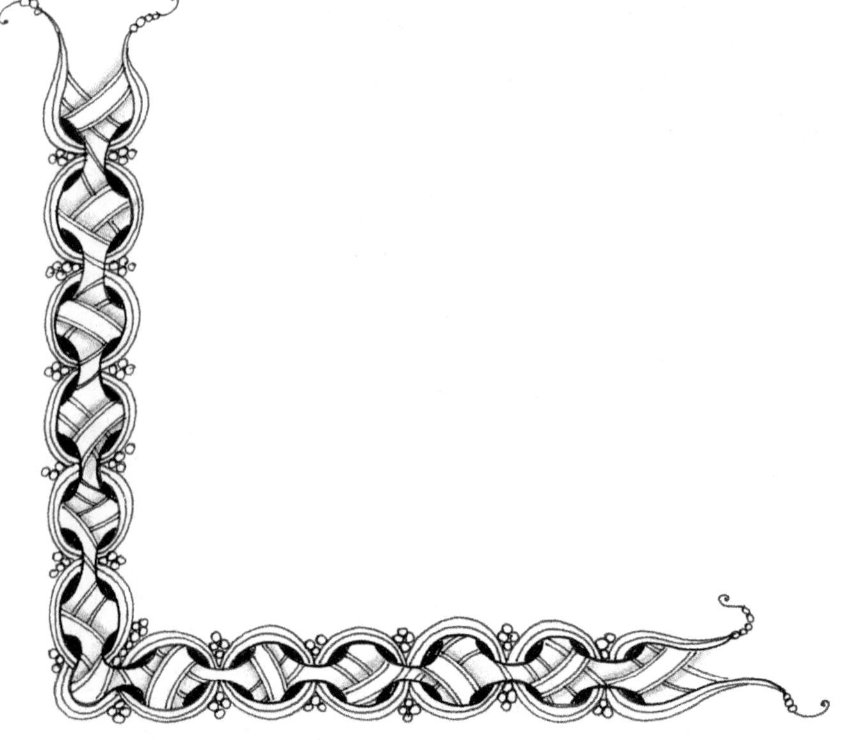

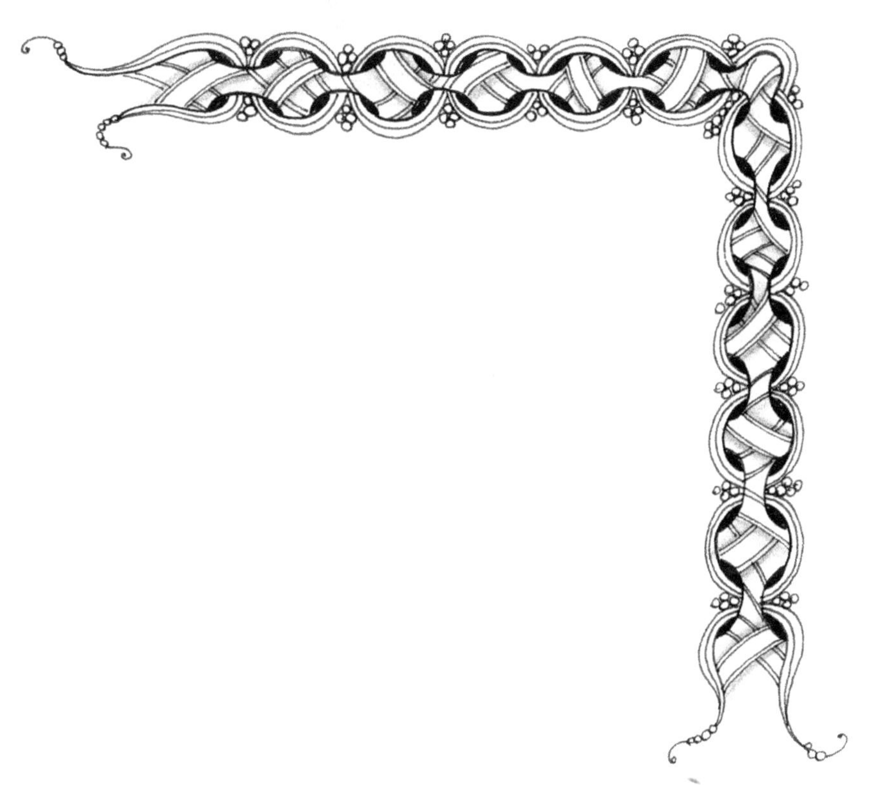

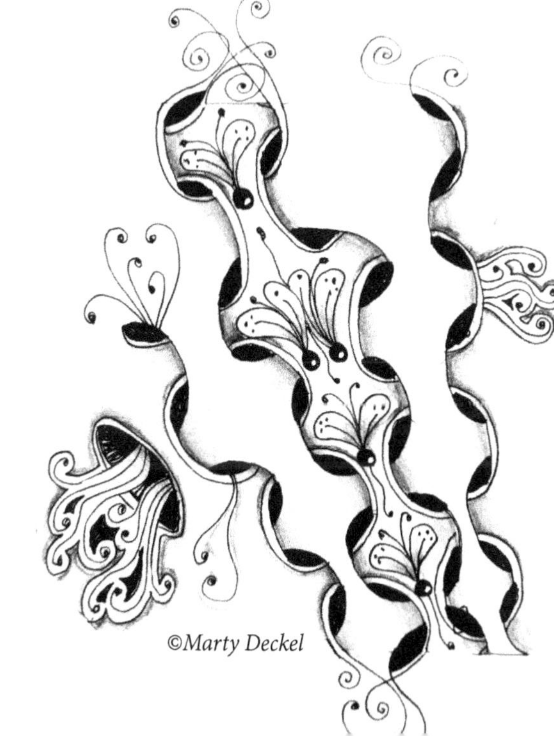

✏ Want a new look? Listen to different styles of music while you tangle. Your art may be influenced by what you hear. Try hard-driving rock, syncopated jazz, or calming classical music.

FALZ

by Sue Clark, CZT

Like water cascading over a tropical waterfall, FALZ has a natural rhythm all its own. This beauty easily flows across your tile, adding a hint of nature everywhere it goes. FALZ breaks up the sharp edges of geometric and graphic tangles, giving softness to your artwork. Is it time you took a dip in FALZ?

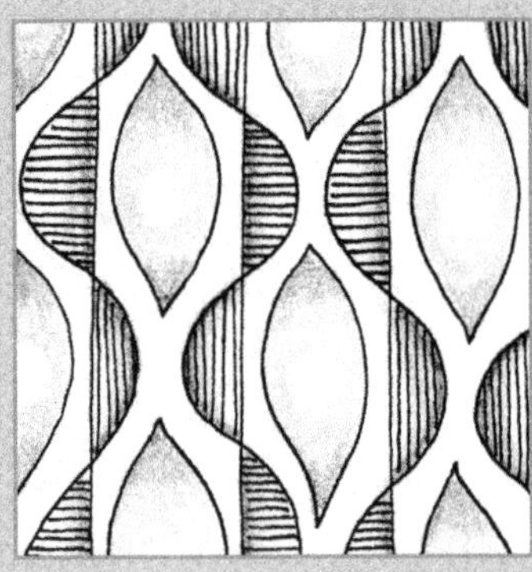

Begin with parallel vertical lines, allowing ample space in between. Overlap a wavy line on each one of the vertical lines. Every time you draw a new wave, alternate the direction of the curves so the waves almost touch from one to the next. Draw pod shapes in the empty spaces. Fill enclosed areas with vertical and horizontal stripes.

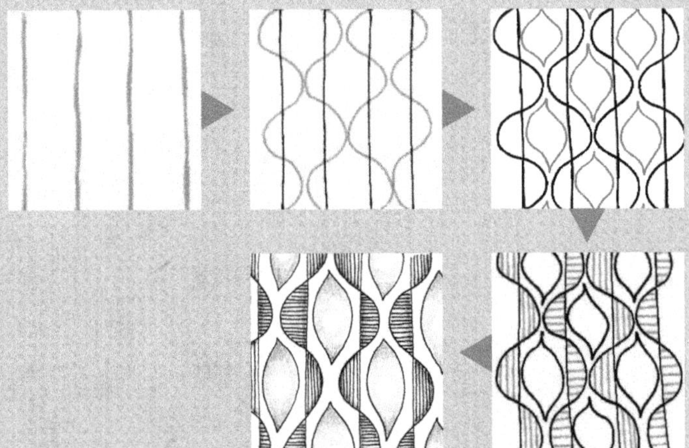

TANGLEATION 1

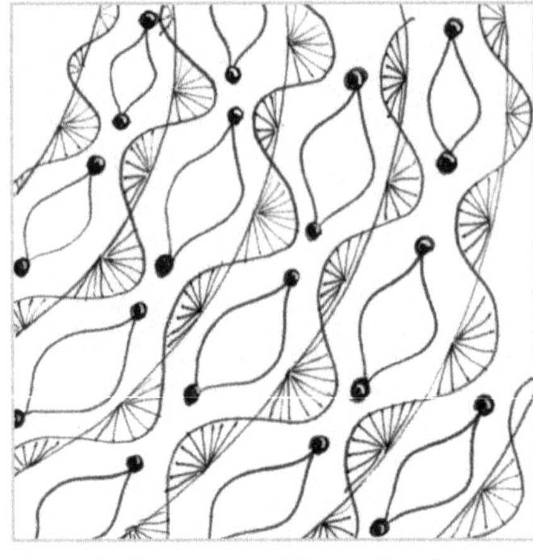

Curve the lines in step 1 for a softer, flowy appearance. Add black pearls to highlight the points at each end of the pod shapes.

TANGLEATION 2

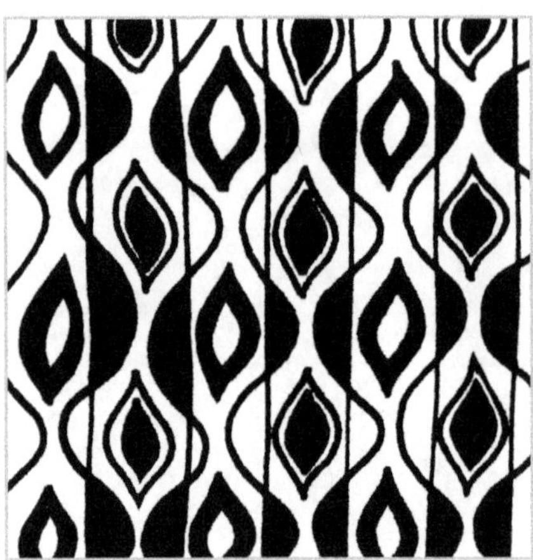

Instead of using lines, fill the overlapping areas with solid black for a bold look. Alternate the fill in every other stripe.

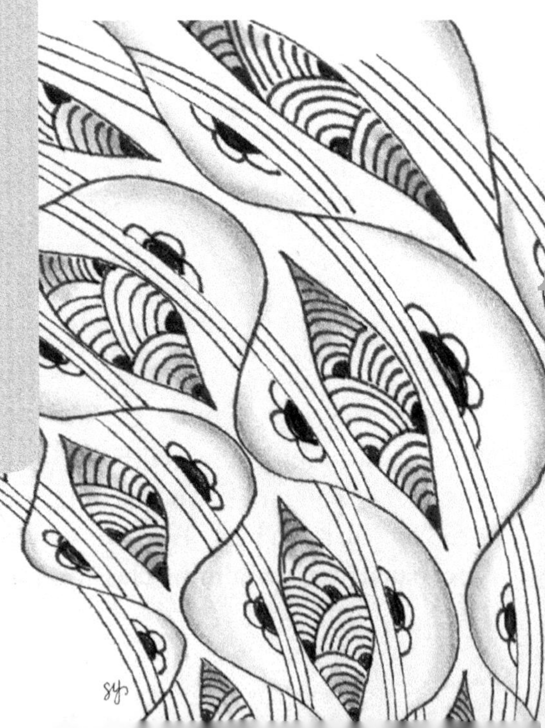

TANGLEATION 3

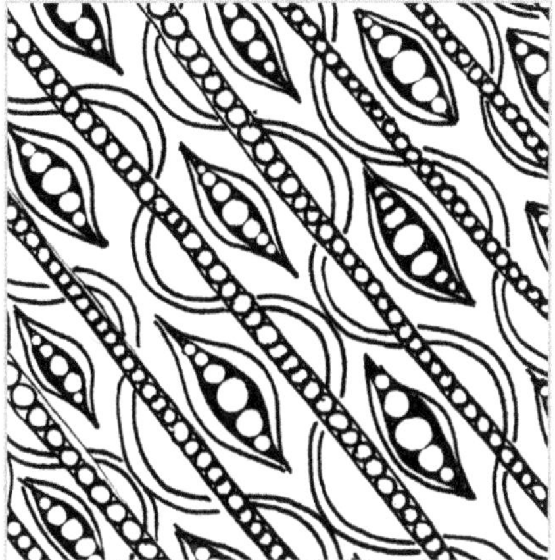

Start with diagonal stripes in step 1 for a new look. Add auras to all curved shapes. Fill lines and pods with orbs to create an elegant look.

TANGLEATION 4

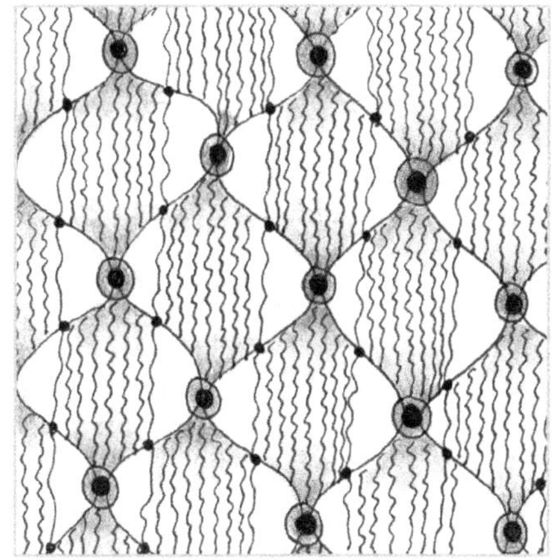

Draw squiggly lines instead of straight. Fill the lines with more squiggly lines. Add orbs at the intersections for interest.

FALZ REALLY SHINES IN THIS FLOWING TANGLEATION. REMINISCENT OF UNDERSEA TENTACLES BURSTING THROUGH BUBBLES. CURLING ENDS AND VARIED FILLS ADD INTEREST AND MOVEMENT.

Tile features: FALZ, PRINTEMPS, MSST, INAPOD, *and* TIPPLE.

TANGLEATION 5

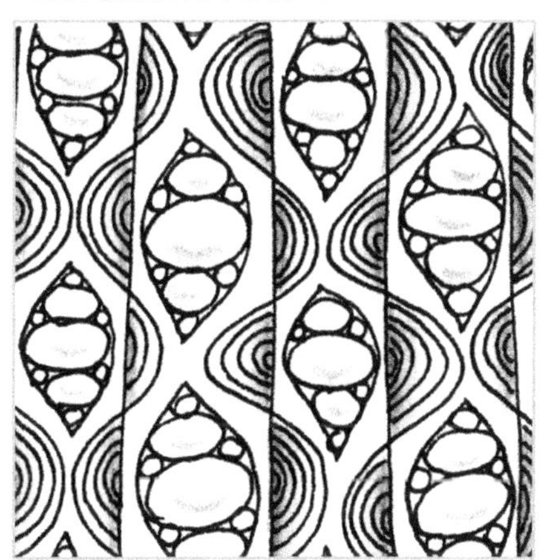

Fill the pods with ONOMATO and the half-moons with auras to achieve a psychedelic look. Shade inside the half-moons and orbs.

TANGLEATION 6

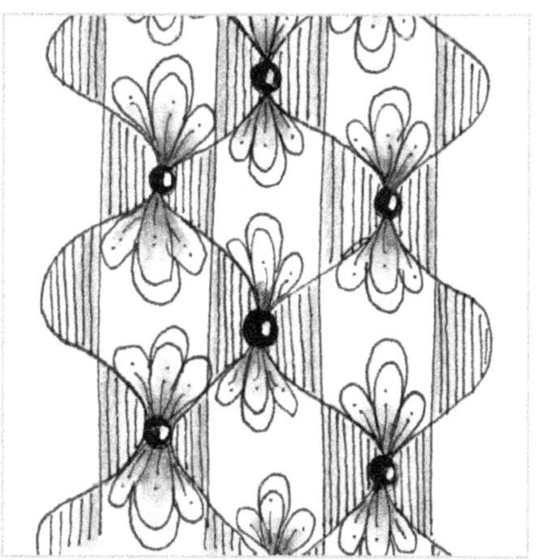

Eliminate the pods. Draw FLUX and a black pearl at every intersection for this beautiful tangleation.

IDEA STARTERS

- Vary the spacing of the vertical lines for dramatic changes.
- Mix very curvy lines and straight, angular ones in the same tangleation of FALZ.
- Fill the pod shapes and half-moon shapes with contrasting tangles, such as KNIGHTSBRIDGE and CRESCENT MOON.
- Substitute a different shape for the pod, such as an orb.

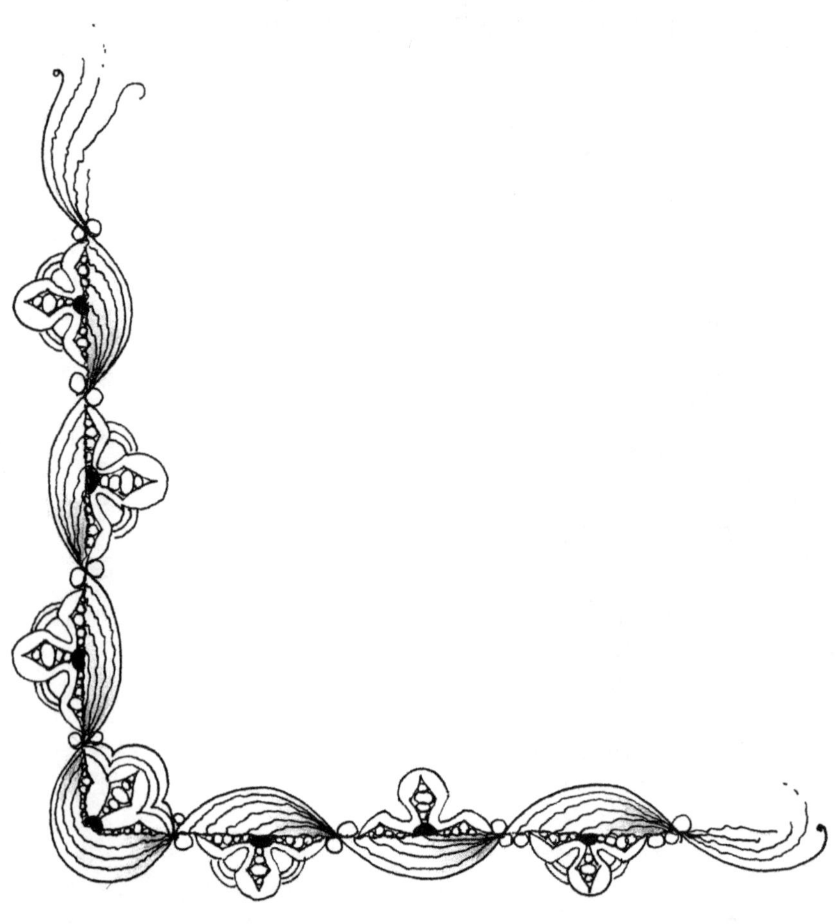

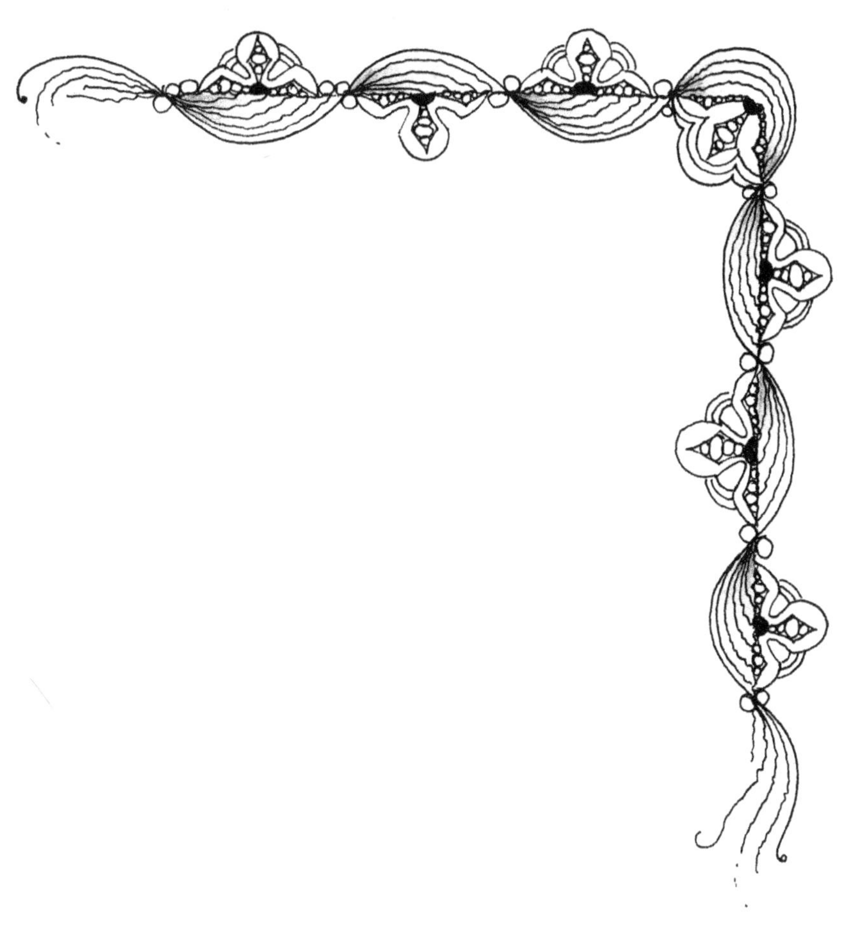

✏ Change your perspective often to encourage creative thinking. Hold your tile (or book) upside down, sideways, closer, or further away.

FALZ

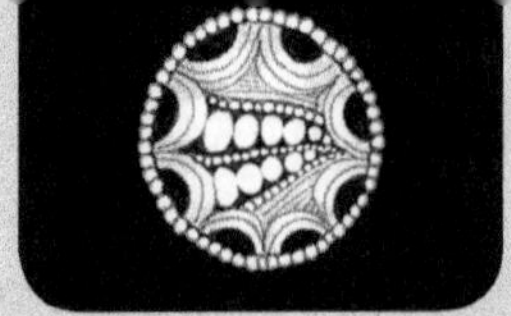

PURK

by Rick Roberts & Maria Thomas

Reminiscent of strands of pearls wound around a drop of water, **PURK** *is a beautiful and elegant focal point to any of your Zentangle art. Its bubbly shape full of puffy orbs provides wonderful dimension. It is truly a fun tangle to play with as small changes make a huge visual difference.*

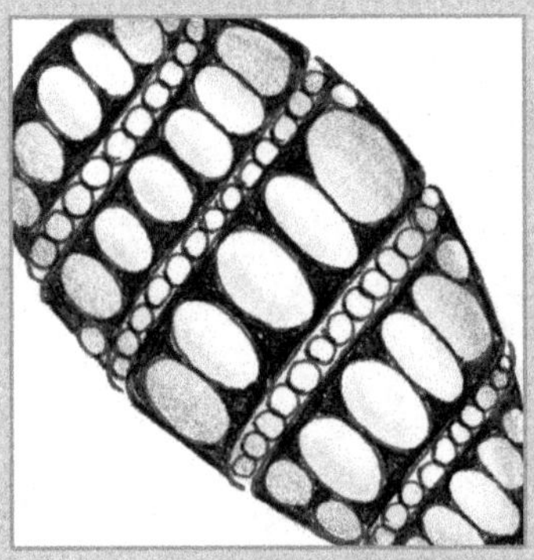

an official Zentangle tangle

PURK is the perfect tangle for round or teardrop shapes, but is not limited to these. Begin by drawing parallel lines (ribbons) wrapping across your shape. Ink the first row of orbs down the center in a line. Complete each row of large orbs. Fill in the ribbons with tiny orbs. Blacken the background and add shading.

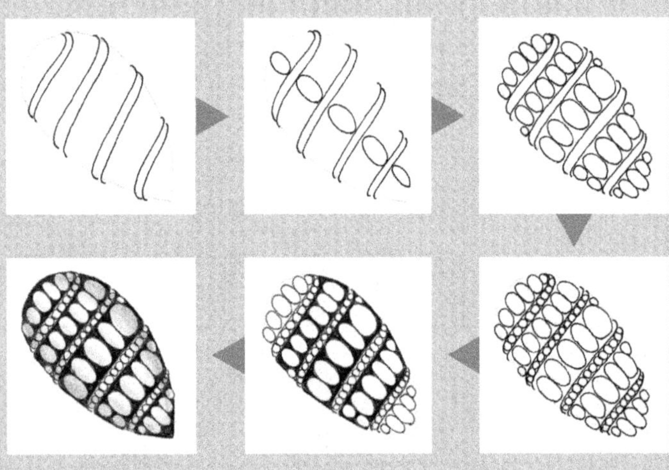

TANGLEATION 1

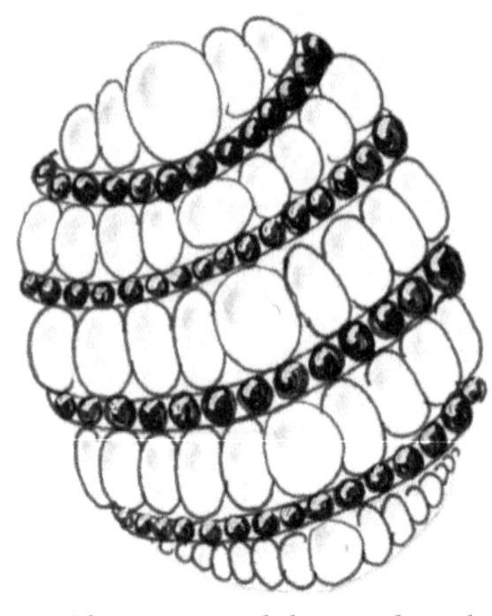

Begin with a very round shape and evenly spaced ribbons. Alternating black and white pearls makes it look even rounder.

TANGLEATION 2

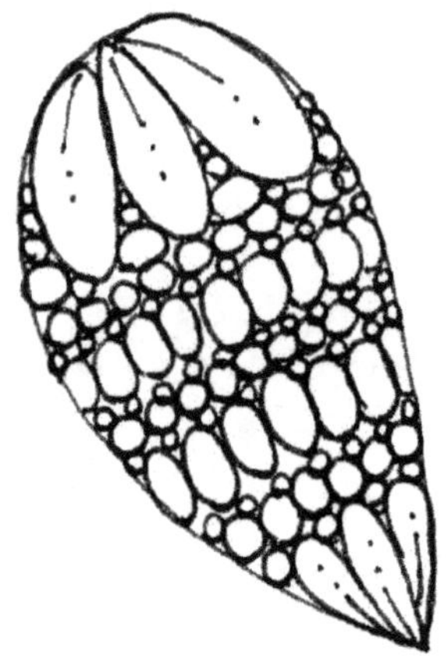

Draw **FLUX** on the top and bottom of the teardrop for a strawberry-inspired look. Ink rows of orbs with no ribbons.

TANGLEATION 3

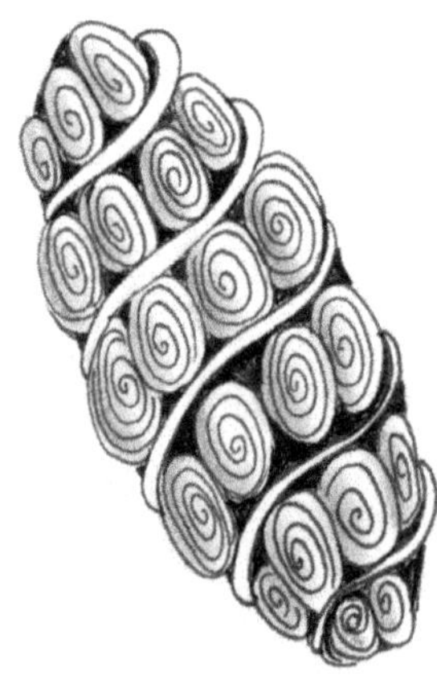

Use spirals instead of orbs. Shade carefully on both the left and bottom of each spiral to create this delightfully different version. (Inspired by Sue Clark)

TANGLEATION 4

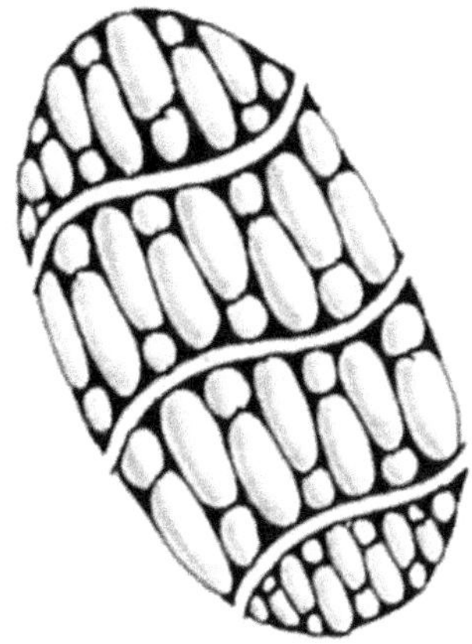

Space thin ribbons widely to allow multiple orbs in between. Stack long and short pill shapes to add an interesting rhythm. *(©Caren Mlot)*

TANGLEATION 5

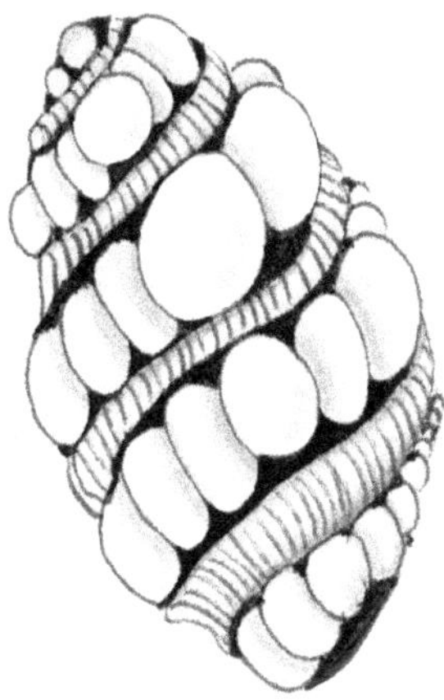

Draw the first row of orbs round; all other orbs should be oblong, behind the first. Shade carefully to achieve this 3D look.

TANGLEATION 6

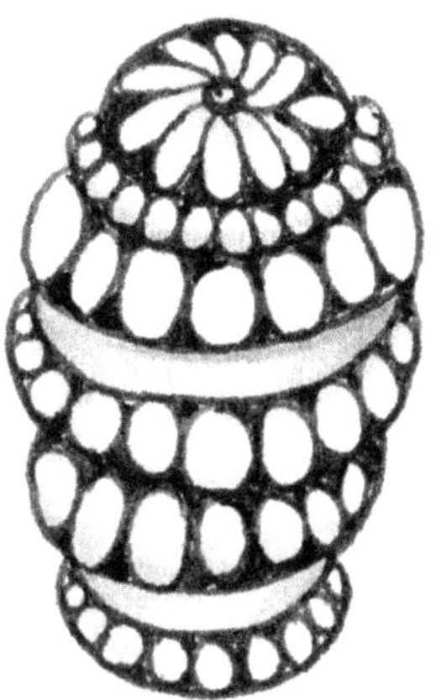

Want a challenge? Change the perspective on PURK. Instead of drawing it from the side, imagine drawing it looking down at the top.

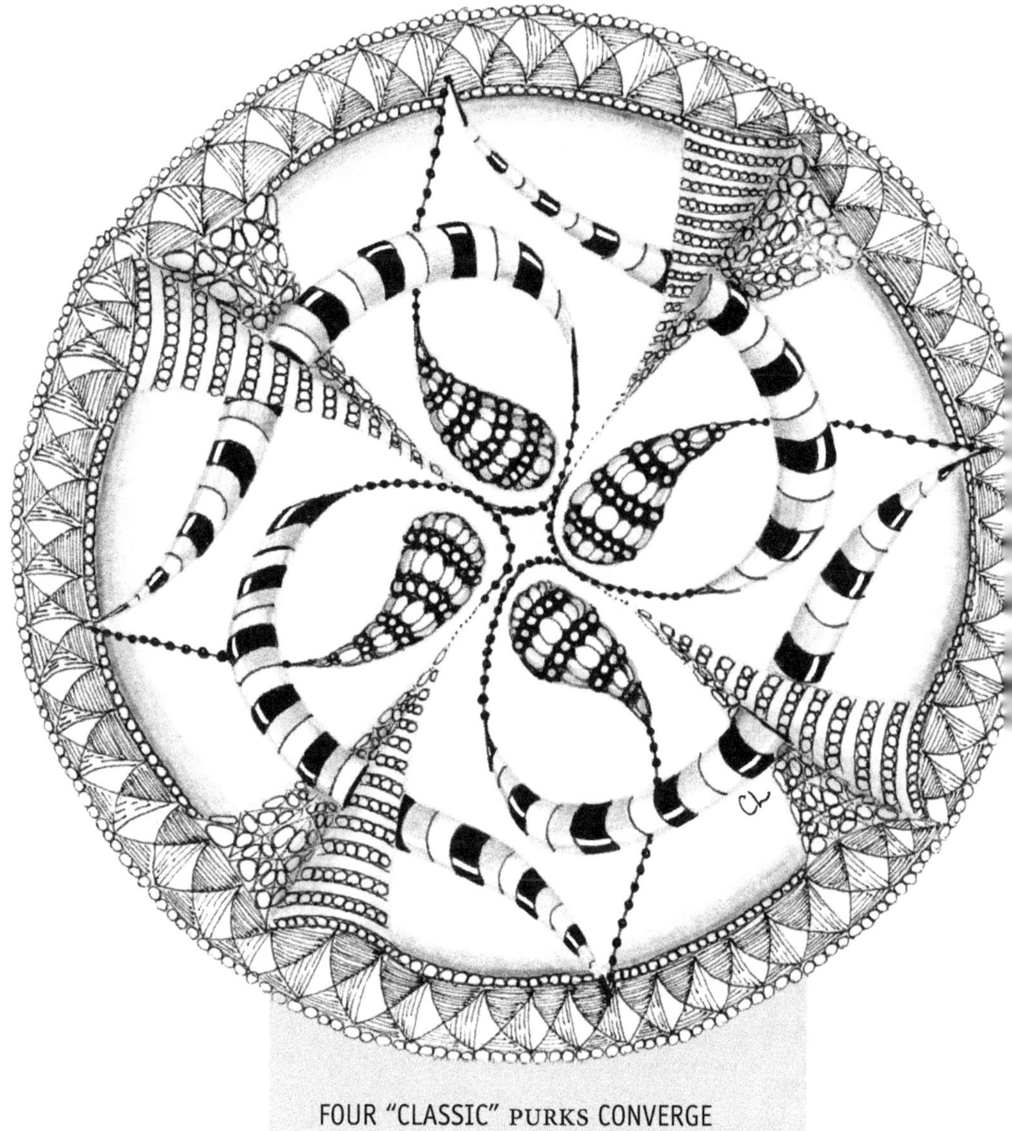

FOUR "CLASSIC" PURKS CONVERGE AT THE CENTER OF THIS BEAUTIFUL ZENDALA TO CREATE THE FOCAL POINT. A SECOND SET OF SIMPLIFIED PURKS DRAWS THE EYE FROM THE OUTSIDE EDGE TOWARD THE CENTER.

Zendala features: PURK, 'NZEPPEL, STRIPING, BEADLINES *and* AVREAL.

IDEA STARTERS

- Instead of a teardrop, start with an orb or maybe even a spiral.
- Add auras around your orbs. If they are large enough, you can decorate them with stripes or dots.
- Reverse the colors so that you have black orbs on a white background. Or maybe alternate black and white pearls instead.
- Change the size of your orbs: tall and skinny, or short and round. All are beautiful.

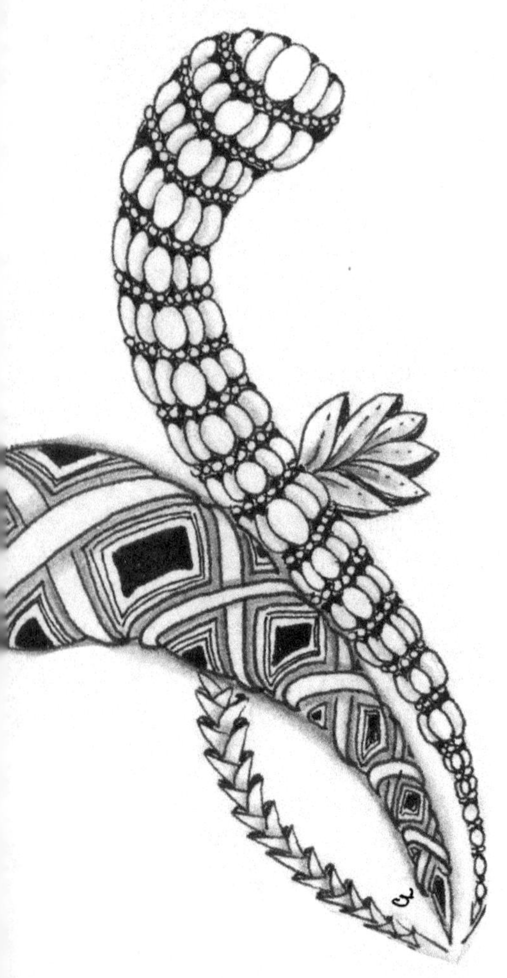

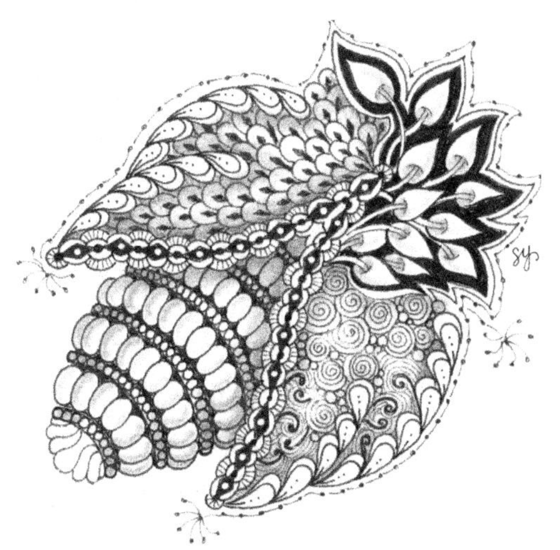

✏ Take a break. Set a timer to go off every 15 minutes (or 10 or 5). When it beeps, close your eyes and take a deep breath. Move your body for a minute and recharge. Do you notice anything different when you return to your tangling?

PAUSHALÖV

by Amy Broady

This soft staircase to heaven is a beautiful addition to any tile. Flowing curls stack up like rungs of a ladder, giving a gentle nod to nature as they climb around with other tangles on the page. PAUSHALÖV *can be used to fill any number of shapes—round, angular or irregular— but can also run in a line as a border.*

Creating PAUSHALÖV is simple. With only three steps, it can be mastered swiftly. Draw a light pencil string in the shape of a teardrop. Beginning on the bottom left, create a curl extending from one side to the other. Stack a second curl on top of the first, alternating the direction. Continue this back and forth stacking until the space is full.

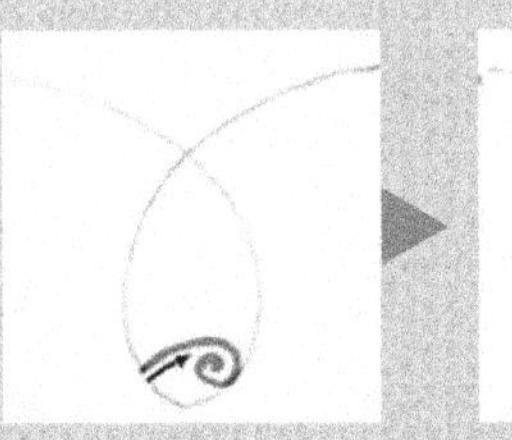

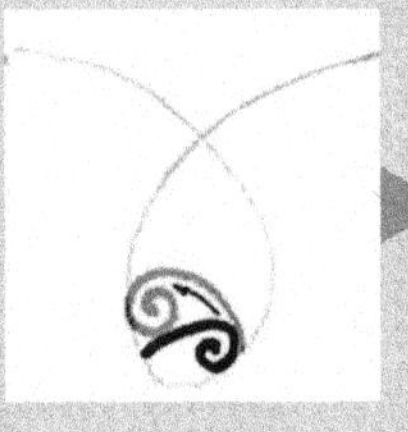

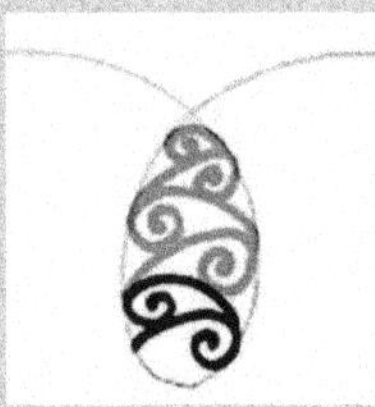

TANGLEATION 1

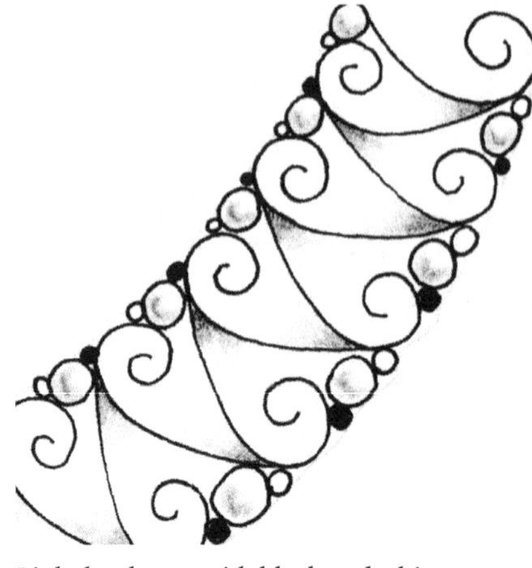

Link the shapes with black and white pearls for an elegant look. Delicate shading at the intersections adds softness.

TANGLEATION 2

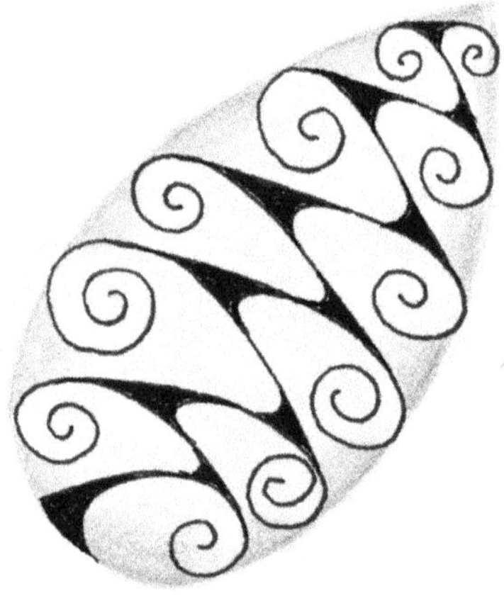

Add rounding for emphasis and boldness. Shade around the edges of the exterior shape to create a soft frame.

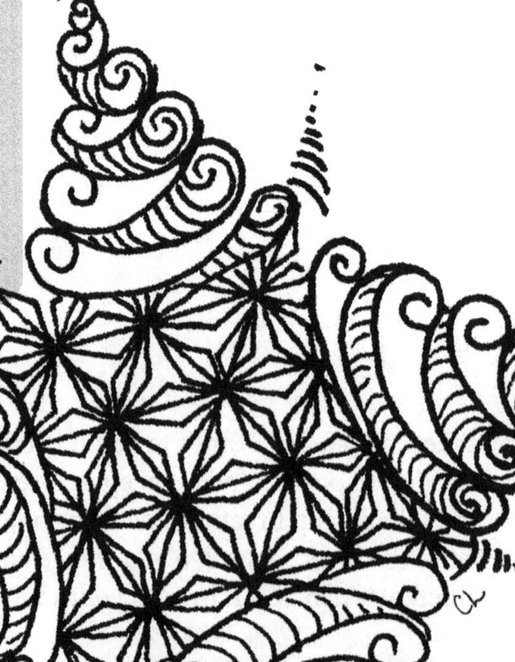

TANGLEATION 3

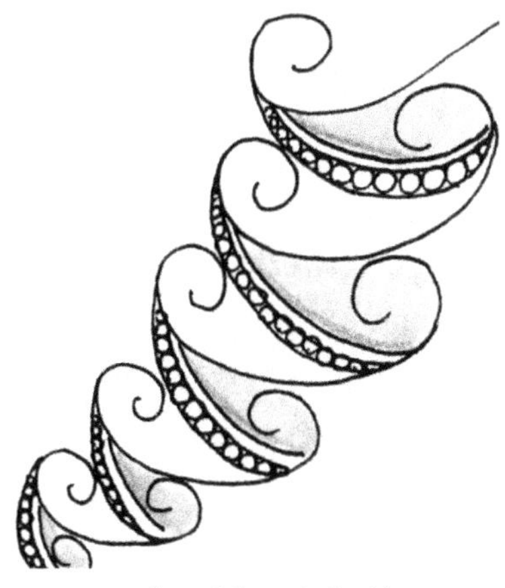

Accent one edge of the spiral with auras, perfs, shading or anything you choose for an new look.

TANGLEATION 6

Consider sprouting flowers from the center of each spiral and aura to turn the lines into leaves, a perfect addition to a tangled garden.

TANGLEATION 4

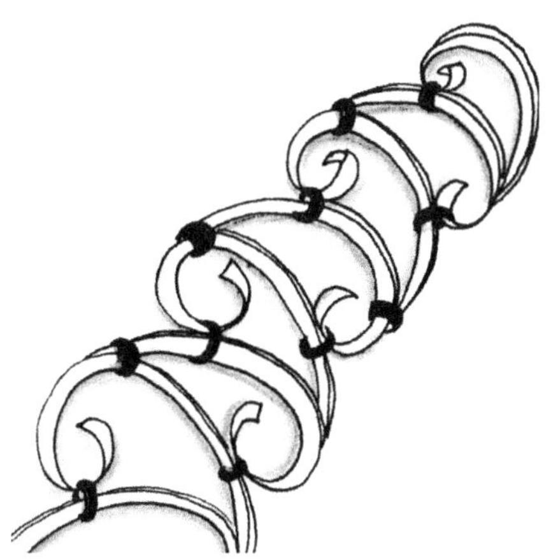

Turn the spirals into wrought iron by adding auras and shading. Embellish the connecting points with black bands to complete the look.

TANGLEATION 5

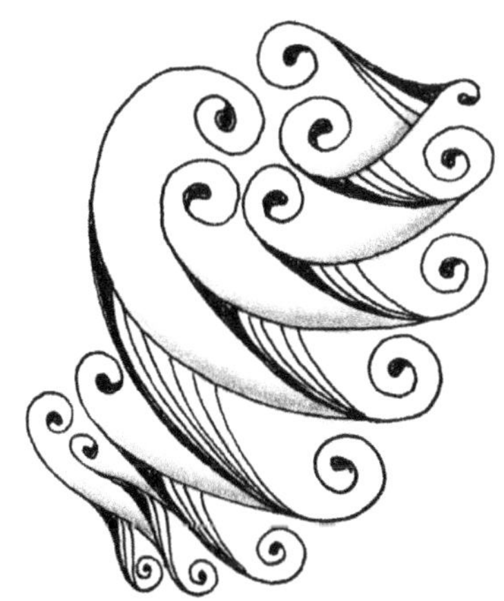

Vary the size and direction of some of the spirals to create a vibrant free-form version. Shading and line work add extra movement.

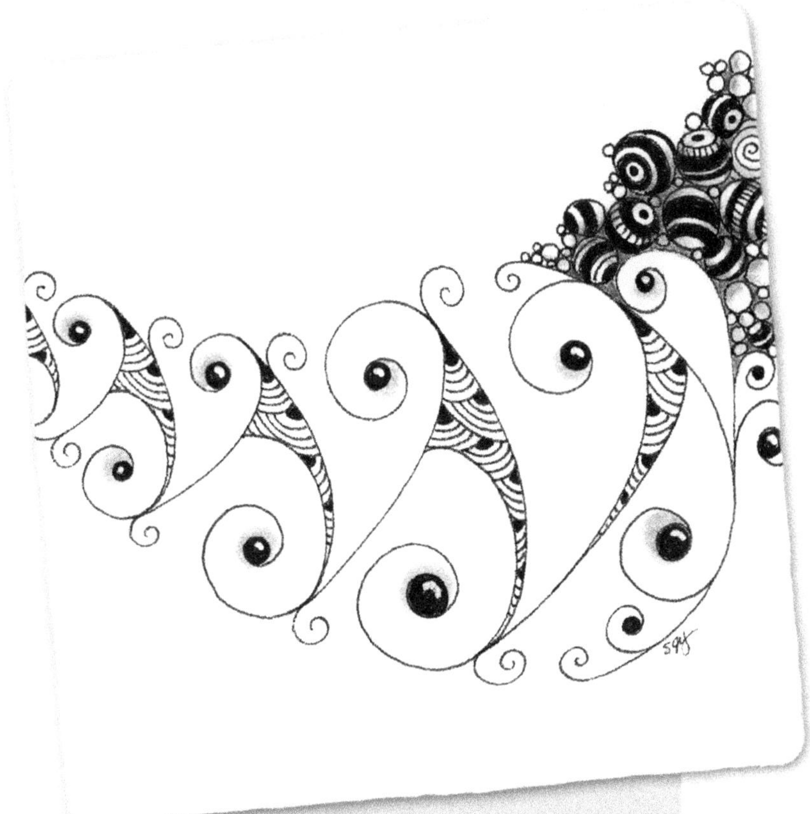

FREE-FORM PAUSHALÖV IS HIGHLIGHTED WITH BLACK PEARLZ AND JETTIES IN THIS LIGHT AND AIRY TILE. THE WHITE SPACE IN THE DESIGN PLAYS A CRITICAL PART IN AN UNEXPECTED COMPOSITION.

Tile features: PAUSHALOV, TIPPLE, SHATTUCK, *and* JETTIES.

IDEA STARTERS

- Make exaggerated spirals similar to tangleation 3 of PURK.
- Draw an aura in the triangular space between the spirals, and tangle there.
- Make the spirals on one side curve downward and those on the other side curve upward.
- Drawing question marks instead of spirals.

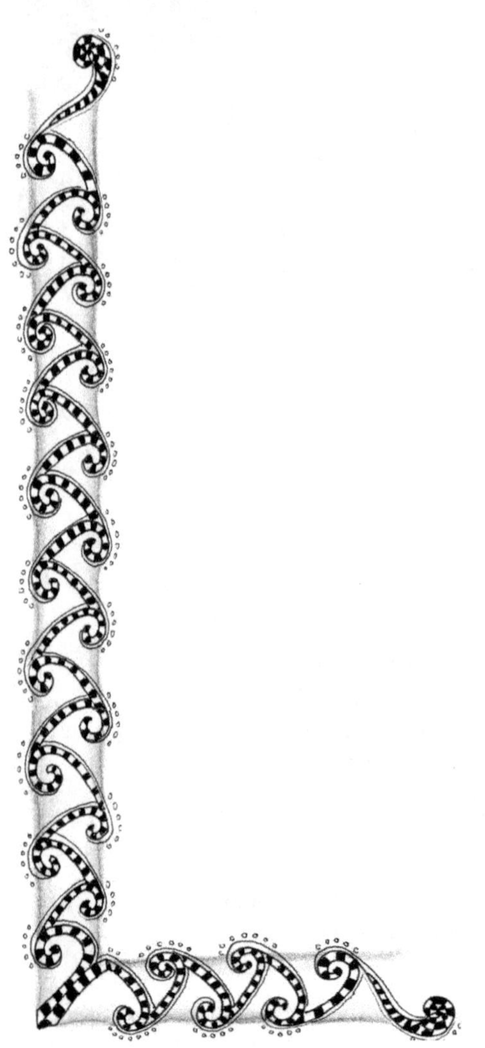

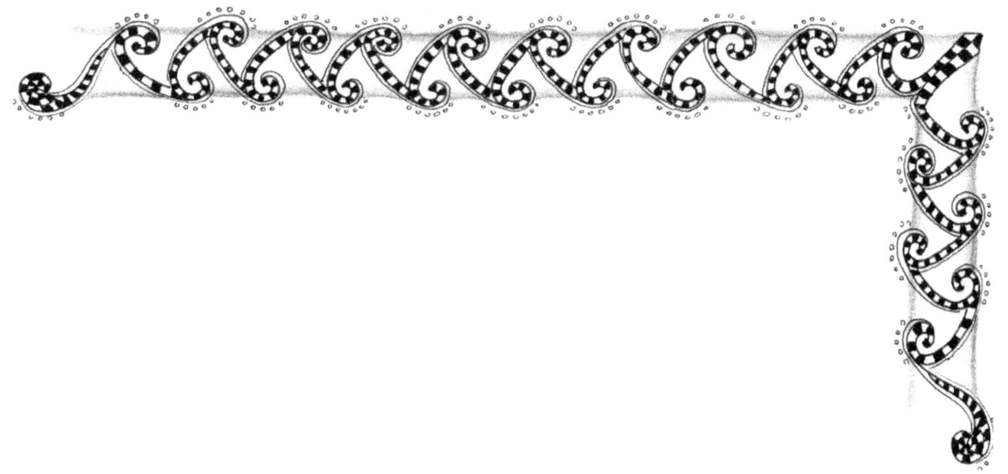

✏ Try something new. Sometimes we get in a rut and tangling loses some of its magic. Learn a new tangle or tangleation.

PAUSHALÖV

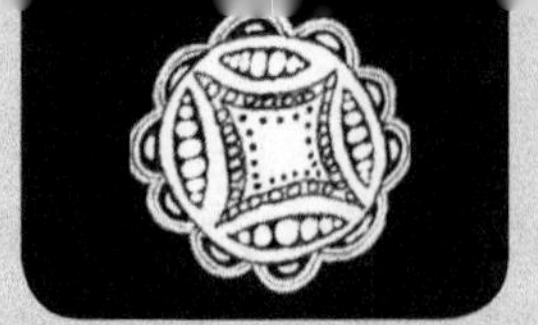

PUBFLEUR

by Cris Letourneau, CZT

Where do you find inspiration? Fabric, architecture, nature? Patterns are everywhere. Pubfleur came from a garland of flowers carved into a wooden bar. Compare the photo on page 113 with the finished tangle. Note that everything except the essential strokes was eliminated to create this beautiful, duplicable tangle.

Like the official tangle MOOKA, PUBFLEUR is a self-contained pod shape that works well as a centerpiece or in a cluster. Start with a teardrop shape in the center and then add a number of hook shapes for petals. Vary the size, width, and spacing, but aim to keep the shape the same. Drawing one side at a time may help keep them consistent.

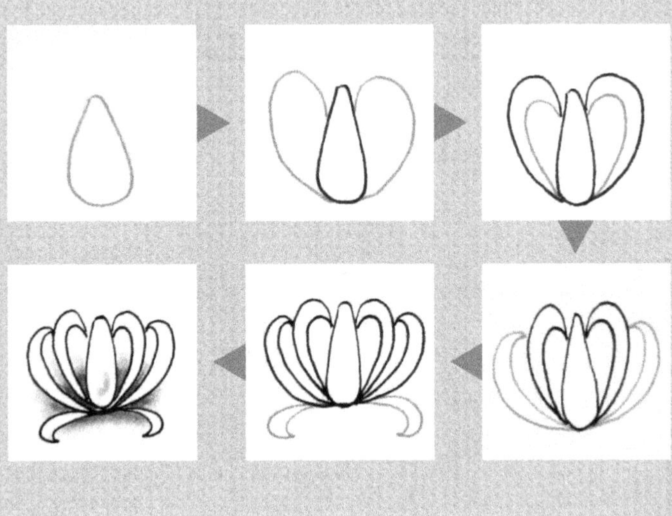

Thanks to Sue Jacobs for drawing the step-outs.

Eliminate the inner hook and decorate alternating with climbing tangles, like FLUX. Curlicues at the top add to the airy effect.

TANGLEATION 2

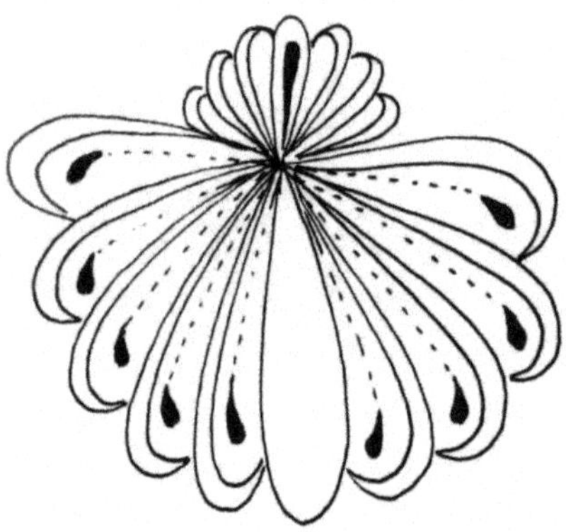

Draw widely-spaced skinny hooks to allow room for embellishing in between. Different-sized pods work together in this version.

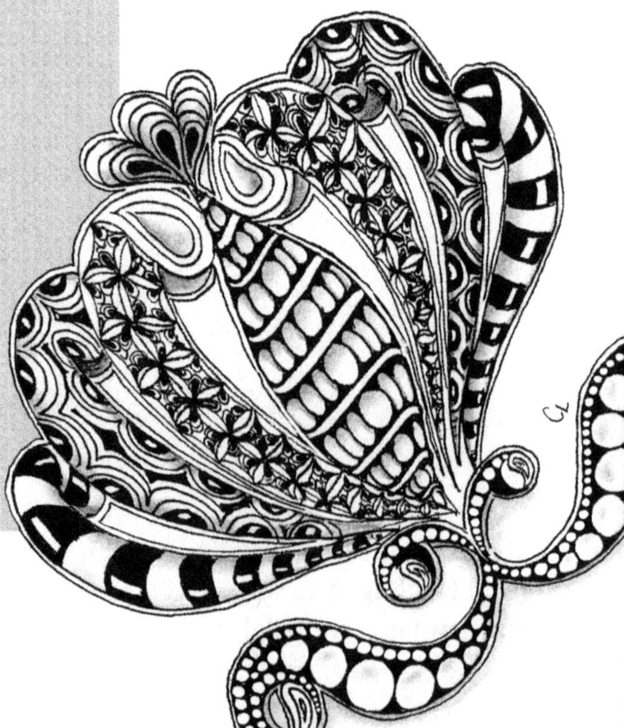

TANGLEATION 3

Use two pods as a base and draw a line coming up between to act as a stem for a third pod. Is this the start of a garden of PUBFLEUR? *(©Sue Jacobs)*

TANGLEATION 4

Fill the teardrop and hooks a solid black for a dramatic, geometric look. Diverging lines add to the effect.

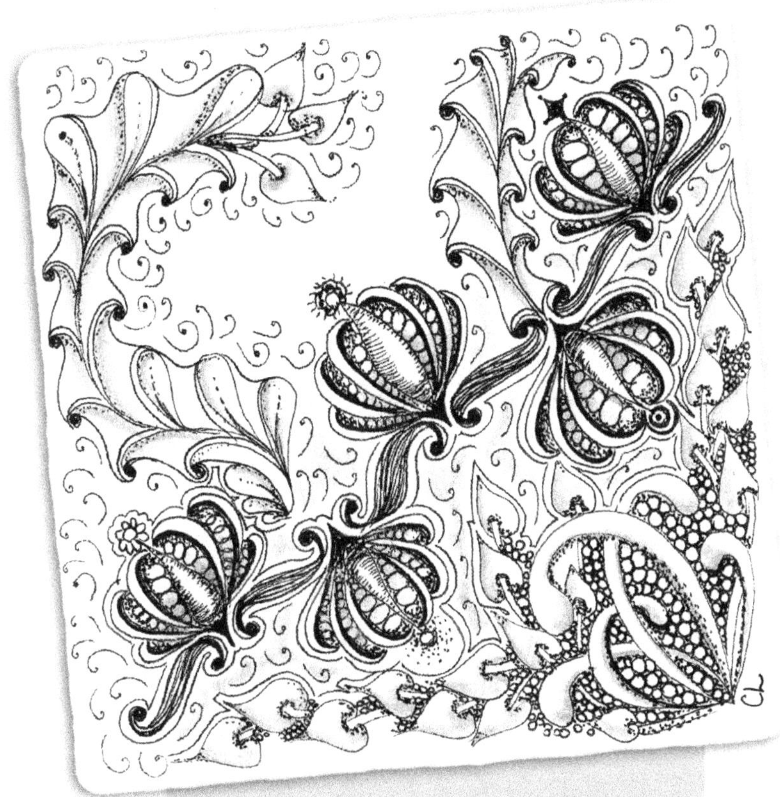

A LINE OF PUBFLEUR DANCES TOGETHER BY CONNECTING CURLICUES AT THE BASE OF EACH POD. CAREFUL SHADING, INCLUDING STIPPLING AND HATCHING, ADDS TO THE SOFTNESS OF THIS PIECE.

Tile features: MOOKA, POKELEAF, ONAMATO, *and* TIPPLE.

TANGLEATION 5

Add a second hook inside and shade for a 3D look similar to the inspiration carving. Varying the amount of curve gives many different looks.

TANGLEATION 6

Twist the bottom of the hooks into spirals and add rounding. Petals, perfs, and auras grace the top.

IDEA STARTERS

- Fill the space between the petals solid black.
- Add auras to each of your hook shapes.
- Alternate black and white fills on the petals.
- Draw several pods together in a cluster, back to back and side to side.
- Tangle inside the beginning teardrop shape.

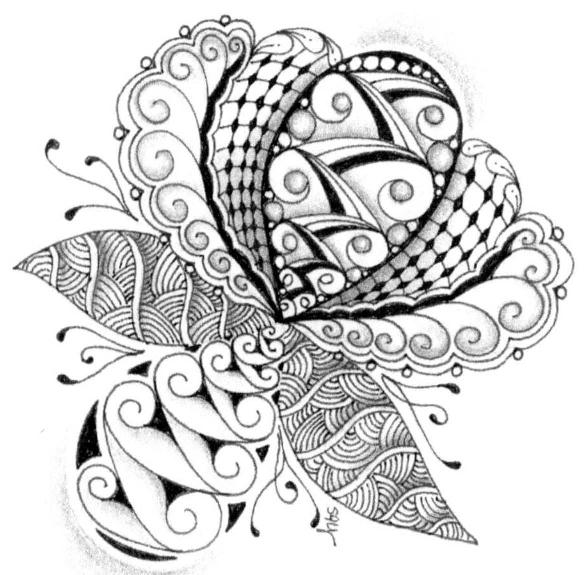

✏ Challenge yourself to step out of your comfort zone. If you prefer straight lines, choose something organic or vice versa. If you usually work small, pick something large.

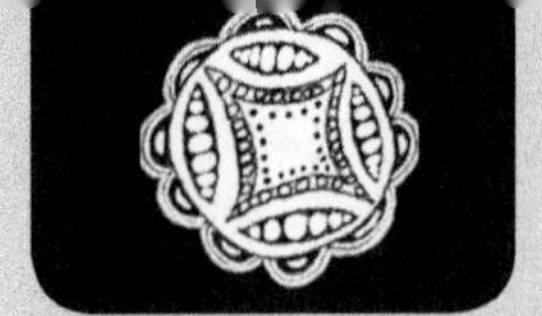

VEEZ

by Alice Hendon

Add a touch of spring to your art with this tulip-inspired tangle. VEEZ *shines in its versatility, lending itself to borders, fillers, or as a string. It looks especially lovely around a circle. It came together as Alice worked on a large-scale geometric drawing, mixing brackets and circles.*

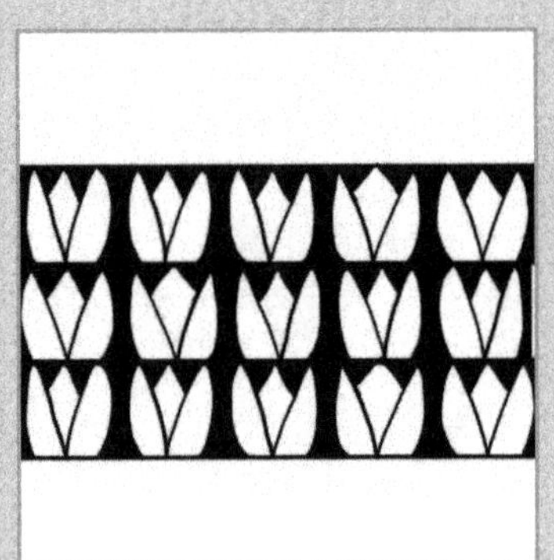

Drawing VEEZ could not be simpler. Simple parenthesis are filled with a large V and then a smaller upside-down V. Change the spacing and amount of curve in your beginning parenthesis strokes and see what happens to the result. Also play with different patterns to fill the Vs.

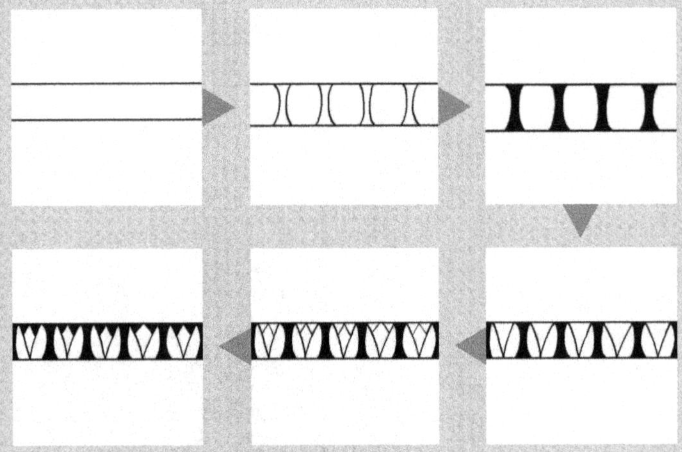

TANGLEATION 1

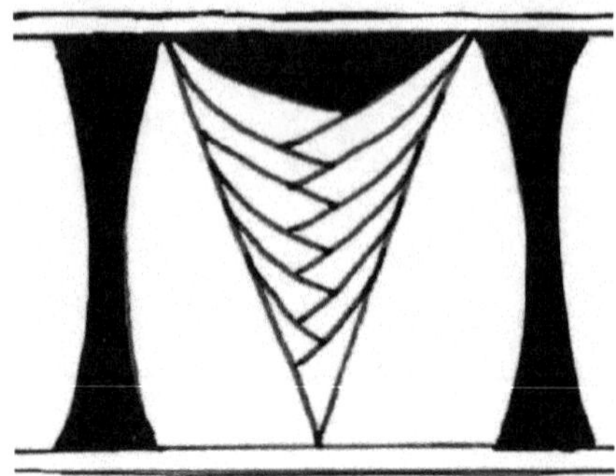

Enlarge the tulip shape, and tangle inside the large V. Here, we used **BETWEED**.

TANGLEATION 2

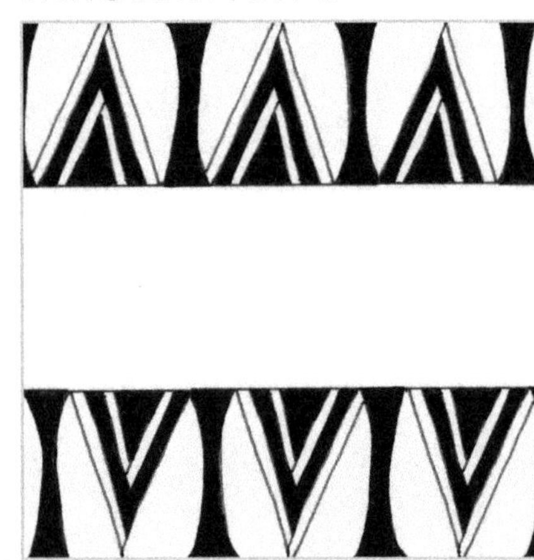

Draw double rows of **VEEZ** facing one another for a lovely frame. Here, stripes take center stage, replacing the small V.

TANGLEATION 3

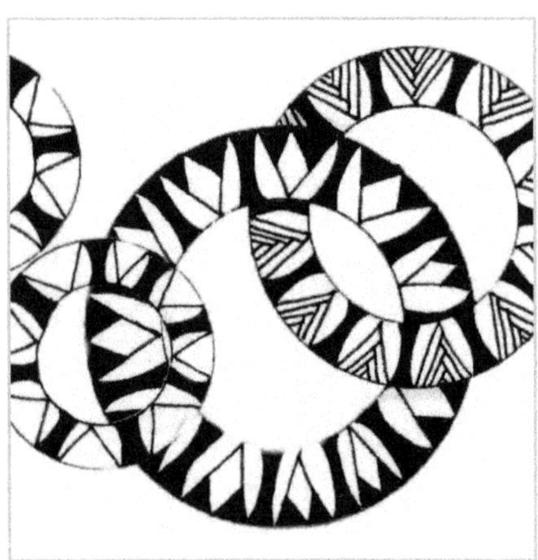

VEEZ works really well in an orb.
(©Alice Hendon)

TANGLEATION 4

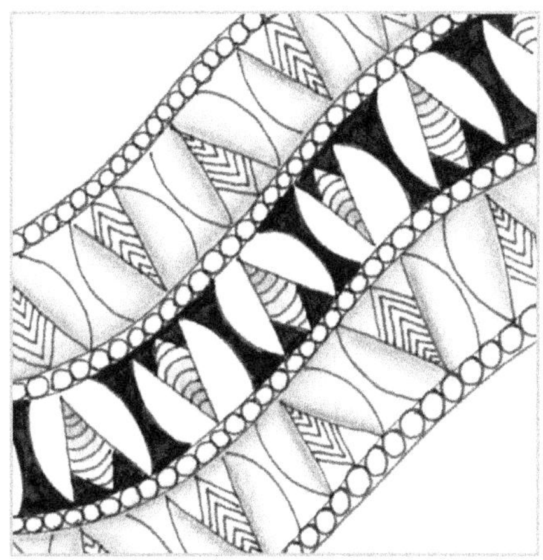

Draw rows of VEEZ separated by orbs to fill a space. Here, alternating light and dark fills add an interesting stripe effect.

TANGLEATION 5

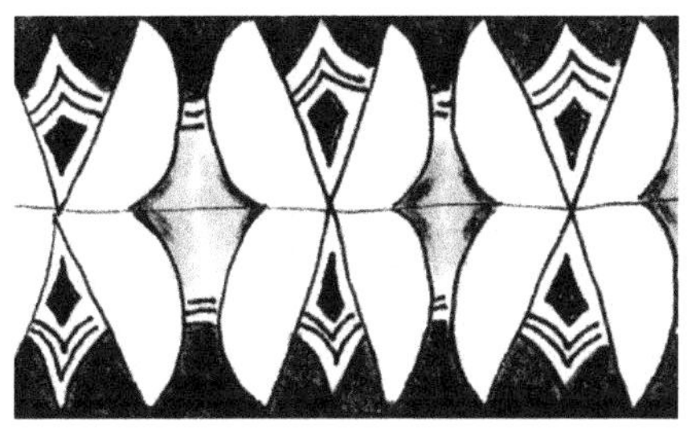

Add auras to the small V, and connect them by drawing behind the petals. Place one on top of the other for a row of butterflies.

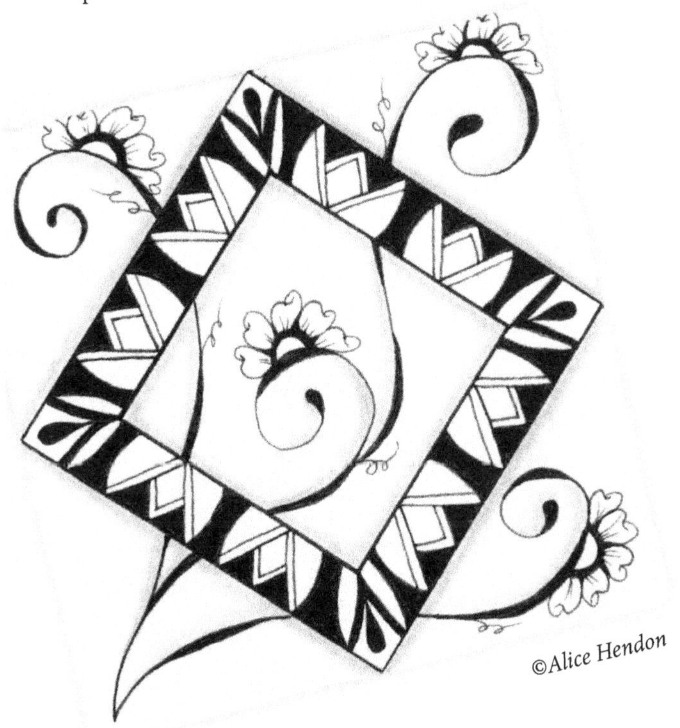

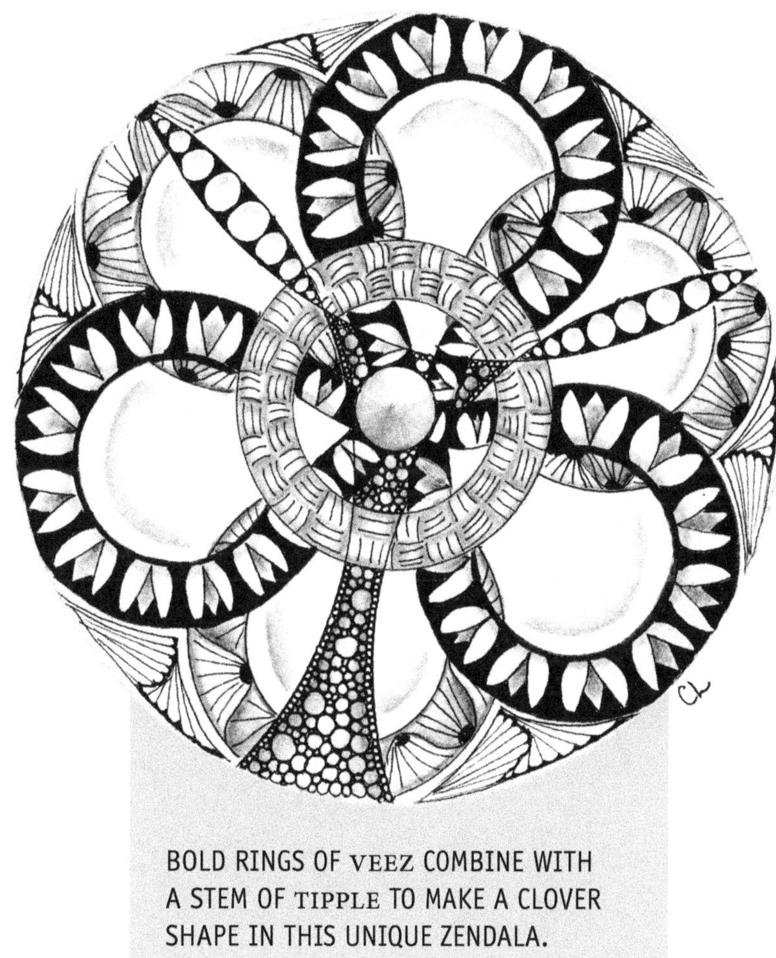

BOLD RINGS OF VEEZ COMBINE WITH A STEM OF TIPPLE TO MAKE A CLOVER SHAPE IN THIS UNIQUE ZENDALA.

Zendala features: KEEKO, FOOTLIGHTS, TIPPLE, PARADOX, ONOMATO, *and* VEEZ.

TANGLEATION 6

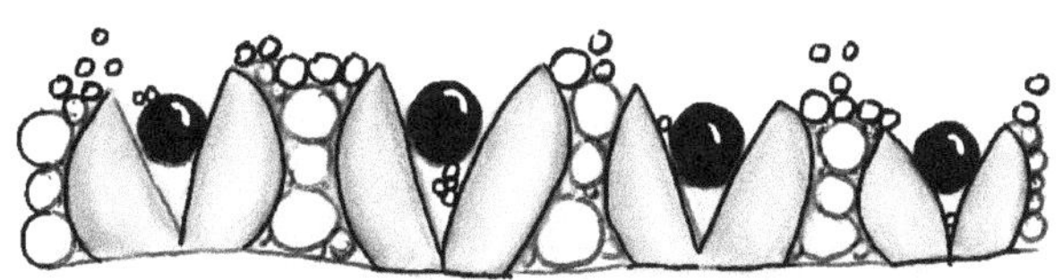

Replace the small v with a pearl, and the petals become clam shells. Add TIPPLE to enhance the underwater illusion.

IDEA STARTERS

- Eliminate the small V for a light and airy look.
- Draw an X instead of the large V for a double-sided tulip.
- Draw the large V only part way down instead of to the opposite side.
- Make some of your Vs "upside-down."
- Use a W instead of a V.

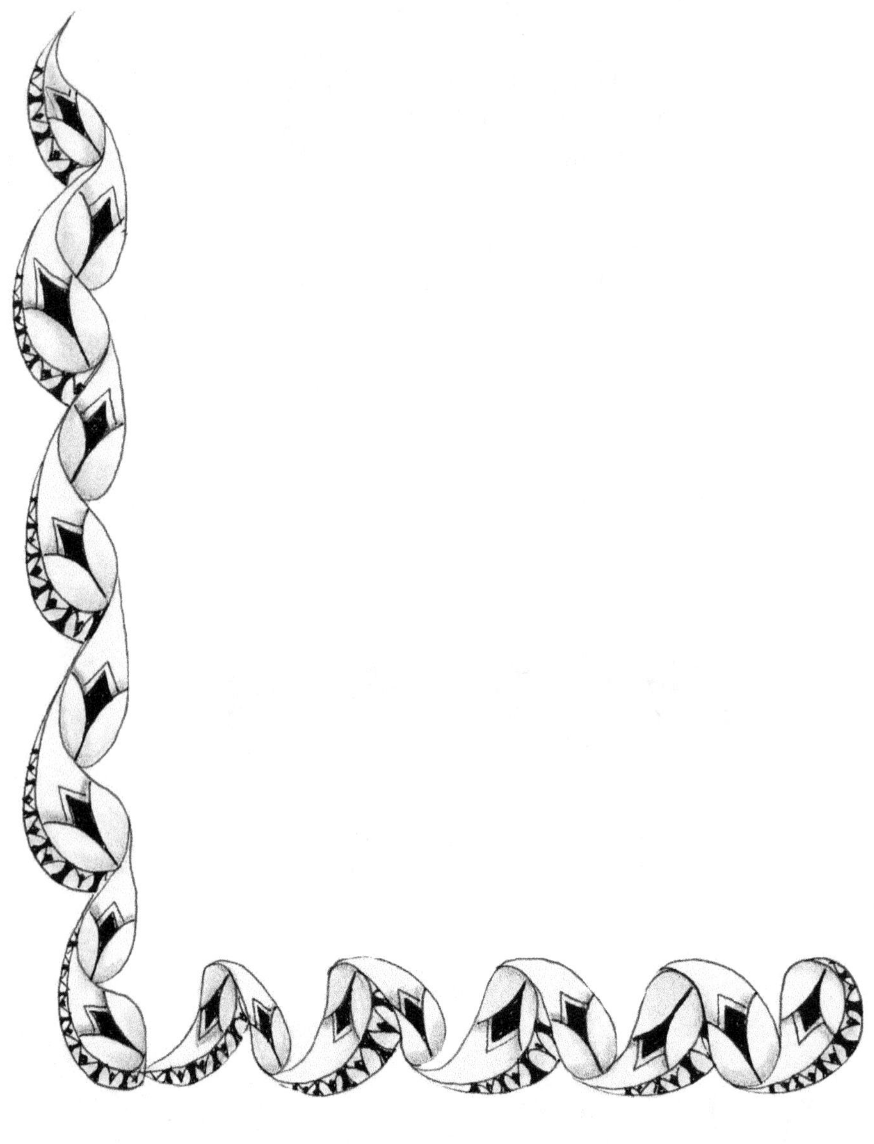

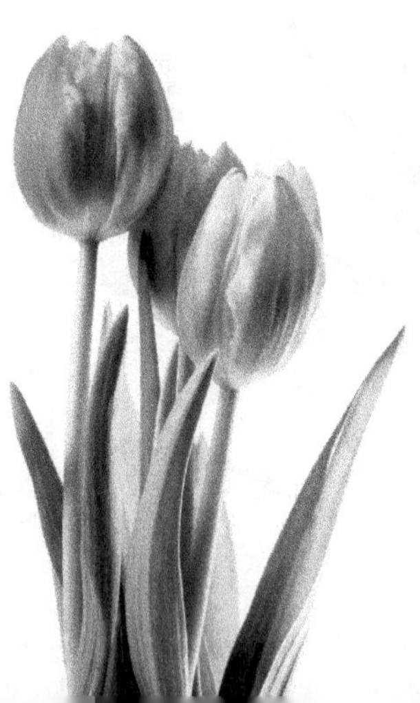

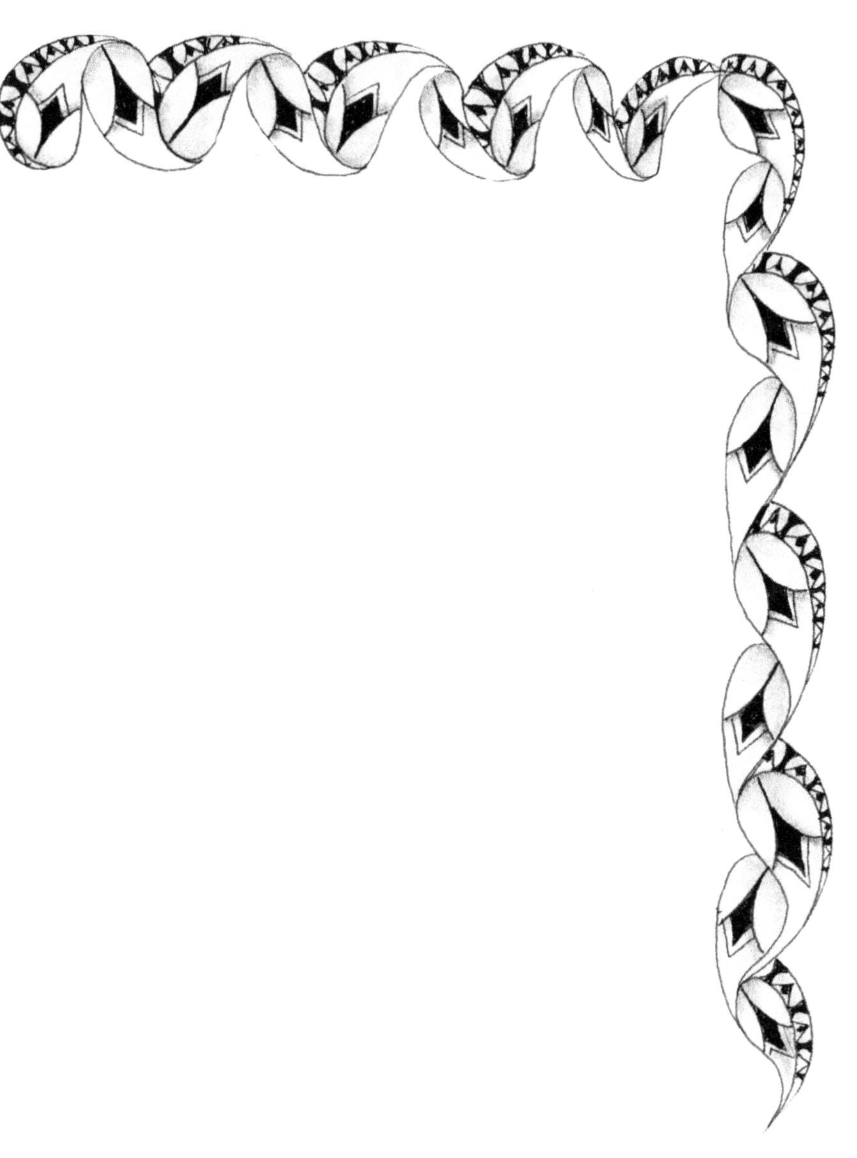

✏ Have trouble with perfectionism? Try tangling with your non-dominant hand. You will naturally slow down and let go of your expectations.

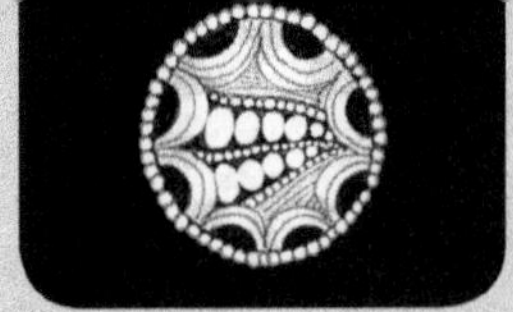

OPUS

by Maria Thomas

Maria is often inspired by the naturally occurring patterns in nature. **OPUS** *is reminiscent of the unfurling fronds of a fiddlehead fern. The swirls and curls of this flowy organic tangle add fluidity, direction, and softness to any Zentangle artwork.*

an official Zentangle tangle

OPUS starts with a single curl that looks like a bass clef. Draw the next curl on top of the first, connecting the stems. Continue adding curls until one side is as large as you want. Then draw curls in the opposite direction, mirroring the first side, until it loosely resembles a central stem and curly branches. Add an aura around the whole thing, then fill the space between the curls with orbs.

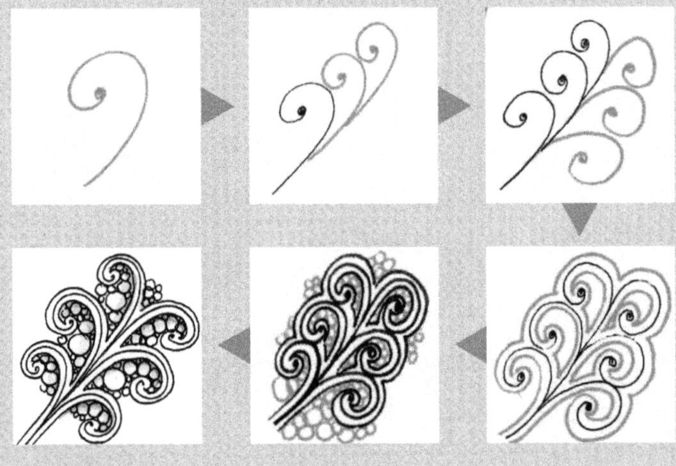

TANGLEATION 1

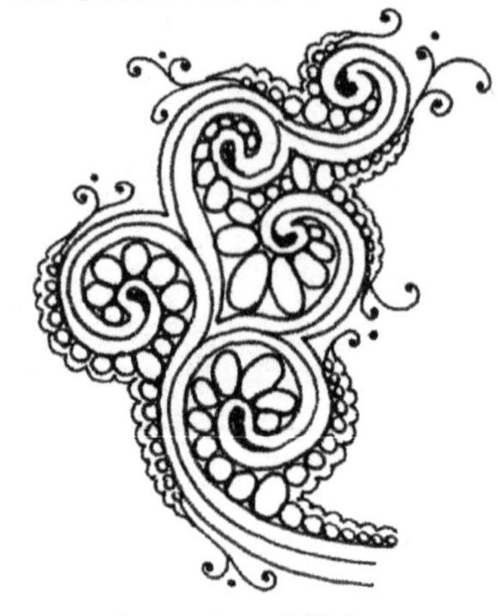

Create random curls, and fill them with a single row of orbs in the tradition of **SNAYLZ TRAYLZ**. Add auras and curlicues for energy.

TANGLEATION 2

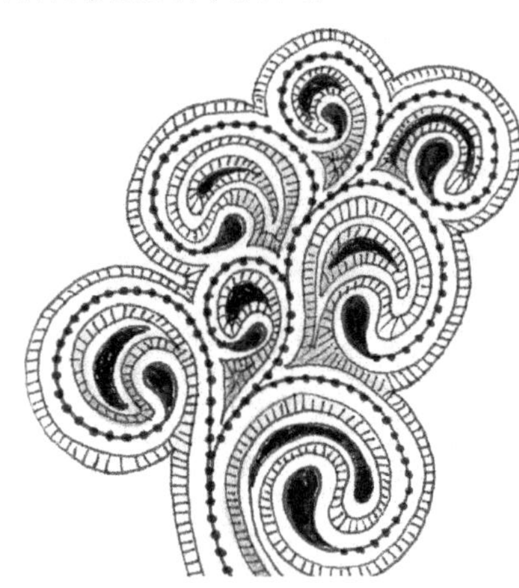

Use **BEADLINES** for the stem. Ink wide auras that can be filled with any variety of patterns and shading.

TANGLEATION 3

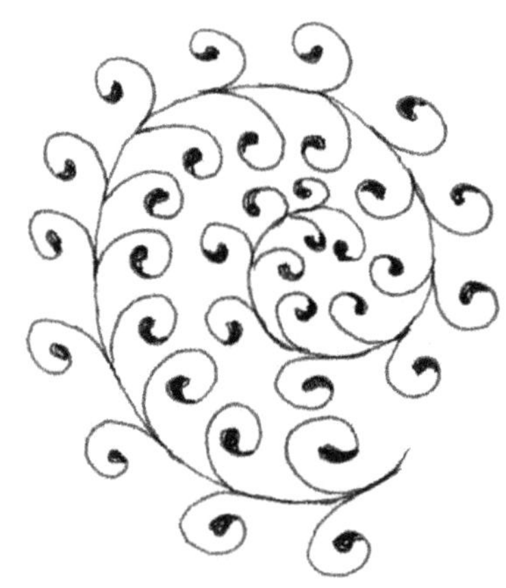

Simplify **OPUS** to its most basic elements. While it contrasts the busier more complicated designs, it is no less elegant.

TANGLEATION 4

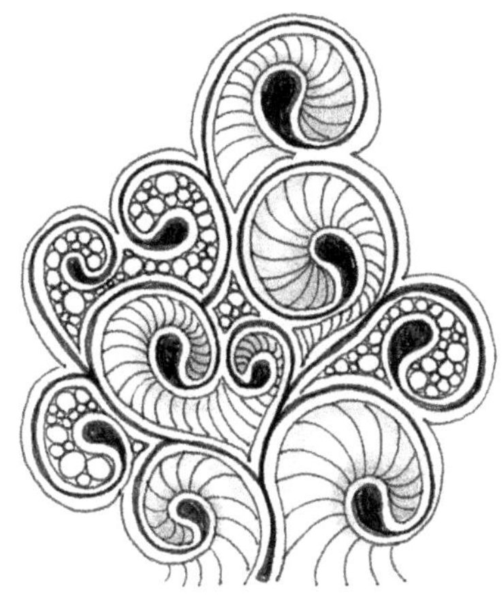

Use heavier strokes to draw multiple stems sprouting in various directions. Add auras and more than one fill pattern.

TANGLEATION 5

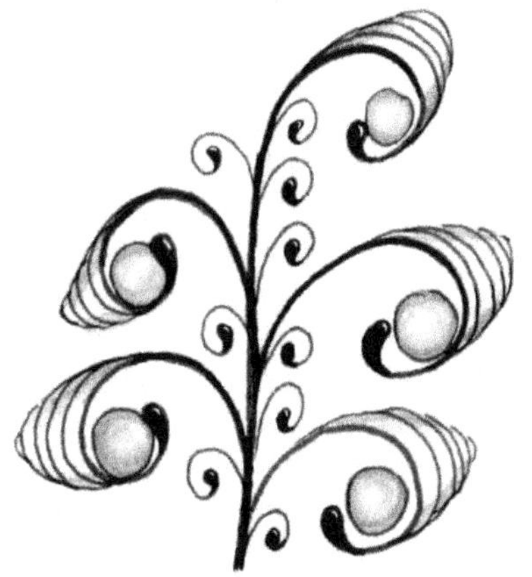

Draw auras on the outside portion of each swirl to create a layered look reminiscent of SPRINGKLE and ZINGER.

TANGLEATION 6

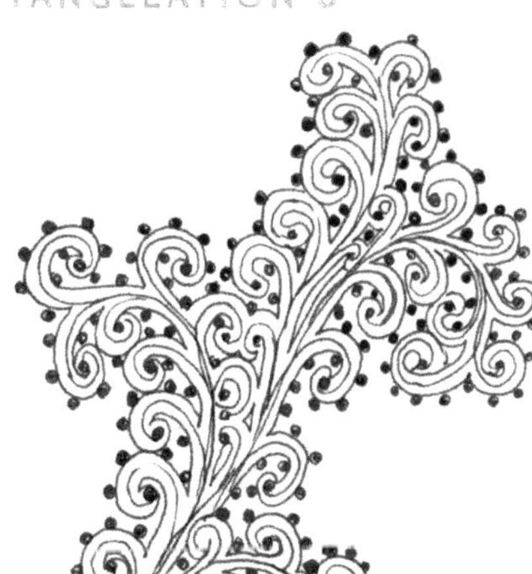

Reverse the order of some of the elements. Accent each swirl with black orbs on the outside for a lacy appearance.

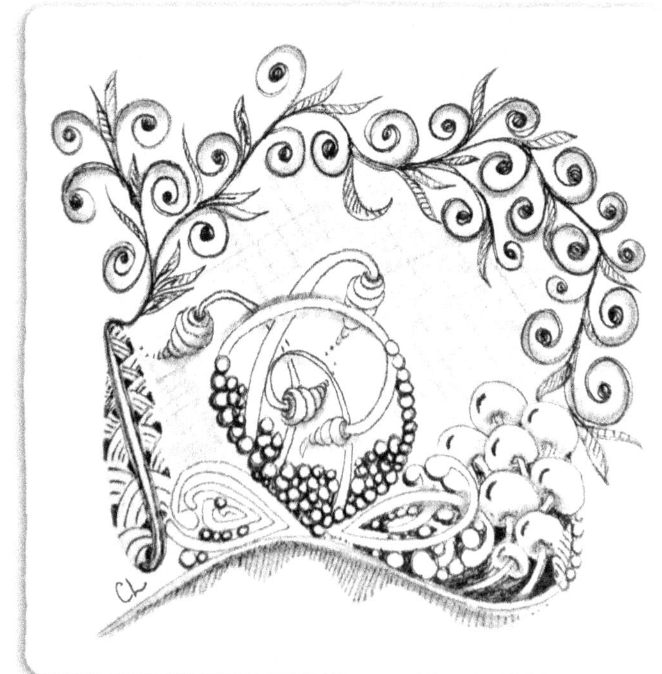

HERE OPUS MARRIES WELL WITH DELICATE LEAVES AND WELL-PLACED SHADOWS, CREATING AN ORGANIC BEAUTY.

Tile features: OPUS, SHATTUCK, ZINGER, MOOKA, POKEROOT, *and* TIPPLE.

IDEA STARTERS

- Instead of filling the empty spaces with orbs, use stripes or KNIGHTSBRIDGE.
- Start with a thick "stem," and add rounding where the curls attach to it.
- End each curl with a round tangle like PEPPER, CIRQUITAL or PRINTEMPS.
- How about using a double or triple stem to add variety?

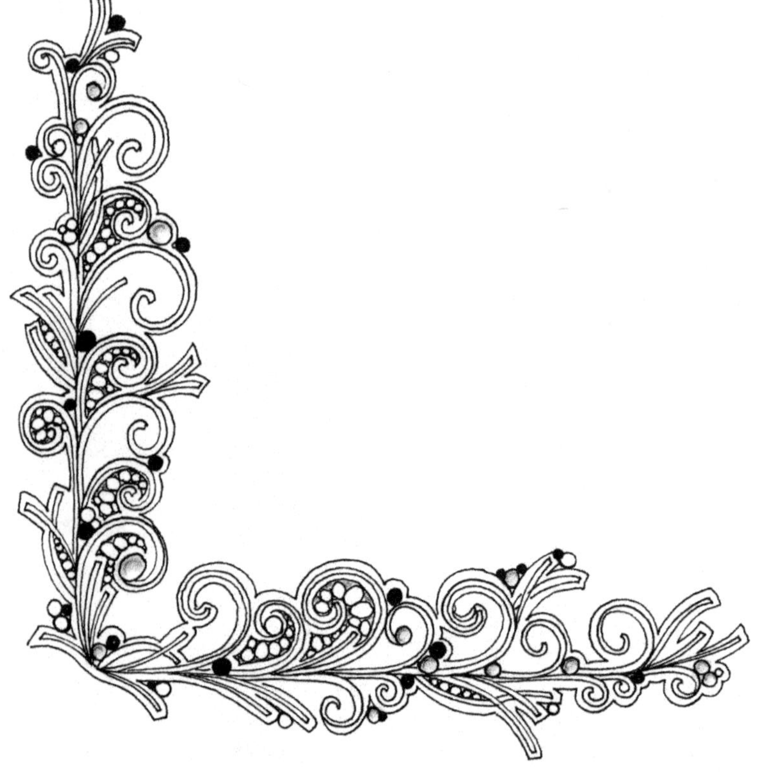

✏ Let go of expectations and planning. Allow yourself to be surprised by the result. "*Let go and let Zentangle.*"

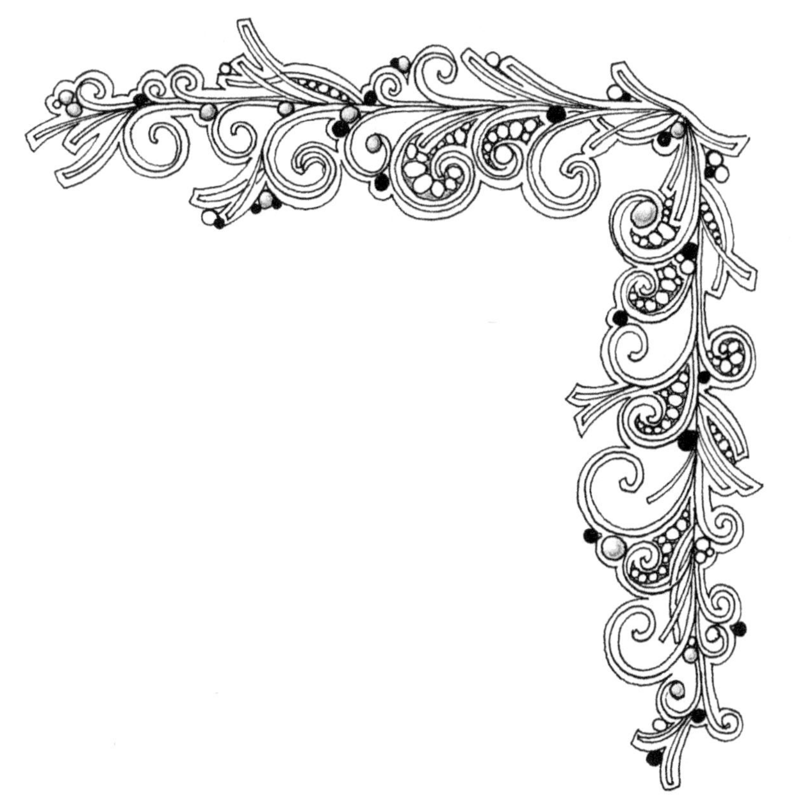

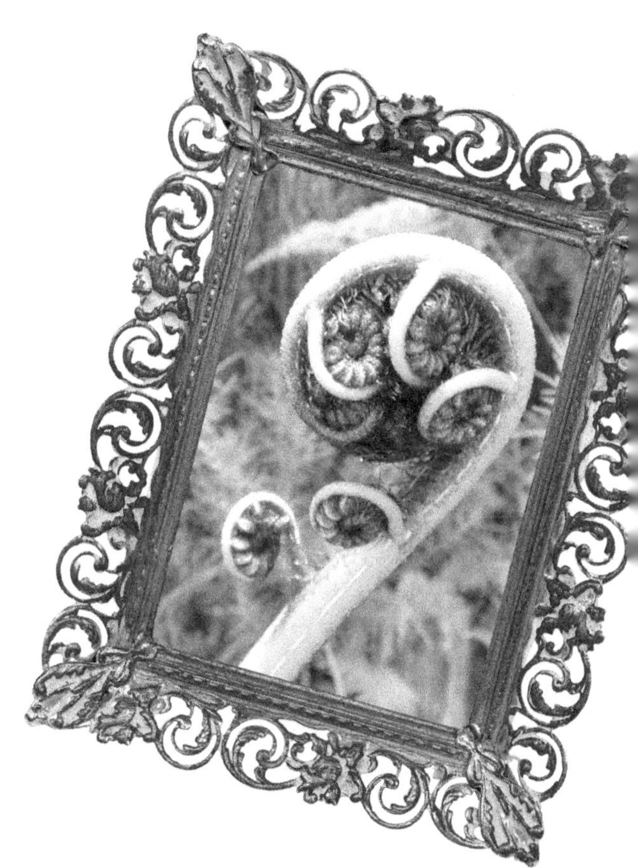

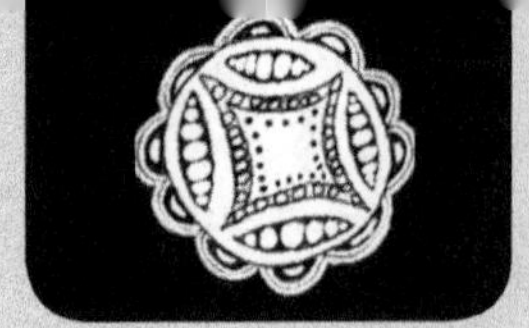

BRAZELET

by Sonya Yencer

Inspired by shiny beads and jewels encircling a friend's wrist, BRAZELET *adds a hint of sparkle and movement to your work. This delicate beauty snakes through Zentangle art, wrapping around other shapes with ease as an interesting border. Mix and match straight or curvy strings of* BRAZELET *to fill large areas with bands of geometric shapes.*

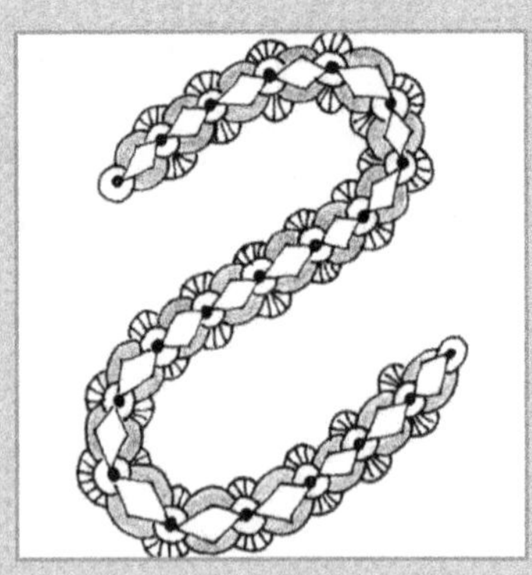

Begin with a line of heavy black dots to create the shape of your BRAZELET. Connect the dots with elongated diamonds. Draw an aura around the dots. Add arcs connecting the auras. Draw another layer of auras around the black dots. Fill the outside aura with stripes in a fan pattern.

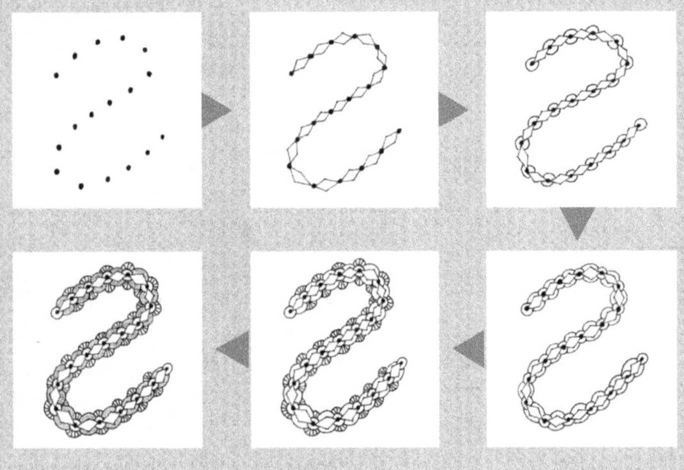

TANGLEATION 1

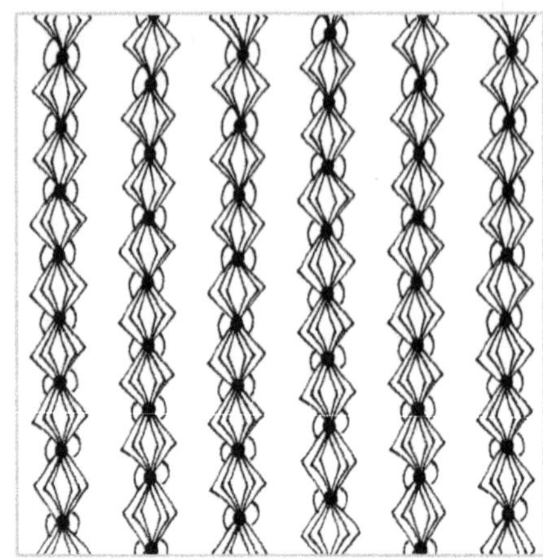

Draw row after row of your favorite BRAZELET to fill a space like the striped wallpaper in grandma's dining room.

TANGLEATION 2

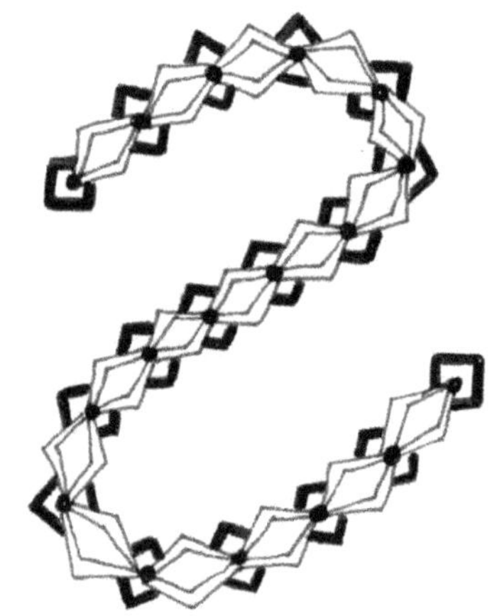

Use only dots and diamonds to create this version. Thick black lines create some of the auras for a more graphic look.

TANGLEATION 3

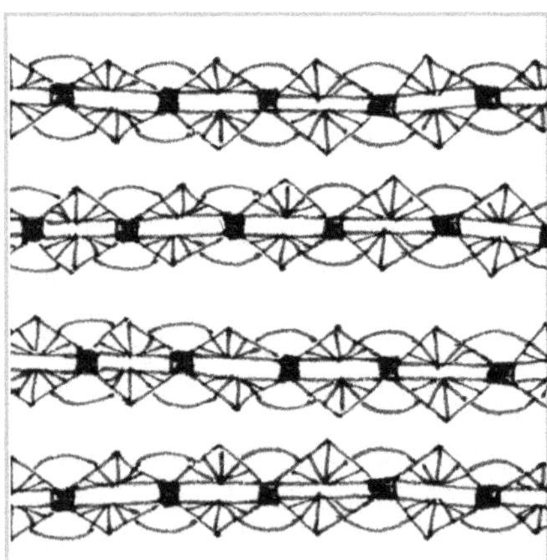

Create horizontal stripes of BRAZELET, beginning with black squares connected by parallel lines. Then add diamonds and auras.

TANGLEATION 4

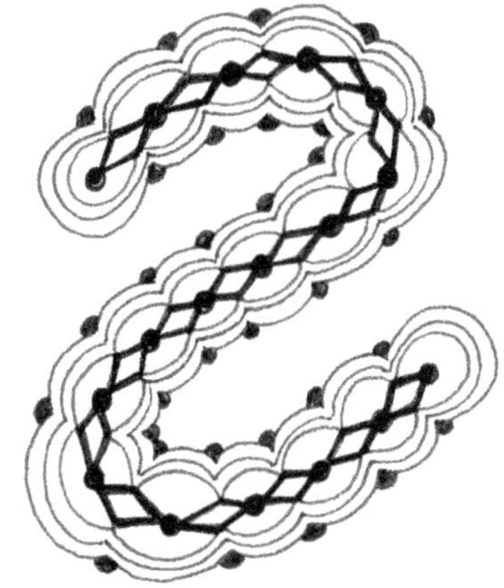

Vary the line weight and layers of connecting auras. At each intersection along the outside, add a ladybug like CRESCENT MOON.

TANGLEATION 5

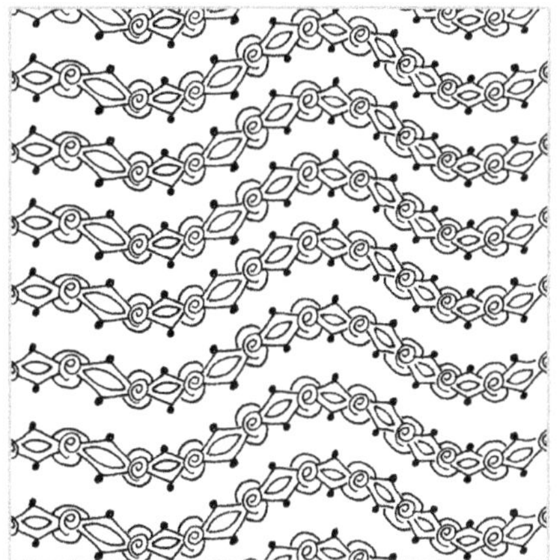

Draw your favorite tangleation in wavy rows for a lovely fill with movement.

TANGLEATION 6

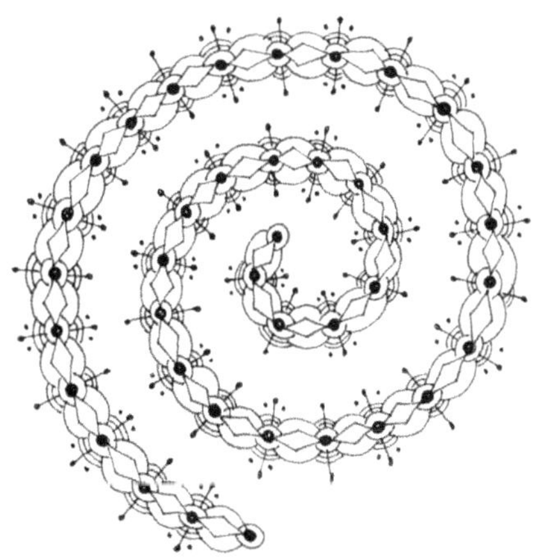

Spiral a line of BRAZELET as a focal point. Multiply some of the auras. Embellish with dots and antennae for interest.

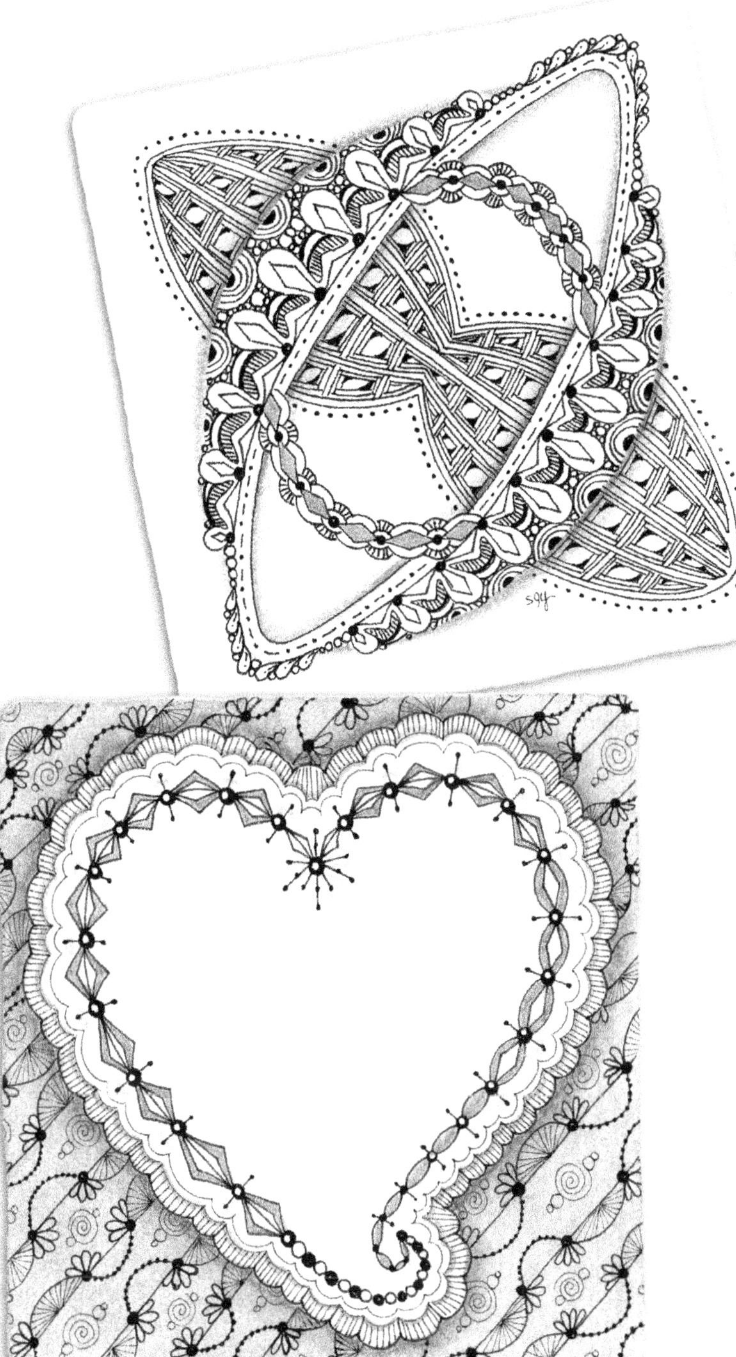

YOUR HEART MAY SKIP A BEAT WHEN BRAZELET TAKES CENTER-STAGE. WHETHER AS A FOCAL POINT OR AN ACCENT, BRAZELET IS A WELCOME ADDITION TO THE TANGLE FAMILY.

Top tile features: BRAZELET, GURTEL, TIPPLE, FLUX, *and* CRESCENT MOON. *Bottom tile features:* BRAZELET *and* FALZ.

IDEA STARTERS

- Draw BRAZELET in a spiral, making the elements smaller in the center. Gradually draw the elements larger as you move toward the outside of the spiral.
- Use all curvy lines, no straight lines. Then do the opposite.
- Enlarge BRAZELET and tangle inside the auras and diamonds.
- Weave BRAZELET in and out of itself like a ribbon, with some parts in front and others behind. Shade to emphasize the depth.

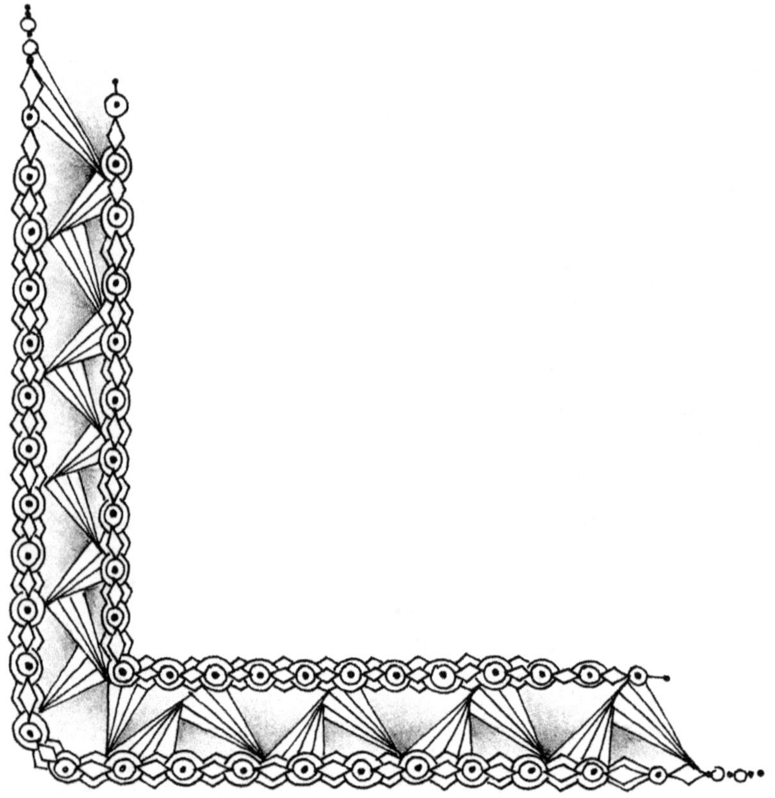

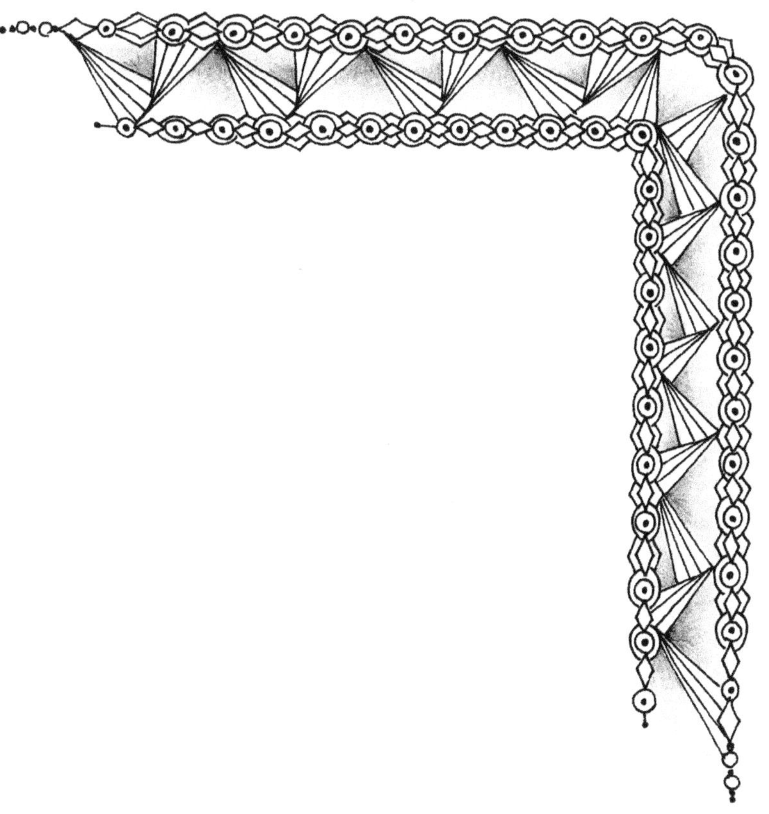

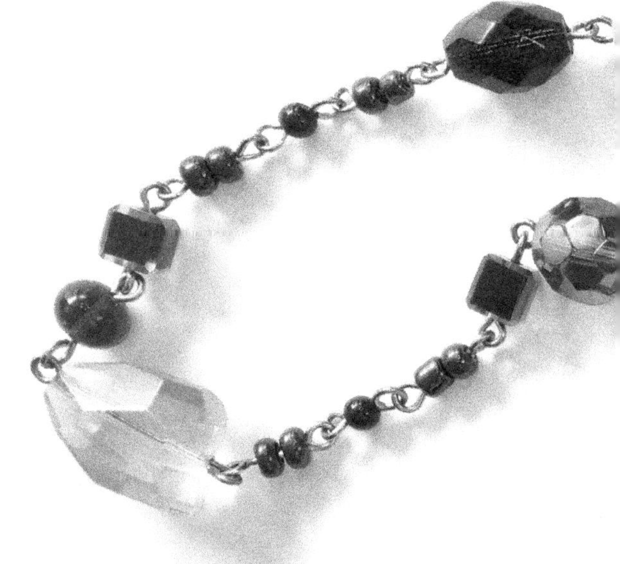

✏ Separate the parts from the whole and examine each for ways to personalize it. This exercise helps you think more creatively and helps you understand the pattern. It is also fun.

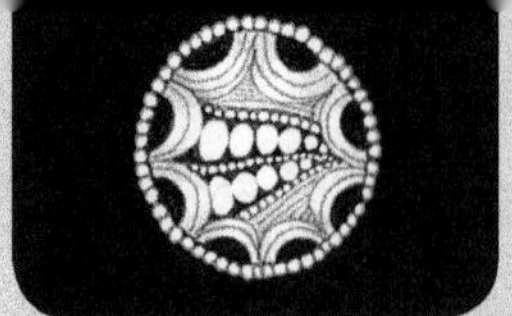

AURAKNOT

by Maria Thomas

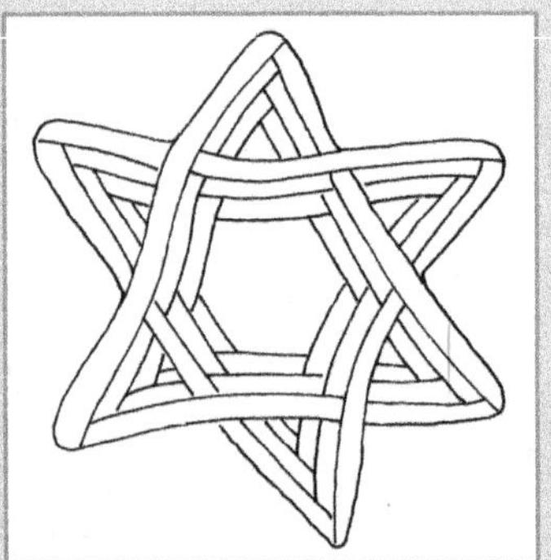

an official Zentangle tangle

Both **AURAKNOT** and **PARADOX** seem complex. But in actuality, they both only require concentration and rhythmic turning of the tile. This tangle is best explained through pictures. Give it a try!

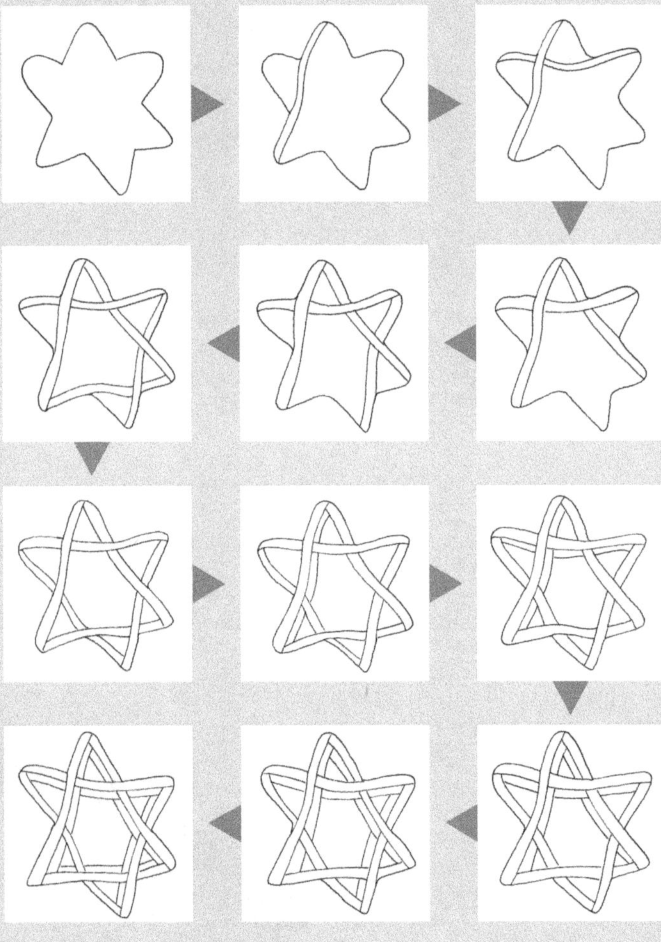

TANGLEATION 1

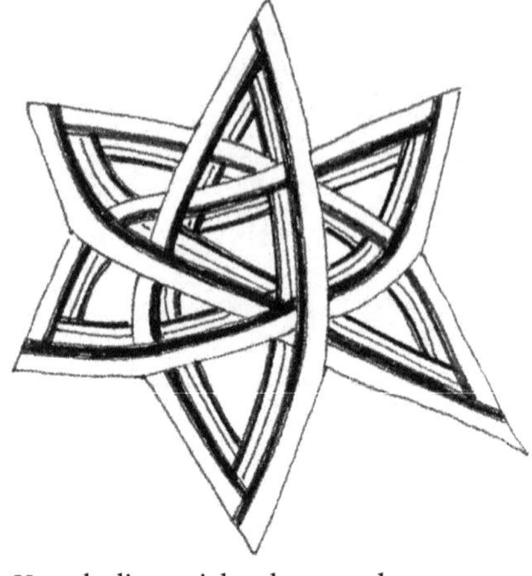

Vary the line weight when you draw **AURAKNOT**. Make the first and last lines the thickest to add boldness.

TANGLEATION 2

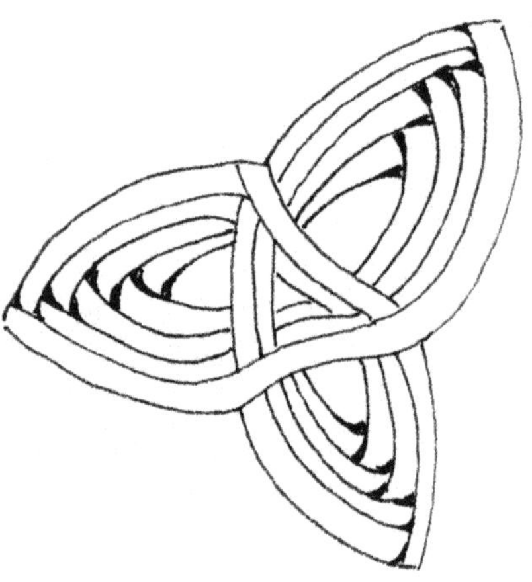

Apply the same technique as **BETWEED**, darkening the spaces where the lines converge, giving weight to the intersections.

TANGLEATION 3

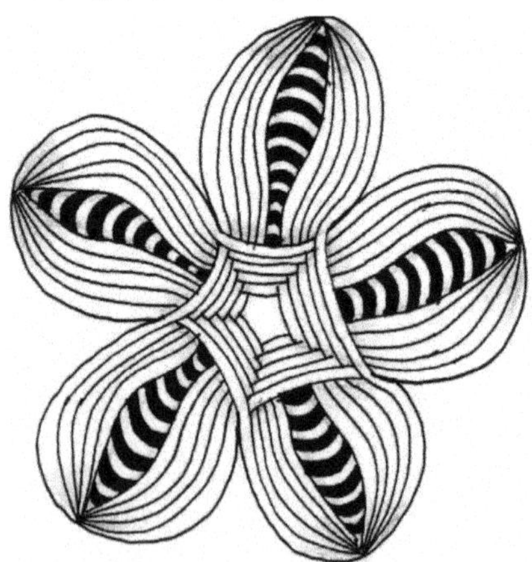

Use curving petals for the outside shape. Draw your ribbons beginning at a single point on the outside edge of each petal. *(©Caren Mlot)*

TANGLEATION 4

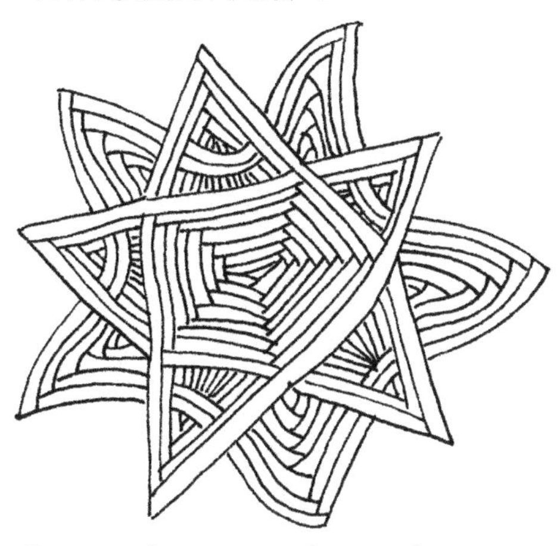

Draw two shapes on top of one another. Follow the step-outs, creating ribbons that flow through from one shape to the next.

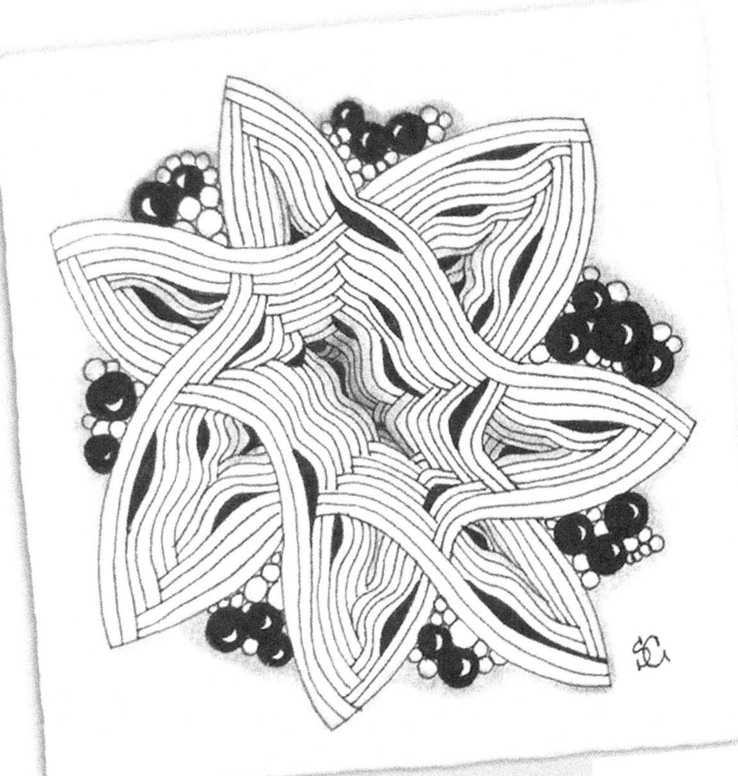

LIKE A DEEP WELL SINKING DOWN INTO THE TILE, THE DEPTH ACHIEVED WITH AURAKNOT AND STRATEGIC SHADING IS AMAZING.

Tile by Sue Clark features: AURAKNOT ,TIPPLE *and a bit of* DIVA DANCE.

TANGLEATION 5

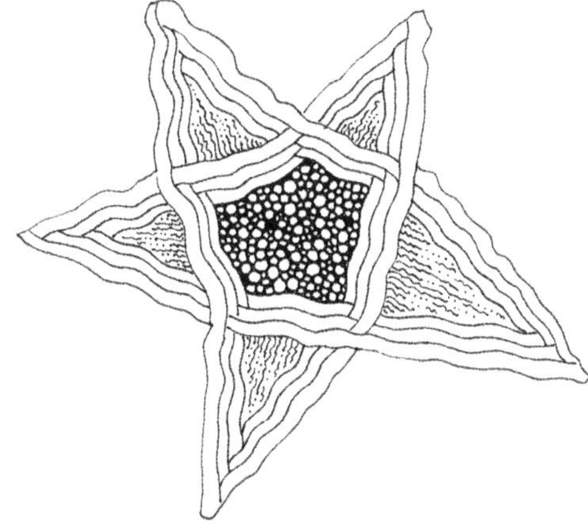

Ink wavy lines for this underwater effect. Leave plenty of open spaces in the center for various tangles.

TANGLEATION 6

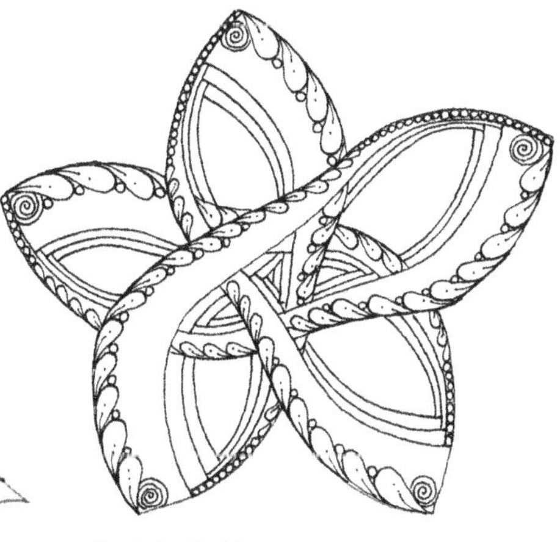

Taper the initial ribbons so they are fat at one end, thin at the other. Fill the wide spaces inside the ribbons with tangles.

IDEA STARTERS

- Vary the number of points on your beginning shape; use both even and odd numbers.
- Make some ribbons wide enough so another tangle can be placed inside them.
- For a high-contrast version, fill every other ribbon solid black or gray.
- Combine AURAKNOT with PARADOX.

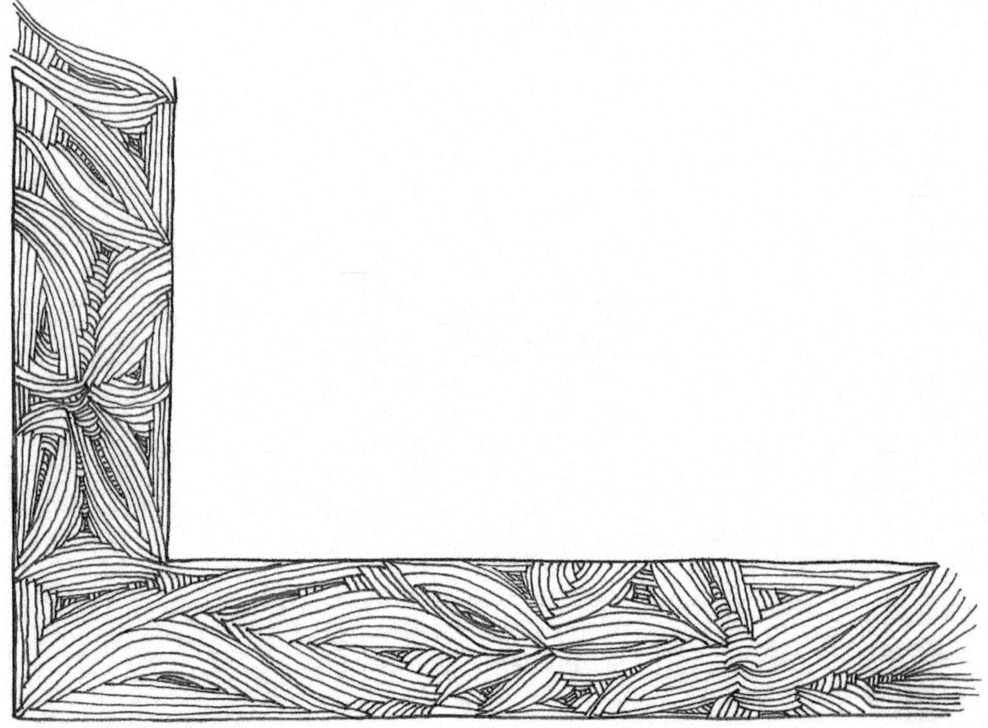

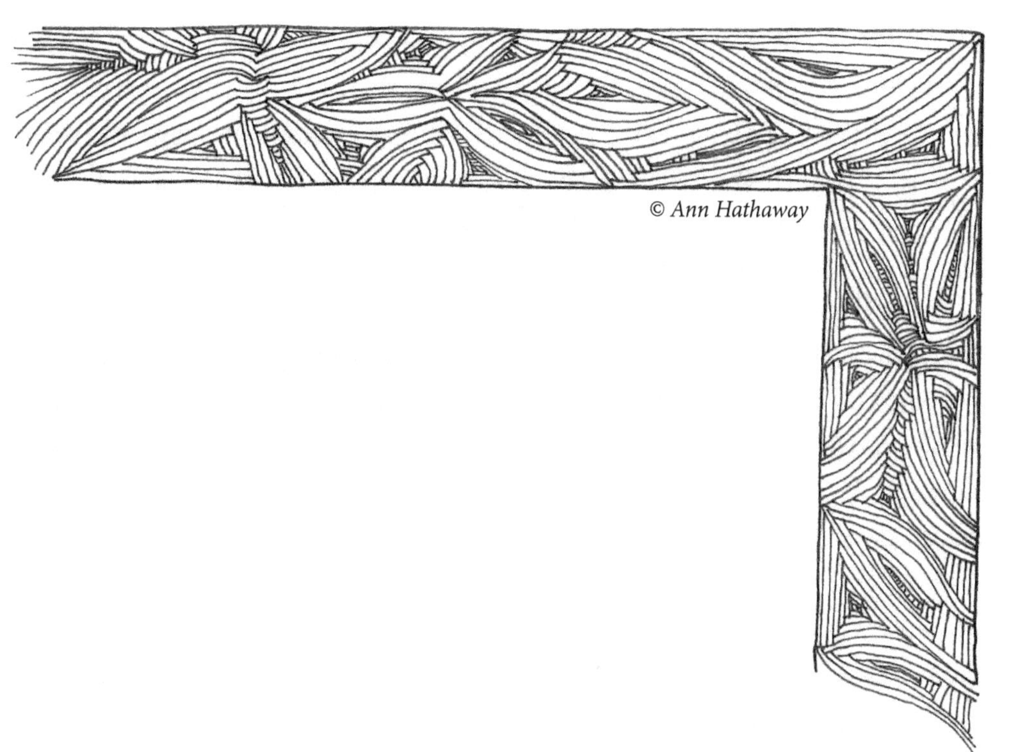

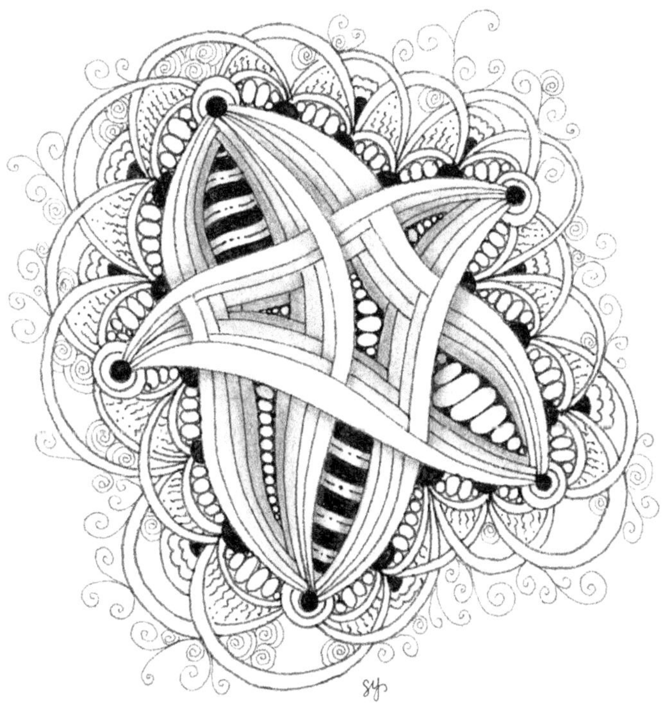

✏ ***Have fun playing with your patterns!***

ETERNAL GRATITUDE

A world of thanks to the folks who believed in us and backed our Kickstarter:

Lorna Aaronson, CZT
Bette Abdu, CZT
Arun Agrawal
Kate Ahrens
Barbara J. Allen, CZT
Jill Barber
Kathy Barringer, CZT
Elizabeth Batten-Carew, CZT
Moo Bishop, CZT
Mary Jane Bohlen, CZT 2
Barbara Bradley
Melanie Bratko
Margaret Bremner, CZT
Amy Broady, CZT
Bonnie Browning, CZT 7
Melissa W. Cahn, CZT
Susan Carr, CZT
Faith K. Cohen
Sue Clark, CZT 4
LeAnna Coetzee
Sherry Cook, CZT
Bonnie Cox, CZT
Geneviève Crabe, CZT
Diana Crick, CZT 9
Joy Crucitti, CZT
Donna J. Cyr, CZT
Nancy Dawes, CZT 13
Martha Deckel
Matt Dressman
Laura Emler
Dorian Eng, CZT 13
Carol Bailey Floyd, CZT
Christina Franks
Julie-Anne Fultz
Breanna Gallagher
Angela Gamble, CZT
Jakki Garlans
Barbara Gill, CZT
Estelle M. Goodnight, CZT
Loretta Gordon
Ann Grasso, CZT 13
Judy Gucker, CZT
Jerryann Haggart, CZT
Christine Halaburka, CZT
Cindy Haller
Paula Harpster
Teresa Hathaway, CZT
Shirl Hawes, CZT
Alice Hendon, CZT 9
Christy Hester, CZT 11
Melissa Hoopes, CZT
Sally Houghton, CZT 7
Sue Jacobs, CZT
Jean Kearney, CZT
Karen Kathryn Keefe, CZT 4
Sandi Kelley, CZT 12
Kelley Kelly, CZT
Natalie Kessler, CZT
Georgianna Klein, CZT
Diane Knauff, CZT
Lynne M. Koliha
Rhonda Koplin
Dianne Krumnow, CZT
Lisa Kruse
Cheryl Kullman
Sheryl Lamarand, CZT
Linda Latham, CZT
Sherri Lee, CZT
Terra Lee
Mimi Lempart, CZT
Kazue Lethin, CZT
Pamela Lisak, CZT
Laura Liu, CZT
Rebecca Loveless, CZT
Nancy Lubin, CZT
Jane MacKugler, CZT 6
Terrie Martin, CZT
Virginia E. Mead
Meg, CZT 9
Dawn Meisch, CZT
Jane Monk, CZT
Judy Montgomery, CZT
Sharon Morris, CZT
Bohdanna Murynec, CZT 7
Chris Myers
David Nelson, CZT
Nysha Nelson, CZT
Cathrine Nicols, CZT
Rita Nikolajeva
Lynn Noga, CZT 8
Janet Nordfors, CZT 9
Susan Nutting, CZT
Lisa Thies Osborne
Denise Henkle Owen, CZT 9
Jane Patrick, CZT
Laurie Patterson, CZT5
Christine Payne, CZT9
Jennifer Perruzzi, CZT
Kathy Phillips, CZT 13
Andrea Porrazzo-Nangle
Ronni Pressman, CZT
Debbie Purpura
Joanne Quesnel, CZT
Cari Raboin, CZT
Karen Radke
Penny Raile, CZT
Judy Reeves
Francie Stone Riley, CZT
Debora Rohly, CZT
Ann Rupley, CZT
MaryAnn Scheblein-Dawson, CZT
Mary Beth Schoonover, CZT
Jennifer Seiger, CZT 12
Carolyn Siccama, CZT
Susan Brust Silk
Susan Silvy, CZT
Jackie Sinkovitz, CZT
Elizabeth Skipper
Jean Smeriglio, CZT
Nancy Smith, CZT 4
Marilyn Stephen
Pamela J. Stevens
Gail Stirnaman
Maureen Stott, CZT 13
Randall Taylor-Craven, CZT
Jean Theurkauf, CZT
Barbara F Valenti, CZT
Nancy Van Slyke, CZT
Andrea Varon
Karen Watts, CZT 13
Rita Waller
Liz Ward
Karen Watts, CZT
Jill E. Webb
Gail West
Yvonne Westover, CZT
Susan E. J. White, CZT
Cristina Williams
Lara Williams, CZT
Lisa Wilson, CZT 12
Lianne Woods, CZT
Cindy J. Worthley
Samantha Wunderlich, CTRS CBIS CZT
Diane Yaciuk, CZT
Rebecca Zelanin

Many thanks to these talented artists for their generous contributions:

Adele Bruno, CZT
Altamonte Springs, FL
tickledtotangle.blogspot.com
Page 59

Amy Broady, CZT
Knoxville, TN
tanglefish.blotspot.com
Pages: 58, 66, 106

Sue Clark, CZT
Loveland, Colorado
TangledInkArt.blogspot.com
Pages: 59, 95, 98, 102, 127

Emily Classon, CZT
Lowell, MA
momzenartist.blogspot.com
Pages: 58, 90, 91

Marty Deckel, CZT
Millbury, MA
mdeckel2@gmail.com
Pages: 17, 32, 47, 63, 78, 97

Mae Furst
Columbus, OH
Page 89

Sue Jacobs, CZT
South Barrington, IL
suejacobs.blogspot.com
Pages: 110, 111

Carla Jennings
Hayle, Cornwall, UK
carlajenningsjewellery.com
Page 10

Anne Hatahway, CZT
Wichita, KS
deepmagictangles.blogspot.com
Page 129

Alice Hendon
Keystone Heights, FL
thecreatorsleaf.blogspot.com
Page 86, 114-115

Lea Howard
Pickerington, Ohio
Page 27

Liv Howard
Pickerington, Ohio
Page 51

Ben Kwok
Pasedena, California
bioworkz.com
Page 7

Alexa Letourneau
Pickerington, OH
Pages 27, 36

Jane MacKugler, CZT
Londonderry, VT
dicksallyjane.blogspot.com
Page 20, 50, 71

Caren Mlot, CZT
Mt. Pleasant, SC
tanglemania.com
Page 34, 103, 126

Maria Vennekens, CZT
Venroy, Netherlands
www.zentangle.eu
Page 94

Patti Wilburn
Pickerington, Ohio
Page 17, 32, 45

Hana Yencer
Pickerington, Ohio
Page 83

Sue Ann Zacariah
Kottayam, India
Page 71

Special thanks to:

Pat Allard, CZT
Amy Broady, CZT
Emily Classon, CZT
Alice Hendon, CZT
Robin Leja
Alexa Letourneau
Patti Wilburn
Hana Yencer

for going above and beyond in their diligence and patience in their comments, suggestion, and attention to detail as they helped us fine tune our wording, fix our grammar, and get this book ready for public consumption. Any errors left are solely the fault of the authors and not our wonderful proofreaders.

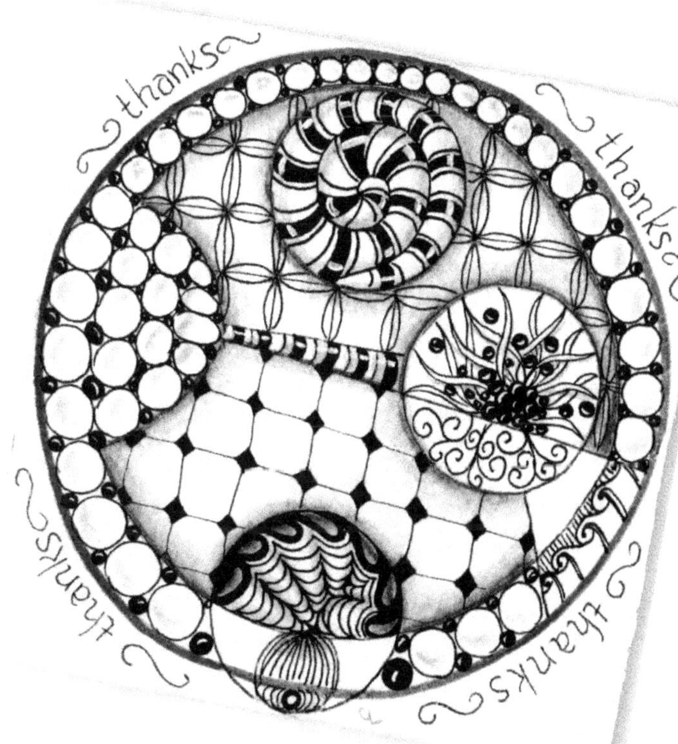

GLOSSARY

A

Abstract: *not imitating external reality or objects in nature*

ATC: *artist trading card*

Aura: *a tanglenhancer consisting of one or more strokes made close to another, like an echo or a halo*

C

Certified Zentangle Teacher: *one who has taken CZT training from Rick and Maria is certified to teach the Zentangle Method*

Chop: *a stylized way of drawing your initials on the front of your tile*

Composition: *the arrangement of objects in a drawing*

Contrast: *calling attention to the difference between values that are next to one another*

CZT: *acronym for Certified Zentangle Teacher*

D

Deckle: *giving the appearance of a rough, untrimmed edge of paper that looks as if it was torn by hand*

Deconstructing: *breaking down a pattern into repeating strokes to turn it into a tangle*

Dewdrop: *a tanglenhancer consisting of enlarging, shading, and highlighting a section of a tangle to make it appear as if you are looking at it through a drop of water*

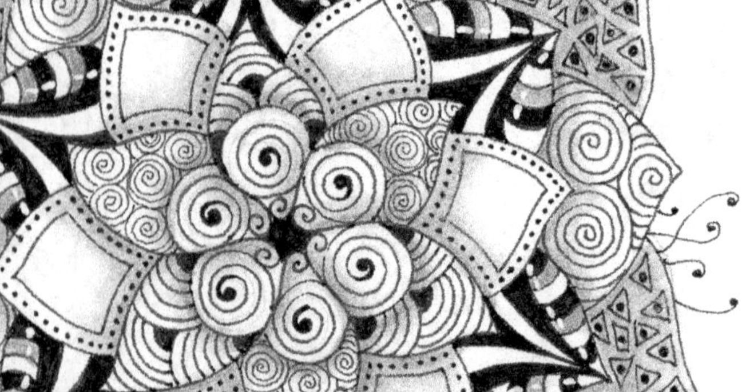

F

Focal point: *the part of a piece of art that draws the eye first*

G

Geometric: *a look characterized predominantly by simple graphic forms, such as circles, rectangles, triangles, straight lines, angles, etc.*

H

Hard edge: *a clear, crisp well-defined line between two shapes or colors*

Hatching: *a series of lines drawn closely together often used to add shading*

L

Loose: *not overly controlled. Loose art is representative instead of photographic*

M

Mandala: *from Sanskrit word for circle. A geometric pattern that represents the cosmos and is used for meditation*

Mindfulness: *a state of active, open attention on the present*

Monotangle: *term coined by Laura Harms CZT to describe a piece of Zentangle art that consists of a single tangle*

Mosaic: *placing two or more tiles next to each other to form a larger piece of art*

Movement: *the path our eyes follow when we look at a work of art*

N

Negative space: *part of a piece of art where the background shows through (see white space)*

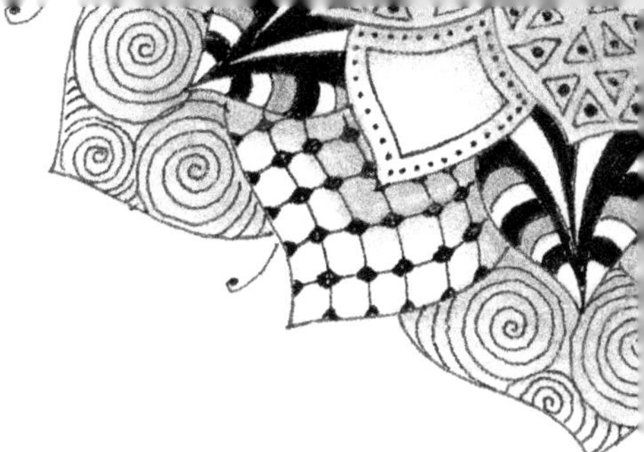

O

Orb: *a round shape, that may or may not be a perfect circle*

Organic: *composed of free-flowing and curvy shapes like those in nature, not rigid and geometric*

P

Pearl: *shading an orb to make it look 3D*

Perf: *a tanglenhancer consisting of tiny circles drawn randomly as an enhancement*

R

Representational: *art intended to look like something in the physical world, e.g. a house or a tree*

Rick & Maria: *Rick Roberts and Maria Thomas, founders of Zentangle*

Rounding: *a tanglenhancer where the crevices of a tangle are darkened*

S

Scale: *size of an object in relation to another*

Shading: *adding shades of gray to artwork to enhance or define it*

Soft edge: *blending one color into another without a clearly defined line*

Sparkle: *a tanglenhancer which is a deliberate break made when drawing a tangle to suggest a highlight*

Stipple: *tiny dots used for shading*

Step-out: *a diagram showing the sequence of strokes to create a tangle*

String: *a line that divides a tile into sections, usually drawn in pencil*

Stroke: *to draw a mark with a single, continuous line*

T

Tangle (n): *a named pattern that can be broken down into simple, repeated strokes*

Tangle (v): *to draw tangles*

Tangleation: *a variation of a tangle*

Tanglenhancer: *one of six basic techniques used to add style to your tangles: aura, dewdrop, sparkle, rounding, shading, and perfs*

Tango: *two or more tangles entangled as if they were dancing with each other*

Tile, Zentangle: *a 3.5 inch square of beautiful printmaking paper used as the surface in the Zentangle Method*

Tooth: *the surface texture of paper. Paper with more tooth will feel bumpier than smooth paper with less tooth*

W

White space: *part of a tile that is intentionally left blank, even if the tile is black or tan*

Z

Zendala: *a ZIA drawn in a circular pattern similar to a mandala*

Zentangle Method: *a trademarked method of creating beautiful images by drawing structured patterns that is easy-to-learn, fun, and relaxing*

ZIA: *an acronym for Zentangle Inspired Art. Any art consisting of tangles that is non-traditional, either larger, containing color, or representational*

RESOURCES

Your best source for information about Zentangle is your local Certified Zentangle Teacher. These are some of the authors' favorite other resources.

BOOKS

The Book of Zentangle
Rick Roberts and Maria Thomas
This book is an amazing collection of wisdom and information in words and pictures, direct from the creators of Zentangle.

The Joy of Zentangle
Design Originals
Inspiration, instruction, and over 100 tangle patterns to keep you tangling for a long time.

Made in the Shade: a Zentangle Workbook
Cris Letourneau, CZT
Shading is another way to add your own personality to your art, and this workbook will help you learn and develop shading skills. It includes both instruction and workbook pages. Available on Amazon.

The Beauty of Zentangle
Design Originals
The tag line is "Inspirational Examples from 137 Gifted Tangle Artists Worldwide." It has stunning and unique Zentangle Inspired Art, including some from the authors.

WEBSITES

zentangle.com
zentangle.blogspot.com
Learn about Zentangle, see the newest products, and keep up to date on what is happening at Zentangle, Inc. This is also where you will find a list of CZTs, links to their websites and contact information.

Zentangle youtube channel: youtube.com/user/Zentangle
Videos of Rick and Maria tangling. The best source for inspiration!

TangleldUpInArt.com
Find out what's happening with Cris. Learn about new books, sign up for classes in central Ohio, buy Zentangle supplies and books.

iamthedivaczt.blogspot.com
Laura Harms, CZT, posts weekly challenges, sure to keep you tangling, and make sure you do not get stuck in a rut. Search her blog for "monotangles" to see tons of tangleations.

Facebook: Zenergize You
Keep up with Sonya's latest Zentangle inspirations.

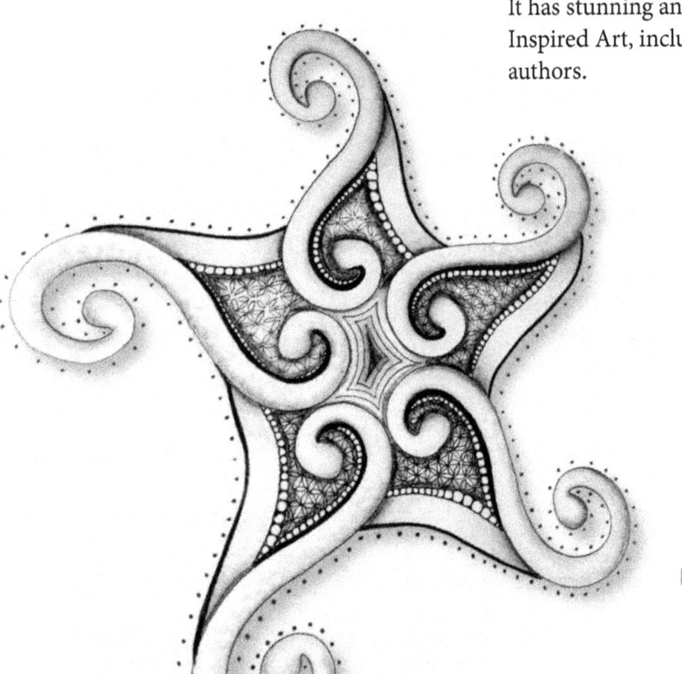

www.ingramcontent.com/pod-product-compliance
Lightning Source LLC
LaVergne TN
LVHW081407110826
845149LV00010B/1664
* 9 7 8 0 9 9 0 3 7 9 8 0 5 *